THE
ILLUSTRATED
COMPUTER
DICTIONARY

The Charles E. Merrill Information Processing Series

INTRODUCTION

Spencer (1983): *Illustrated Computer Dictionary*

Spencer (1983): *An Introduction to Computers: Developing Computer Literacy*

Spencer (1982): *Data Processing: An Introduction (2d Edition)*

Spencer (1982): *Data Processing: An Introduction with BASIC (2d Edition)*

Spencer (1981): *Introduction to Information Processing (3d Edition)*

Spencer (1976): *Computer Science Mathematics*

LANGUAGES

Thompson (1981): *BASIC—A First Course*

Richards and Cheney (1981): *COBOL—A Structured Approach*

SYSTEMS/MIS

Thierauf and Reynolds (1982): *Effective Information Systems Management*

Thierauf and Reynolds (1980): *Systems Analysis and Design*

THE
ILLUSTRATED

COMPUTER
DICTIONARY

DONALD D. SPENCER

Computer Science Consultant

CHARLES E. MERRILL PUBLISHING CO.
A Bell & Howell Company
Columbus   Toronto   London   Sydney

Published by
Charles E. Merrill Publishing Company
A Bell & Howell Company
Columbus, Ohio 43216

This book was set in Palatino and Moore Computer.
Production Editor: Rex Davidson.
Cover Design Coordination: Tony Faiola.
Cover Photos: Ampex Corporation; Richard Feldman, National Institute of Health,
Bethesda, Maryland; The Goodyear Tire and Rubber Company; Honeywell Information
Systems; MATRIX Instruments, Inc.; and Tektronix.

Library of Congress Catalogue Card Number: 83-60392

International Standard Book Number: 0-675-20075-X

1 2 3 4 5 6 7 8 9 10—86 85 84 83

Printed in the United States of America

CONTENTS

DEDICATION

To Sherrie and John

The primary objective of *The Illustrated Computer Dictionary* is to present compactly and concisely the most common terms currently used by computer scientists, data processing personnel, and other computer users. The book is for anyone who is using or studying about computers.

Familiarity with the vocabulary of any academic course, business, organization, or profession is absolutely mandatory if people working in those areas expect to succeed. Lack of knowledge can cause anger, failure, frustration, and loss of time and effort. This book should help students and other computer users overcome many of the problems associated with learning the terminology of an unfamiliar field. It may be used as a personal reference book or as a text in a course, workshop, or seminar to teach students about the vocabulary of computer users. Managers, professionals, teachers, technical people, and others should find this a helpful resource.

The keynote of this book is clarity—without any sacrifice of authority or definitional precision. All definitions are simply stated, and they stand as independent units of explanation. Many important terms, such as artificial intelligence, BASIC, data, hardware, industrial robot, microcomputer, network, software, and source program are explained in nontechnical language, simply and tersely. In those few cases that require special terminology, the expressions used are carefully defined, and cross-references indicate related terms or concepts. The book also contains many illustrations that will aid the reader in understanding many of the terms presented.

Special features of the book include the following:

COMPUTER ORGANIZATIONS   Short descriptions are given to acquaint the reader with professional organizations such as ACM, AEDS, AFIPS, BEMA, DPMA, ICCE, IEEE-CS, IFIPS, and SPA.

METRIC SYSTEM   Since the United States will eventually go metric, it is essential that everyone learn how to use metric measurements. This book contains definitions of important metric terms and uses metric values throughout.

BIOGRAPHIES   This book presents notes on the life histories of the most important people of computer science, with emphasis given to their influence on the development of computer techniques and equipment. Examples: Aiken, Atanasoff, Babbage, Boole, Eckert, Hollerith, Hopper, Leibniz, Mauchly, Napier, Pascal, Turing, von Neumann, Watson, Wiener, and Zuse. Birth and death dates, where available, are given.

PROGRAMMING LANGUAGES   Included in the book are definitions of the important languages, Ada, APL, BASIC, C, COBOL, COGO, FORTH, FORTRAN, GPSS, LOGO, Pascal, PILOT, PL/C, PL/I, RPG, SNOBOL, and WATFOR, as well as many others.

HISTORICAL   In addition to short sketches of famous people, the book also includes descriptions of many famous computers. Examples: ABC, ASCC, COLOSSUS, EDSAC, EDVAC, ENIAC, STRETCH, and UNIVAC I.

COMPUTERS IN SOCIETY   Readers will become aware of the effects of computers on society by reading the definitions of terms such as cashless society, computer applications, computer literacy, and privacy.

MANAGEMENT   Business people will find terms to aid them in their everyday activities. Examples: centralized data processing, computer security, data base, distributed data processing, feasibility study, information retrieval, management information system, and microcomputer.

EDUCATION   Computers are now being used in all aspects of education, both administrative and instructional. Educators will find descriptions for many useful terms and acronyms, such as CAI, CMI, computer literacy, LOGO, and PILOT.

COMPUTER PROFESSIONALS   Programmers and analysts will find many useful terms. Examples: algorithm, artificial intelligence, byte, data base, heuristic, intelligent terminal, laser storage, multiprocessing, operating system, point-of-sale terminal, simulation, structured programming, time-sharing, and virtual storage.

I am indebted to my wife, Rae, for typing the manuscript and to Linda King and John Beatty, who drew many of the illustrations that appear in the book. I also thank the many educators, engineers, scientists, researchers, and writers who have identified new terms and written about new computer equipment and techniques. Only through the works of these people can I keep up-to-date with the ever growing vocabulary of computer terminology. Finally, I should like to express the hope that readers who find mistakes will be so kind as to let the publisher or author know so that errors may be corrected in future printings and editions.

Donald D. Spencer

Ormond Beach, Florida

HOW TO USE THIS DICTIONARY

Most terms appear in alphabetical order rather than under a general heading. For example, the terms **floppy disk** and **moveable-head disk unit** appear under *F* and *M*, although they are mentioned and cross-referenced under the general description of **magnetic disk unit.**

All *italicized* words within this dictionary are defined within. Cross-references that are important to an understanding of any term are usually given in italics. If you are unfamiliar with descriptions of modern computer terms, you might find it helpful to begin by looking up some of these words that appear over and over again, although not always as cross-references.

assembler	microcomputer
binary	microprocessor
cathode ray tube	object program
central processing unit	off-line
compiler	on-line
computer	output
data	program
debug	programming language
digital	PROM
flowchart	RAM
hardware	ROM
input	simulation
input/output	software
instruction	source program
loop	symbolic programming
machine language	terminal

If you cannot find a word, it might be listed in a slightly different form. For example, you might try looking for the term *flowcharting* and find your description under the term *flowchart*.

AAAI An acronym for American Association for Artificial Intelligence. A professional organization concerned with advancing artificial intelligence.

abacus An ancient device for doing simple calculations that uses movable beads threaded on a grid of wires. Still widely used in many oriental countries.

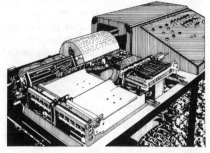

ABC machine

absolute address An address that is permanently assigned by the machine designer to a particular storage location. For example, the addresses, 0000, 0001, 0002, and 0003 might be assigned to the first four locations in a computer's storage. Also called *machine address.*

absolute coding Coding that uses machine instructions and absolute addresses; therefore, it can be directly executed by a computer without prior translation to a different form. Contrast with *symbolic coding.*

absolute value The magnitude of a number without regard to sign.

abstract A summary of a document.

AC An acronym for *Automatic Computer.*

acceptance test A test used to demonstrate the capabilities and workability of a new computer system. It is usually conducted by the manufacturer to show the customer that the system is in working order.

access Generally, the obtaining of data. To locate the desired data.

access arm A mechanical device in a disk file storage unit that positions the reading and writing mechanisms.

abacus

ABC An acronym for the Atanasoff-Berry Computer. An early electronic digital computer built in 1942 by Dr. John V. Atanasoff and his assistant, Clifford Berry.

abort The procedure for terminating a program when a mistake, malfunction, or error occurs.

access method Any of the data management techniques available to the user for transferring data between internal storage and an input/output device.

access time The time interval between the instant data are called for from the storage unit and the instant data are delivered. The time interval between the instant data are requested to be stored and the instant at which storage is completed. See also *seek time* and *transfer rate*.

accounting The interpretation and organized method of recording all the transactions affecting the financial condition of a business.

accumulator A register or storage location that forms the result of an arithmetic or logic operation.

accuracy The degree of exactness of an approximation or measurement. Accuracy normally denotes absolute quality of computed results; precision usually refers to the amount of detail used in representing those results. Thus, four-place results are less precise than six-place results; nevertheless a four-place table might be more accurate than an erroneously computed six-place table. See *precision*.

ACM An acronym for Association for Computing Machinery, a professional computer science organization. Its function is to advance the design, development, and application of information processing and to promote the interchange of such techniques between computer specialists and users.

ACMST An acronym for Association for Computers in Mathematics and Science Teaching. This professional organization directs itself toward college and secondary school mathematics, and science teachers interested in educational uses of computers.

acoustic coupler A data communications device that converts electrical data signals to/from tones for transmission over a telephone line using a conventional telephone headset.

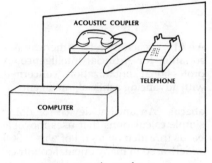

acoustic coupler

ACPA An acronym for Association of Computer Programmers and Analysts, a professional computer science organization.

acronym A word formed from the first letter (or letters) of each word in a phrase or name (e.g., BASIC from Beginner's All-purpose Symbolic Instruction Code; RPG from Report Program Generator; CPU from Central Processing Unit).

action (1) The performance of a particular operation or set of operations in response to a stimulus. (2) The resulting activity of a given condition.

activity A term used to indicate that a record in a master file is used, altered, or referred to.

activity ratio When a file is processed, the ratio of the number of records in a file that have activity to the total number of records in that file.

ACU An acronym for Automatic Calling Unit. A device that allows a business machine to make dial calls on a telephone network.

Ada A high-level programming language developed by the Department of Defense for use in military systems. The language was named after Ada Augusta Lovelace, the first woman programmer.

ADAPSO An acronym for Association of Data Processing Service Organizations. A trade association for vendors of computer systems, software, and services.

adapter A device that allows compatibility between different equipment.

adaptive systems Systems displaying the ability to learn, change their state, or otherwise react to a stimulus. Any system capable of adapting itself to changes in its environment.

A-D converter See *analog-to-digital converter*.

addend A number of quantity to be added to another, the augend, to obtain a result called the sum.

adder A device capable of forming the sum of two or more quantities. See *parallel adder* and *serial adder*.

adding wheel A toothed gear that allows the process of "carrying" to be accomplished mechanically. Adding wheels were used in Pascal's calculator.

GEAR ARRANGEMENT FOR AUTOMATIC CARRYING

adding wheel

addition record A record that results from the creation of a new record during the processing of a file.

address An identification (e.g., a label, number, or name) that designates a particular location in storage or any other data destination or source.

address modification An operation that causes an address to be altered in a prescribed way by a stored program computer.

address register A register containing the address of the instruction currently being executed.

address space The complete range of addresses that is available to a computer user.

address translation The process of changing the address of an instruction or item of data to the address in internal memory at which it is to be loaded or relocated.

add time The time required for a computer to perform an addition, exclusive of the time required to obtain the quantities from storage and put the sum back into storage.

administrative data processing The field of data processing concerned with the management or direction of an organization. See *business data processing*.

administrative management A general term for such functions as bookkeeping, payroll, inventory control, and budget preparation.

ADP An acronym for Automatic Data Processing. Data processing performed largely by automatic means.

AEDS An acronym for Association for Educational Data Systems. A professional organization interested in sharing information related to the effect of data processing on the educational process.

AFCET An acronym for Association Francaise pour la Cybernetique Economique et Technique. A professional organization whose purpose is to bring together French scientists, computer

3

users, computer manufacturers, and engineers who work or are interested in computer technology and applied mathematics.

AFIPS An acronym for American Federation of Information Processing Societies. A society whose primary purpose is to advance understanding and knowledge of the information processing sciences through active engagement in various scientific activities and through cooperation with state, national, and international (called *IFIPS*) organizations on information processing.

Aiken, Howard Hathaway (1900–1973) Headed the team of people who designed and built the first electromechanical computer, the Automatic Sequence Controlled Calculator (commonly called the Mark I), at Harvard University. See *Mark I*.

Howard Hathaway Aiken

airline reservation system An on-line, direct access application in which a computing system is used to keep track of seat inventories, light sched-

ules; and other information required to run an airline. The reservation system is designed to maintain up-to-date data files and to respond, within seconds or less, to inquiries from ticket agents at locations remote from the computing system.

airline reservation system

AL An acronym for Assembly Language. A programming language used at Stanford University for controlling robots.

algebra The study of mathematical structure. Elementary algebra is the study of numeral systems and their properties. Algebra solves problems in arithmetic by using letters or symbols to stand for quantities.

algebra of logic A system of logical relations expressed as algebraic formulas; first introduced by George Boole. See *Boole, George* and *Boolean algebra*.

ALGOL An acronym for ALGOrithmic Language—an international high-level programming language used to code problem-solving algorithms.

algorithm A prescribed set of well-defined, unambiguous rules or processes for the solution of a problem in a finite number of steps; for example, a full statement of an arithmetic procedure for evaluating cosine x to a stated precision. Contrast with *heuristic*.

algorithmic language A language designed for expressing algorithms.

aligning edge That edge of a form which, in conjunction with the leading edge, serves to correctly position the document that is to be scanned by an OCR device.

allocate To assign a resource for use in performing a specific job.

allocation The process of reserving computer storage areas for instructions or data.

alphabetic Pertaining to a character set that includes the letters of the alphabet.

alphameric A contraction of alphanumeric.

alphanumeric A general term for alphabetic letters (A through Z), numerical digits (0 through 9), and special characters (−, /, *, $, (,), +, etc.) that are machine-processable.

alteration switch An actual switch on the computer console or a program-simulated switch that can be set on or off to control coded machine instructions.

alternate routing Assignment of a secondary communications path to a destination if the primary path is unavailable.

ALU Abbreviation for Arithmetic Logic Unit—a computational subsystem that performs the mathematical and logical operations of a digital system. A basic element of a central processing unit (CPU). Same as *arithmetic unit*.

ambient temperature The temperature of the environment surrounding an element of a computer system.

AMBIT A string processing language oriented toward algebraic manipulation. See *string processing languages*.

American Standard Code for Information Interchange See *ASCII*.

ampere Base unit of electric current in the SI metric system.

amplifier An electronic circuit that increases the voltage, current, or power of an input signal, or that isolates one part of a system from another.

analog Pertaining to representation by means of continuously variable physical quantities. Contrast with *digital*.

analog computer A devise that operates on data in the form of continuously variable physical quantities. See *computer*. Contrast with *digital computer*.

analog data A physical representation of information such that the representation bears an exact relationship to the original information. For example, the electrical signals on a telephone channel are analog data representation of the original voice data.

analog model A model that relates physical similarity to the actual situation.

analog-to-digital converter A mechanical or electrical device used to convert continuous analog signals to discrete digital numbers. Abbreviated A-D converter. Opposite of *digital-to-analog converter*. See *digitize*. *(Illus. p. 6)*

analysis The investigation of a problem by some consistent, systematic procedure. See *systems analysis*.

analyst A person skilled in the definition of and development of techniques for solving a problem, especially those techniques for solutions on a computer. See *programming analyst* and *systems analyst*. *(Illus. p. 6)*

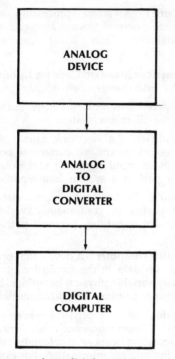

analog-to-digital converter

analyst

analytical engine A device invented in the mid 1800s by Charles Babbage, a British mathematician, to solve mathematical problems. This machine was a forerunner of the modern digital computer. See *Babbage, Charles.*

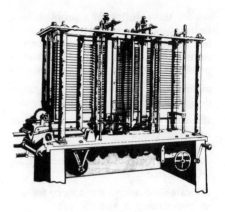

analytical engine

AND A logical connection, as in the statement A AND B, which means that the statement is true if, and only if, A is true and B is true simultaneously.

AND-gate (1) A binary circuit with two or more inputs and a single output, in which the output is logic 1 only when all inputs are logic 1, and the output is logic 0 if any one of the inputs is logic 0. (2) In a computer, a gate circuit with more than one input terminal. No output signal will be produced unless a pulse is applied to all inputs simultaneously.

annotation A description or explanation usually in the form of a comment or note.

annotation symbol A flowcharting symbol used to add messages or notes to a flowchart.

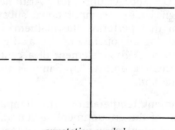

annotation symbol

ANSI An acronym for American National Standards Institute. An organization that acts as a national clearinghouse and coordinator for voluntary standards in the United States.

aperture card A punched card with an opening specifically prepared for the mounting of a frame or frames of microfilm.

APL An acronym for A Programming Language. A mathematically-structured programming language developed by IBM Corporation. In its simplest mode of operation, APL performs the functions of an intelligent calculator. The power of the language is demonstrated by its extended single operators that allow a user to directly perform such calculations as taking the inverse of a matrix or solving a set of linear equations.

Apple II A popular microcomputer system manufactured by Apple Computer, Inc. See *microcomputer*.

application Task to be performed by a computer program or system. Broad examples of computer applications are engineering design, numerical control, airline seat reservations, business forecasting, and hospital administration.

Apple II microcomputer

application-oriented language A problem-oriented programming language whose statements contain or resemble the terminology of the computer user.

applications programming The preparation of programs for application to specific problems in order to find solutions. Contrast with *systems programming*.

applications programs The programs normally written by the using organization that enable the computer

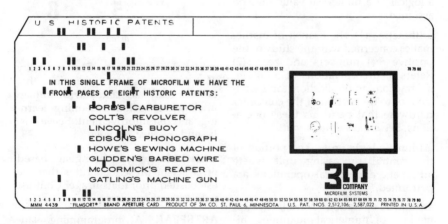

aperture card

to produce useful work; for example, inventory control, attendance accounting, linear programming, and medical accounting.

applied mathematics Mathematics put to practical use, as in mechanics, physics, or computer science, among others.

approximation A number that is not exact, but has been rounded off to a prescribed decimal place. An approximation of π is 3.14.

APT An acronym for Automatic Programmed Tool. A programming system that is used in numerical control applications for the programmed control of machine functions. The APT language allows a user to define points, lines, circles, planes, conical surfaces, and geometric surfaces. See *numerical control* and *parts programmer*.

architecture The physical structure of a computer's internal operations, including its registers, memory, instruction set, input/output structure, and so on.

area search The examination of a large group of documents to select those that pertain to one group, such as one category, class, and so on.

argument A variable to which either a logical or a numerical value may be assigned.

arithmetic (1) The branch of mathematics concerned with the study of the positive real numbers and zero. (2) Refers to the operations of addition, subtraction, multiplication, and division, or to the section of the computer hardware that performs these operations. See *arithmetic-logic unit*.

arithmetic-logic unit The portion of the central processing unit where arithmetic and logical operations are performed.

arithmetic operation Various manipulations of numerical quantities, including the fundamental operations of

addition, subtraction, multiplication, and division.

arithmetic shift To multiply or divide a quantity by a power of the number base; for example, if binary 1101, representing decimal 13, is arithmetically shifted twice to the left, the result is 110100, representing 52, which is also obtained by multiplying 13 by 2 twice; on the other hand, if the decimal 13 were to be shifted to the left twice, the result would be the same as multiplying by 10 twice, or 1300.

arithmetic unit Same as *arithmetic-logic unit*.

ARQ An acronym for Automatic Repeat ReQuest. A data transmission checking function.

arrangement Order of index terms or items of data in a system.

array (1) A series of related items. (2) An ordered arrangement or pattern of items or numbers, such as a determinant, matrix, vector, or a table of numbers. See *matrix* and *vector*.

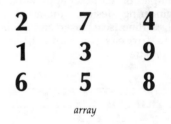

array

artificial intelligence The capability of a device to perform functions that are normally associated with human intelligence, such as reasoning, learning, and self-improvement. See *heuristic* and *machine learning*.

artificial language A language based on a set of prescribed rules that are established prior to its usage. Contrast with *natural language*.

ARTSPEAK A programming language designed to help beginning users

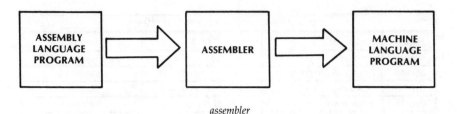

assembler

produce computer drawings on digital plotters.

ASA An acronym for American Standards Association. Replaced by *ANSI.*

ASCC An acronym for Automatic Sequence Controlled Calculator. First electromechanical computer developed under the direction of Howard Aiken at Harvard University. Also called the *Mark I.*

ascending Increasing. In $x^1 + x^2 + x^3 + x^4$, the exponents are in ascending order.

ASCII An acronym for American Standard Code for Information Interchange. Acronym pronounced "asskey." A 7-bit standard code adopted to facilitate the interchange of data among various types of data processing and data communications equipment.

ASIS An acronym for American Society for Information Science. This professional organization provides a forum for librarians, information specialists, scientists, and others who seek to improve the communication of information.

ASM An acronym for Association of Systems Management. This organization represents members of the industry who are concerned with the promotion of effective management of people and equipment in data processing fields.

aspect card A card containing the accession numbers of documents in an information retrieval system.

ASR An acronym for Automatic Send/Receive. A teletypewriter with keyboard, printer, paper tape reader, and paper tape punch that allows tape to be produced and edited off-line for automatic transmission. An input/output device for minicomputers, personal computers, and remote time-sharing terminals.

assemble To gather, interpret, and coordinate data required for a computer program, translate the data into computer language, and project it into the final program for the computer to follow.

assembler A computer program that takes nonmachine language instructions prepared by a computer user and converts them into a form that may be used by the computer.

assembling The automatic process by which a computer converts a symbolic source language program into a machine language usually on an instruction-by-instruction basis. See *cross compiling/assembling.*

assembly language A programming language that allows a computer user to write a program using mnemonics instead of numeric instructions. It is a low-level symbolic programming language that closely resembles machine code language. Same as *low-level language.* Contrast with *problem-oriented language* and *procedure-oriented language.*

assembly listing A listing of the details of an assembly procedure. *(Illus. p. 10)*

MACHINE LANGUAGE CODING FORM			
Oper	OP 1	OP 2	Comments
100010	000 000 000 000 011	010 110 100 000 000	Load register with C
001100	000 000 000 000 011	011 010 000 000 000	Multiply by B
011100	000 000 000 000 011	010 101 011 000 000	Add A
010111	000 000 000 000 011	100 001 000 000 000	Store as D

assembly listing

Association for Computing Machinery The major professional organization for computer scientists. See *ACM*.

associative storage A storage device whose storage locations are identified by their contents (rather than by names or positions, as in most computer storage devices). Same as *content-addressable memory* and *search memory*.

asynchronous computer A computer in which each operation starts as a result of a signal generated by the completion of the previous operation or by the availability of the equipment required for the next operation. Contrast with *synchronous computer*.

asynchronous input Input data having no time-dependable pattern or cycle when related to the computer system.

asynchronous transmission Transmission of data that requires the use of start and stop elements for each character because the interval of time between characters can vary.

Atanasoff, John V. (born 1903) Designed an electronic digital computer in 1942. He was interested in finding faster ways of performing computations for physics problems. See *ABC*.

Atari 800 A popular microcomputer system developed by Atari. The sys-

John V. Atanasoff

Atari 800

tem uses preprogrammed ROM cartridges as well as other forms of input. See *microcomputer, solid state cartridge,* and *read-only memory.*

ATLAS The third in a series of early computers designed in the United Kingdom.

atom The elementary building block of data structures. An atom corresponds to a record in a file and may contain one or more fields of data.

attenuation The decrease in the strength of a signal as it passes through a control system. Opposite of *gain.*

attribute A word that describes the manner in which a variable is handled by the computer.

audible Capable of being heard.

audio device Any computer device that accepts sound and/or produces sound. See *voice recognition* and *voice synthesis.*

audio response device An output device that produces a spoken response. See *voice output.*

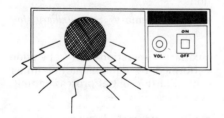

audio response device

audio-visual The nonprint materials such as films, tapes, cassettes, and other media that record information by sound and sight.

audit trail A means for identifying the actions taken in processing input data or in preparing an output. By use of the audit trail, data on a source document can be traced to an output, and an output can be traced to the

source items from which it was derived.

author language A programming language that is used for designing instructional programs for computer-assisted instruction (CAI) systems. See *PILOT* and *PLANIT.*

authors People who design instructional material for *computer-assisted instruction* (CAI) systems.

autochart A type of documentor used for the automatic production and maintenance of charts, principally flowcharts.

AUTODIN An acronym for AUTOmatic DIgital Network. The data handling portion of the military communications system.

auto indexing A system of indexing that superimposes additional information at any of several given addresses.

automata The theory related to the study of the principles of operation, the application, and the behavioral characteristics of automatic devices.

automated office A general term that refers to the merger of computers, office electronic devices, and telecommunications technology in an office environment.

automatic Pertaining to a process or device that, under specified conditions, functions without intervention by a human operator.

automatic carriage See *carriage.*

automatic check An equipment check built in specifically for checking purposes. Also called *built-in check.*

automatic coding See *automatic programming.*

automatic computer A computer that can process a specified volume of work, its assigned function, without requiring human intervention except for program changes. See *computer.*

automatic controller A device or instrument that is capable of measuring and regulating by receiving a signal from a sensing device, comparing this data with a desired value, and issuing signals for corrective action.

automatic data processing Abbreviated *ADP*. See *data processing*.

automatic error correction A technique for detecting and correcting errors that occur in data transmission or within the system itself.

automatic loader A hardware loader program, usually implemented in a special ROM, that allows loading of information from paper tapes or an auxiliary storage unit (disk or magnetic tape). See *bootstrapping*.

automatic message switching See *message switching*.

automatic programming (1) The process of using a computer to perform some stages of the work involved in preparing a program. (2) The production of a machine language computer program under the guidance of a symbolic representation of the program.

automatic quality control Technique for evaluating the quality of a product being processed by checking it against a predetermined standard, and then automatically making the proper corrective action if the quality falls below the standard.

Automatic Sequence Controlled Calculator See *ASCC*.

automation (1) The implementation of processes by automatic means. (2) Automatically controlled operation of an apparatus, process, or system by mechanical or electronic devices that take the place of human observation, effort, and decision.

automaton A machine designed to simulate the operations of living things.

automonitor (1) A computer's record of its functions. (2) A computer program that records the operating functions of a computer.

autopolling A contraction for automatic polling. Polling is a process whereby terminals in a computer network are scanned periodically to determine whether they are ready to send information. Autopolling is a combination of hardware and software that polls the terminals in a computer network.

autorestart A capability of a computer to perform automatically the initialization functions necessary to resume operation following an equipment or power failure.

auxiliary equipment Equipment not under direct control of the central processing unit. See *off-line*.

auxiliary function In automatic machine tool control, a machine function other than the control of the motion of a work-piece or cutter. Control of machine lubricating and cooling equipment are typical auxiliary functions.

auxiliary memory See *auxiliary storage*.

auxiliary operation An operation performed by equipment not under control of the central processing unit. See *off-line*.

auxiliary storage A storage that supplements the primary internal storage of a computer. Same as *secondary storage*. (*Illus. p. 13*)

availability The ratio of the time that a hardware device is known or believed to be operating correctly to the total hours of scheduled operation. Often called *operating ratio*.

available time The time that a computer is available for use. Synonymous with *uptime*. Contrast with *downtime*.

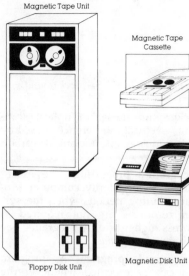

Magnetic Tape Unit

Magnetic Tape Cassette

Magnetic Disk Unit

'Floppy Disk Unit

auxiliary storage

average The statistical mean. The arithmetic mean.

average search length An anticipated time or number of functions to be performed to locate an address.

AWC An acronym for Association for Women in Computing. The AWC has these purposes: to promote communication among women in computing; to further the professional development and advancement of women in computing; and to promote the education of women and girls in computing.

B

Babbage, Charles (1792–1871) A British mathematician and inventor. He designed a "difference engine" for calculating logarithms to 20 decimal places and an "analytical engine" that was a forerunner of the digital computer. Babbage was a man ahead of his time, and engineering techniques of his day were not advanced enough to successfully build his machines. See *analytical engine; difference engine; Scheutz, George;* and *Stibitz, George.*

Charles Babbage

babble The cross talk from a large number of channels in a system. See *cross talk.*

background In multiprogramming, the environment in which low priority programs are executed.

background job See *background program.*

background noise In optical scanning, electrical interference caused by such things as ink tracking or carbon offsetting.

background processing The execution of lower-priority computer programs during periods when the system resources are not required to process higher-priority programs. See *background program.*

background program A program that can be executed whenever the facilities of a multiprogramming computer system are not required by other programs of higher priority. Contrast with *foreground program.*

backlash In a mechanical operation, the "play" between interacting parts, such as two gears, as a result of tolerance.

backplane The circuitry and mechanical elements used to connect the boards of a system. Also called *motherboard.*

backspace tape The process of returning a magnetic tape to the beginning of the preceding record.

backtracking The operation of scanning a list in reverse.

backup Pertaining to procedures or equipment that are available for use in the event of failure or overloading of the normally used equipment or procedures. See *fail-safe system, fail-soft system, fall-back,* and *father file.*

backup copy A copy of a file or data set that is kept for reference in case the original file or data set is destroyed.

Backus Normal Form A language used for describing languages. Abbreviated *BNF.*

backward read A feature available on some magnetic tape systems whereby the magnetic tape units can transfer data to computer storage while moving in a reverse direction.

badge reader A terminal equipped to read credit cards of specially coded badges.

Baldwin, Frank Stephen In 1875, he invented the first practical reversible four-process calculator in the United States.

Frank Stephen Baldwin

band (1) In communications, a range of frequencies, as between two specified limits. (2) Range, or scope, of operation. (3) A group of circular recording tracks on a storage device such as a disk or drum.

bandwidth In data communications, the difference (expressed in hertz) between the highest and lowest frequencies of a band.

bank A unit of *internal storage*.

Bardeen, John (born 1908) A Bell Laboratories scientist who along with William Shockley and Walter Brattain invented the transistor. See *transistor.*

bar printer A printing device that uses several type bars positioned side-by-side across the line.

base (1) The radix of a number system. (2) The region between the emitter and collector of a transistor that receives minority carriers injected from the emitter. (3) On a printed circuit board, the portion that supports the printed pattern.

Base 2 See *binary.*

Base 8 See *octal.*

Base 10 See *decimal.*

Base 16 See *hexadecimal.*

base address A specified address that is combined with a relative address to form the absolute address of a particular storage location.

baseline document A document that is a reference for changes to a data processing system.

BASIC An acronym for Beginner's All-purpose Symbolic Instruction Code. An easy-to-learn, easy-to-use,

```
10 PRINT "DO YOU LIKE STEAK"
20 INPUT A$
30 IF A$ = "NO" THEN 70
40 IF A$ = "YES" THEN 90
50 PRINT "NOT AN ACCEPTABLE
   ANSWER"
60 GOTO 99
70 PRINT "THE STEER LOVES YOU"
80 STOP
90 PRINT "THE STEER HATES YOU"
99 END
```

BASIC

algebraic programming language. BASIC has a small repertory of commands and simple statement formats. For this reason, BASIC is widely used in programming instruction, in personal computing, and in business and industry. The BASIC language has been implemented on most microcomputers, minicomputers, and larger machines. See *BASIC-PLUS, integer BASIC,* and *floating point BASIC.*

Basic FORTRAN An approved American Standard version of the FORTRAN programming language. See *FORTRAN.*

basic linkage A linkage that is used repeatedly in one routine, program, or system and that follows the same set of rules each time. See *calling sequence* and *linkage.*

BASIC-PLUS An extension of the BASIC programming language. The language includes more powerful capabilities, especially for data manipulation.

batch A group of records or programs that is considered as a single unit for processing on a computer.

batch processing A technique by which programs that are to be executed are coded and collected together into groups for processing in groups or batches. The user gives the job to a computer center where it is put into a batch of programs and processed, and then the data are returned. The user has no direct access to the machine. See *remote batch processing.*

batch total A sum of a set of items in a batch of records that is used to check the accuracy of operations involving the batch.

Batten system A method of indexing invented by W.E. Batten that uses the coordination of single attributes to identify specific documents. Sometimes called the ''peek-a-boo'' system because of its method of comparing

holes in cards by superimposing cards and checking the coincidence of holes.

baud A unit for measuring data transmission speed. One baud is one bit per second.

Baudot code A code for the transmission of data in which five bits represent one character. It is named for Emile Baudot, a pioneer in printing telegraphy. The name is usually applied to the code used in many teleprinter systems.

Baudot, Emile (1845–1903) Invented the Baudot code (also called the International Telegraph Code Number 1) in 1880. By 1950 this code had become one of the standards for international telegraph communications.

Baum, L. Frank (1856–1919) Shared the turn-of-the-century optimism about machines as a positive force. An admired (but not beloved) character in his famous *Oz* series was Tik-tok, the

L. Frank Baum

clockwork copper man who "was sure to do exactly what he was wound up to do, at all times and in all circumstances."

BCD An acronym for *Binary Coded Decimal.*

BCS An acronym for British Computer Society. A professional computer society in the the United Kingdom.

bedlam Wild uproar and confusion.

bells-and-whistles An informal description of the special or extra features of a computer system; for example, graphics, color displays, sound, many peripherals, etc.

BEMA An acronym for Business Equipment Manufacturers Association. This organization's main functions are to guide information processing equipment users in solving problems and applying information for general benefit, and to sponsor the settings of standards for computers and information processing.

benchmark A point of reference from which measurements can be made, as the use of a program to evaluate the performance of a computer.

benchmark problem A problem used to evaluate the performance of digital computers relative to each other.

benchmark tests Tests used in the measurement of computer equipment performance under typical conditions of use (i.e., a computer program run on several different computers for the purpose of comparing execution speed, throughput, etc.).

bias The amount by which the average of a set of values departs from a reference value.

bibliography (1) An annotated catalog of documents. (2) An enumerative list of books. (3) A list of documents pertaining to a given subject or author.

(4) The process of compiling catalogs or lists.

bifurcation A condition where two, and only two, outcomes can occur (e.g., on or off, 0 or 1).

BINAC An acronym for BINary Automatic Computer. Built by the Eckert-Mauchly Corporation in 1949.

binary Pertaining to the number system with a radix of 2, or to a characteristic or property involving a choice or condition in which there are two possibilities.

binary arithmetic A mathematical numeration system equivalent to our decimal arithmetic system but involving only two digits: 1 and 0.

binary code A coding system in which the encoding of any data is done through the use of bits—that is, 0 or 1.

binary coded character One element of a notation system representing alphanumeric characters such as decimal digits, alphabetic letters, and special symbols by a predetermined configuration of consecutive binary digits.

binary coded decimal A computer coding system in which each decimal digit is represented by a group of four binary ones and zeros. Abbreviated BCD.

binary coded decimal number A number usually consisting of successive groups of figures in which each group of four figures is a binary number that represents, but does not necessarily equal arithmetically, a particular figure in an associated decimal number; for example, the decimal

binary coded decimal number

17

number 264 is represented as the binary coded number 0010 0110 0100.

binary device (1) A device that can register two conditions; for example, an electrical switch that can be ON or OFF. (2) In computer science, equipment that records data in binary form or that reads the data so coded.

binary digit Either of the characters 0 or 1. Abbreviated *bit*.

binary notation A numeral system written in base two notation.

binary point The radix point in the binary numeral. The point that separates the fractional part of a mixed binary numeral from the integer part. In the binary numeral 110.011, the binary point is between the two zeros.

binary search A search in which the series of items is divided into two parts, one of which is rejected, and the process repeated on the unrejected part until the item with the desired property is found. Also known as *dichotomizing search*.

binary system A numeral system with a base or radix of two; for example, the numeral 111 represents the quantity 1, plus 1×2^1, plus 1×2^2—i.e., 7.

binary-to-decimal conversion The process of converting a numeral written to the base two to the equivalent numeral written to the base ten.

binary-to-gray code conversion A gray code equivalent of a binary numeral can be obtained by applying the following rule: The most significant gray code digit equals the corresponding binary digit, and the following gray code digit is 1 if the binary digit changes and 0 if it does not. For example, the binary value 0110100 equals the gray code value 0101110.

binary-to-hexadecimal conversion The process of converting a numeral written to the base two to the equiva-

lent numeral written to the base sixteen.

binary-to-octal conversion The process of converting a numeral written to the base two to the equivalent numeral written to the base eight.

binding time The stage at which a compiler replaces a symbolic name or address with its machine language form.

bionics The study of living systems for the purpose of relating their characteristics and functions to the development of mechanical and electronic hardware (hardware systems).

bipolar The most popular fundamental kind of integrated circuit, formed from layers of silicon with different electrical characteristics. Bipolar literally means "having two poles" and is used to distinguish the earlier transistor from the MOS Field Effect Transistor (MOSFET), which is unipolar (having one pole). As in MOSFET, the current flow of majority carriers goes in one direction only—for example, from source to drain. In a bipolar transistor, the current in the emitter region splits and flows toward two terminals (poles), the base and the collector.

bipolar read only memory See *BROM*.

biquinary code A 7-bit weighted code used primarily to represent decimal numbers. It is a redundant code that may be used to provide error-checking features. A pair of bits represents the decimal number 5 or 0, and the remaining five bits are used to represent the decimal numbers 0 through 4.

bistable device A device with only two stable states, such as "on" and "off."

bit A binary digit; a digit (1 or 0) in the representation of a number in binary notation. Several bits make up a byte, or a computer word.

bit density A measure of the number of bits recorded per unit of length or area.

bit rate The rate at which binary digits, or pulse representations, appear on communication lines or channels.

bit-slice processor This approach to microprocessors allows microcomputer organizations of variable word sizes, with processor units separated into 2-, 4-, or 8-bit slices on a single chip. These devices can be paralleled to yield an 8-, 12-, 16-, 24-, or 32-bit microcomputer when assembled with the other necessary overhead components of the system.

bit stream Referring to a binary signal without regard to groupings by character.

bit transfer rate The number of bits transferred per unit time, usually expressed in bits per second.

black box An electronic or mechanical device that alters input signals in a predictable manner but whose inner workings are often a mystery to the user.

blank character A character used to produce a character space on an output medium.

block A group of digits, characters, or words that are held in one section of an input/output medium and handled as a unit (e.g., the data recorded between two interblock gaps on a magnetic tape).

block diagram A graphic representation showing the logical sequence by which data is processed. See *flowchart*.

blocking Combining two or more records into one block usually to increase the efficiency of computer input and output operations.

blocking factor The number of logical records per physical record on a magnetic tape or disk.

block length A measure of the size of a block, usually specified in units such as records, words, characters, or bytes.

block sorting A sorting technique used to break down a file into related groups.

block structure A programming concept that allows related declarations and statements to be grouped together.

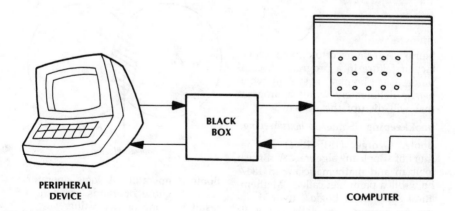

PERIPHERAL DEVICE

BLACK BOX

COMPUTER

black box

BNF An acronym for Backus Normal Form. A notation for describing the syntax of programming languages.

board A card that contains circuitry for one or more specific functions.

Bollee, Leon In 1886, Bollee of Mans, France, designed the first machine to perform multiplication successfully by a direct method instead of repeated addition.

Leon Bollee

bomb A term used to denote a spectacular failure in a program. A computer user "bombs" a system when he/she deliberately writes a program that will disrupt the system.

bookkeeping Same as *housekeeping*.

Boole, George (1815–1864) The father of Boolean algebra. A British logician and mathematician. In 1847, he wrote a pamphlet called "Mathematical Analysis of Logic." In 1851, he wrote a more mature statement of his logical system in a larger work, "An Investigation of the Laws of

Thought," in which are founded the mathematical theories of logic. Boolean algebra lay dormant until it could be usefully applied to the fields of relay switching and electronic computers. It has now become an important subject in logic design of electronic computers. See *Boolean algebra*.

George Boole

Boolean algebra A branch of symbolic logic that is similar in form to algebra but, instead of dealing with numerical relationships, it deals with logical relationships. An algebra named for *George Boole*.

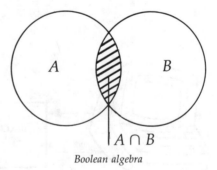

Boolean algebra

Boolean operator A logic operator, each of whose operands and whose result has one of two values.

bootstrapping The process of using a small initialization program (bootstrap) to load another program and start up an inactive computer.

bore The diameter of a hole; for example, the diameter of the hole on a floppy disk or magnetic tape reel.

borrow An arithmetically negative carry. It occurs in direct subtraction by raising the low order digit of the minuend by one unit of the next higher order digit.

bottleneck See *limiting operation*.

bpi An abbreviation for bits per inch or bytes per inch.

bps An abbreviation for bits per second or bytes per second.

branch The selection of one or more possible paths in the flow of control, based on some criterion. See *conditional transfer*, *jump*, and *unconditional transfer*.

branch instruction An instruction to a computer that enables one to instruct the computer to choose between alternative program paths depending upon the conditions determined by the computer during the execution of the program.

branchpoint A place in a program where a branch is selected.

Brattain, Walter Houser (born 1902) A Bell Laboratories scientist who along with William Shockley and John Bardeen invented the transistor. See *transistor*.

breadboard Usually refers to an experimental or rough construction model of a process, device, or construction.

breakpoint A specified point in a program at which the program may be interrupted by manual intervention or by a control routine. Breakpoints are generally used as an aid in testing and debugging programs.

broadband As applied to data communications, used to denote transmission facilities capable of handling fre-

quencies greater than those required for high-grade voice communications.

broadcast In data communications, the dissemination of information to a number of stations simultaneously.

BROM An acronym for Bipolar Read Only Memory. A read only memory with no write function, using bipolar semiconductor devices.

brute-force technique Any mathematical technique that depends on the raw power of a computer to arrive at a nonelegant solution to a mathematical problem. Most computer users try to avoid brute-force techniques unless they have no practical alternative.

BSC An acronym for Binary Synchronous Communication. Procedure used for data transmission.

BTAM An acronym for Basic Telecommunications Access Method. An access method that permits read/write communications with remote devices.

bubble memory A method by which information is stored as magnetized dots (bubbles) which rest on a thin film of semiconductor material. Offers a compact storage capability. *(Illus. p. 22)*

bubble sort A sort achieved by exchanging pairs of keys, which begins with the first pair and exchanges successive pairs until the list is ordered. Also called ripple sort.

bucket A term used to indicate a specific portion of storage.

buffer A temporary storage area that is used to equalize or balance the different operating speeds. For example, a buffer can be used between a slow input device, such as a typewriter, and the main computer, which operates at a very high speed.

buffered computer A computer that provides for simultaneous input/output and process operations.

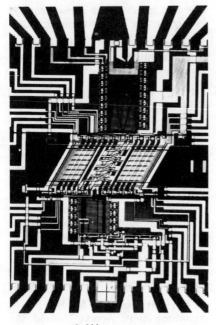

bubble memory

bug A term used to denote a mistake in a computer program or system or a malfunction in a computer hardware component. Hence debugging means removing mistakes and correcting malfunctions. See *malfunction* and *mistake*.

bug

built-in check See *automatic check*.

bulk eraser See *degausser*.

bulk memory See *auxiliary storage*.

bundled The position of a computer manufacturer who includes the entire line of computer products and services in a single price. Contrast with *unbundled*.

burning The process of programming a read-only memory. See *PROM programmer*.

Burroughs, William Seward (1857–1898) Invented the first commercial adding machine on which the fortune of the present Burroughs Corporation is based. See *Burroughs' adding machine*.

William Seward Burroughs

Burroughs' adding machine The first commercially practical adding-listing machine was invented in 1884 by William Burroughs. The keyboard and mechanism remain practically unchanged in some of today's manual machines. See *Burroughs, William Seward*.

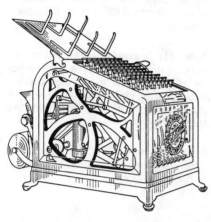

Burroughs' adding machine

burst In computer operations, to separate continuous-form paper into discrete sheets. In data transmission, a sequence of signals counted as one unit.

burst mode A method of reading or writing data that does not permit an interrupt to occur.

bus A channel or path for transferring data and electrical signals. A bus structure would consist of many bus wires that carry many different signals.

Bush, Vannevar (1890–1974) In the late 1920s, Bush was trying to solve equations associated with power failures. To handle such "differential equations," he built, in 1930, the first automatic computer that was general enough to solve a wide variety of problems. He called it a "differential analyzer." This machine, a forerunner of present-day analog computers, weighed 100 tons and used thousands of vacuum tubes.

Vannevar Bush

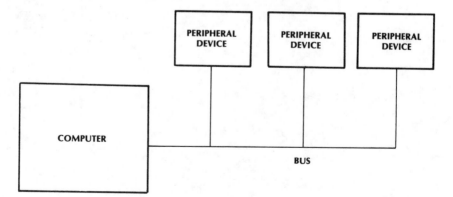

bus

business applications Computer systems involving normal day-to-day accounting procedures such as payroll, accounts receivable, accounts payable, and inventory.

business data processing Data processing for business purposes (e.g., payroll, scheduling, accounting). See *administrative data processing*.

business programming A branch of computer programming in which business problems are coded for computer solution. Business programming usually involves relatively few calculations with a large number of data inputs and outputs. See *business applications*.

bypass A parallel path around one or more elements of a circuit.

bypass capacitor A capacitor used to reduce electrical noise from the power supply.

byte (1) A grouping of adjacent binary digits operated on by the computer as a unit. The most common size byte contains eight binary digits. (2) A group of binary digits used to encode a single character.

bytes per inch (BPI) The number of bytes that can be contained on one inch of magnetic tape.

C

C The full name of a programming language designed for use on microcomputers. The language combines high-level statements with low-level machine control to deliver software that is both easy to use and highly efficient.

cache memory A small, high-speed buffer memory used in modern computer systems to hold temporarily those portions of the contents of main memory which are (believed to be) currently in use.

CAD An acronym for *Computer-Aided Design*.

CAD/CAM An acronym for Computer-Aided Design/Computer-Aided Manufacturing. A term applied to efforts to automate design operations and manufacturing operations.

cage A chassis in which printed circuit cards are mounted.

CAI An acronym for *Computer-Assisted Instruction*.

CAI authors See *authors*.

CAL An acronym for *Computer-Augmented Learning*.

calculating Reconstructing or creating new data by compressing certain numeric facts.

calculating punch A machine designed to perform arithmetic operations with punch cards.

calculator Any mechanical or electronic machine used for performing calculations. Calculators, as distinguished from computers, usually require frequent human intervention. See *calculating punch* and *hand calculator*.

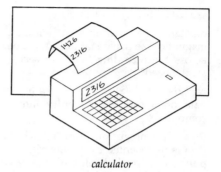

calculator

calculator mode Some interactive computer systems have an operating mode that allows the terminal (or keyboard/display in case of microcomputer systems) to be used as a desk calculator. The user types an expression, and the computer evaluates it and returns the answer immediately.

call (1) To transfer control to a specific closed subroutine. (2) In communications, the action performed by the calling party, or the operations necessary in making a call, or the effective use made of a connection between two stations. Synonymous with cue.

calling sequence A specified set of instructions and data necessary to call a given subroutine.

CAM An acronym for Computer-Aided Manufacturing.

Canadian Information Processing Society An organization formed to bring together Canadians with a common interest in the field of information processing. Abbreviated CIPS.

canned routines Programs prepared by the computer manufacturers or another supplier and provided to a user in a machine-readable form.

25

capacitance In a capacitor or a system of conductors and dielectrics, that property which permits the storage of electrically separated charges when potential differences exist between the conductors.

capacity See *storage capacity*.

capstan The rotating shaft within a magnetic tape drive that pulls the tape across the recording heads at a constant speed.

capture (of data) The recording of data on a form or its entry into a computer.

card A storage medium in which data is represented by means of holes punched in vertical columns in a 18.7 cm by 8.3 cm (7⅜ inches by 3¼ inches) paper card. See *Hollerith card, punched card, ninety-six column card*.

card code The combinations of punched holes that represent characters in a punch card. See *Hollerith code*.

card column One of the vertical lines of punching positions on a punch card.

card deck A set of punch cards.

card face The printed side of a punch card.

card feed A mechanism that moves cards into a machine one at a time.

card deck

card field A fixed number of consecutive card columns assigned to a unit of information.

card frame An enclosure that holds a computer system's circuit boards in place.

card hopper A device that holds cards and makes them available for the feeding mechanism of card handling equipment.

card image A representation in storage of the holes punched in a card.

card punch An output device that accepts information from the computer's memory and punches it into cards. A keyboard device by which an operator can punch cards. Also known as a *keypunch*.

card punching See *keypunching*.

card random access method See *CRAM*.

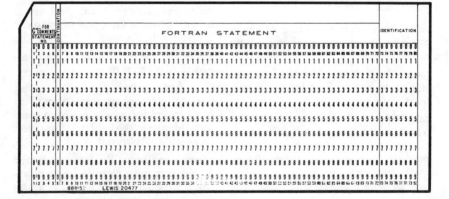

card

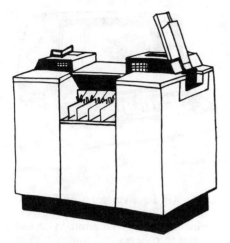

card reader

card reader An input device that reads information punched into cards. The information read is transferred into the computer's memory.

card reproducer A device that reproduces a punch card by punching a similar card. See *reproducing punch*.

card row One of the horizontal lines of punching positions on a punch card.

card sorting Separating a deck of punch cards into stacks in accordance with the holes punched into the individual cards.

card stacker The receptacle into which cards are accumulated after passing through a punch card data processing machine.

card-to-disk converter A device that converts data directly from punch cards to disk storage.

card-to-tape converter A device that converts data directly from punch cards to magnetic or paper tape.

card verification A means of checking the accuracy of keypunching. A second operator verifies the original punching by depressing the keys of a verifier while reading the same source data. The machine compares the key depressed with the hole already punched in the card and, if they are not identical, indicates an error.

caret A symbol used to indicate the location of the radix point of a number. See *radix point*.

123.40

RADIX POINT ↑

caret

carriage A control mechanism for a typewriter or printer that automatically feeds, skips, spaces, or ejects paper forms.

carriage control tape A tape that is punched with the information that is needed to control line feeding on a *line printer*.

carriage return In a character-by-character printing mechanism, the operation that causes the next character to be printed at the left margin. Abbreviated CR.

carrier A continuous frequency capable of being modulated with a signal.

carry A process of bringing forward. The carry digit, or the digit that is to be added to the next higher column, or a special condition that occurs when the sum of two digits in a single column is equal to or greater than the numbering base.

cartridge See *magnetic tape cartridge*.

cascade control An automatic control system in which the control units are linked chain-fashion, each feeding into (as well as regulating) the next stage.

cascade sort An external tape sort that sorts by merging strings from all but one tape onto the remaining tape. Subsequent passes merge fewer tapes until one tape contains all items.

cashless society A conceptual computerized system in which credit transactions would be settled instantaneously by transferring credits from the customer's bank account to the store's account via a point-of-sale terminal.

cassette A small, self-contained volume of magnetic tape used for data storage.

cassette recorder A device designed to use cassettes to record and store digital data and, at a later time, reload this data into the computer's internal storage. Used widely with microcomputers.

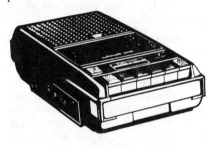

cassette recorder

catalog An ordered compilation of item descriptions and sufficient information to afford access to the items.

catena A connected series. See *concatenate*.

cathode ray tube An electronic tube with a screen upon which information may be displayed. Abbreviated CRT. See *display*, *screen*, and *video terminal*.

CBI See *Charles Babbage Institute*.

CBL An acronym for *Computer-Based Learning*.

CCD An acronym for Charge Coupled Device. A memory device within which stored information circulates, rather than remaining in fixed locations.

cathode ray tube

CCP An acronym for Certificate in Computer Programming. The CCP examinations are given annually at test centers in colleges and universities in the U.S.A., Canada, and several international locations. There are three separate examinations. Each of the three examinations tests a common core of programming knowledge and an area of specialization. The three areas of specialization are Business Programming, Scientific Programming, and Systems Programming. The common core of knowledge emphasizes such areas as data and file organization, techniques of programming, programming languages, interaction with hardware and software, and interaction with people.

CDC An acronym for Call Directing Code. Two or three character code used to route automatically a message or command.

CDP An acronym for Certificate in Data Processing. The CDP examination is given annually at test centers in colleges and universities in the U.S.A., Canada, and several international locations. This broad-based examination consists of five sections and requires one-half day to complete. In addition to experience requirements and an espousal to the Code of Ethics, the CDP candidates must successfully complete all five sections of the examination to receive the certificate.

CE See *customer engineer*.

cell The storage for one unit of information, usually one character, one byte, or one word. A binary cell is a cell of one binary digit capacity. Also called *storage location*.

Celsius Alternate of the *Kelvin*, the base unit of temperature in the SI metric system. Celsius is a basic method for measuring or recording temperature.

centisecond One hundredth of a second.

central information file The main data storage system.

centralized data processing A concept by which a company has all its computing equipment located at the same site, while field-office operations have no effective data processing capability. Contrast with *distributed data processing*.

central processing unit (CPU) The component of a computer system with the circuitry to control the interpretation and execution of instructions. The CPU includes the arithmetic-logic and control sections. Synonymous with *central processor* and *mainframe*.

central processor See *central processing unit*.

Certificate in Computer Programming See *CCP*.

certification Acceptance of software by an authorized agent, usually after the software has been validated by the agent, or after its validity has been demonstrated to the agent.

chad A piece of material removed when forming a hole or notch in punched paper tape.

chadded tape Perforated tape with the chad completely removed.

chain (1) Linking of records by means of pointers in such a way that all like records are connected, the last record pointing to the first. (2) A set of

operations that are to be performed sequentially.

chain field A field in a record that defines the location and storage device of other data items logically related to the original record but not physically attached.

chaining A process of linking a series of records, programs, or operations together.

chaining search A technique that is used for retrieving data from a file by using addresses in the records that link each record to the next in the chain.

chain printer A line printer in which the type slugs are carried by the links of a revolving chain. See *line printer*.

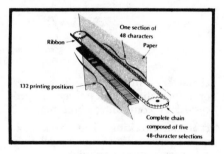

chain printer

channel (1) A path for electrical transmission between two or more points. Also called a path, link, line, facility, or circuit. (2) A transmission path that connects auxiliary devices to a computer.

channel capacity In data communications, a term used to express the maximum number of bits per second that can be accommodated by a channel. This maximum number is determined by the band width modulation scheme and certain types of noise. The channel capacity is most often measured in bauds or bits per second.

chaos Utter confusion and disorder.

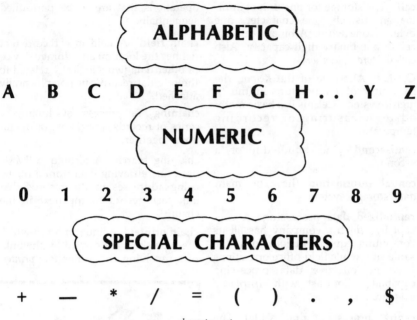

character set

character Any symbol, digit, letter, or punctuation mark stored or processed by computing equipment.

character checking The checking of each character by examining all characters as a group or field.

character code A code designating a unique numerical representation for a set of characters.

character density A measure of the number of characters recorded per unit of length or area.

characteristic That part of a floating point number which represents the size of the exponent.

character printer A printer in which only a single character is composed and determined within the device prior to printing.

character reader See *optical character reader*.

character recognition The identification of phonic, graphic, or other characters by automatic means. See *magnetic ink character recognition* and *optical character recognition*.

character set Comprises the numbers, letters, and symbols associated with a given device or coding system.

character string A string of alphanumeric characters.

character template A device used to shape an electron beam into an alphanumeric character for a CRT display.

charactron A special type of cathode ray tube that displays alphanumeric and special characters on its screen.

charge A quantity of unbalanced electricity in a body.

charged coupled device (CCD) A memory device within which stored information circulates.

Charles Babbage Institute An organization for the study of the "information revolution" from a historical perspective. Intended as a clearing-house for information about research resources related to this history and a repository for archival materials.

chart See *flowchart*.

chassis The metal upon which the wiring, sockets, and other electronic parts of an electronic assembly are mounted.

check bit A binary check digit. See also *parity checking*.

check digits One or more digits carried within a unit item of information that provide information about the other digits in the unit in such a manner that, if an error occurs, the check fails, and an indication of error is given. See *check bit* and *parity checking*.

checkout See *debug*.

checkpoint A specified point at which a program can be interrupted either manually or by a control routine. Used primarily as an aid in debugging programs.

check problem A testing problem designed to determine whether the computer or a computer program is operating correctly. See *bug, debug,* and *test data*.

check sum A summation of digits or bits used primarily for checking purposes and summed according to an arbitrary set of rules.

chip A common term for an integrated circuit etched on a tiny piece of silicon or germanium.

churning See *thrashing*.

CICS An acronym for Customer Information Control System. A widely used teleprocessing monitor.

CIM An acronym for Computer Input Microfilm. A technology that involves using an input device to read the contents of microfilm directly into the computer.

CIPS An acronym for the Canadian Information Processing Society. An organization formed to bring together Canadians with a common interest in the field of information processing.

circuit A pathway designed for the controlled flow of electrons. A system of conductors and related electrical elements through which electrical currents flow. A communication link between two or more points.

circuit board A special board on which specific circuits have been etched or "printed."

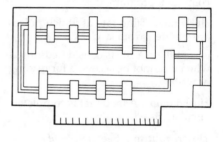

circuit board

circuitry A complex of circuits describing interconnection within or between systems.

circular list A linked list in which the last element points to the first one. Also called a *ring*.

circular shift A shifting operation where bits or characters shifted off one end of a register enter the register on the opposite end. Also called *end-around shift*.

CIU See *computer interface unit*.

class A group having the same or similar characteristics.

classify To arrange into classes of information according to a system or method.

clearing Replacing the information in a register, storage location, or storage unit with zeros or blanks.

CLIP An acronym for Coded Language Information Processing. A scheme used by radiologists for entering their X-ray reports into a computer.

clipping The process of removing portions of an image which are outside the boundaries of the display screen.

clock (1) A timing device that generates the basic periodic signal used to control the timing of all operations in a synchronous computer. (2) A device that records the progress of real time, or some approximation of it, and whose contents are available to a computer program.

clock rate Time rate at which pulses are emitted from a clock.

closed file A file is considered closed when it cannot be accessed for reading or writing.

closed loop A loop that is completely circular. See *loop*.

closed routine See *closed subroutine*.

closed shop The operation of the data processing center by professional operators. Programs and data are carried by messengers or transmitted over telephone lines, avoiding the necessity of users entering the computer room. This enables a very much more efficient use of the computer and is the opposite of the "open shop" in which each user puts her or his own program in the machine and fiddles with the switches on the console. Contrast with *open shop*.

closed subroutine A subroutine that can be stored at one place and can be linked to one or more calling routines. Contrast with *open subroutine*.

clustering Refers to the process of grouping things with similar characteristics.

CMI An acronym for *Computer-Managed Instruction*.

CML An acronym for *Current Mode Logic*. See *ECL*.

CMOS An acronym for Complementary MOS. A method of making MOS (metallic oxide semiconductor) chips that uses almost no power and works faster than MOS. CMOS is not very good for LSI (large scale integration) but is used in electronic watches and clocks where power has to come from a battery.

coaxial cable A specific cable consisting of one conductor, usually a small copper wire within, that is insulated from another conductor of larger diameter, usually copper braid.

COBOL An acronym for COmmon Business Oriented Language, a higher-level language developed for business data processing applications. Every COBOL source program has four divisions, whose names and functions are as follows: (1) Identification Division, which identifies the source program and the output of a compilation; (2) Environment Division, which specifies those aspects of a data processing problem that are dependent upon the physical characteristics of a particular computer; (3) Data Division, which describes the data that the object program is to accept as input, manipulate, create, or produce as output; and (4) Procedure Division, which specifies the procedures to be performed by the object program by means of English-like statements.

CODASYL An acronym for COnference of DAta SYstem Language. The conference that developed the COBOL programming language.

code (1) A set of rules outlining the way in which data may be represented. (2) Rules used to convert data from one representation to another. (3) To write a program or routine (i.e., a programmer generates code). Same as *encode*.

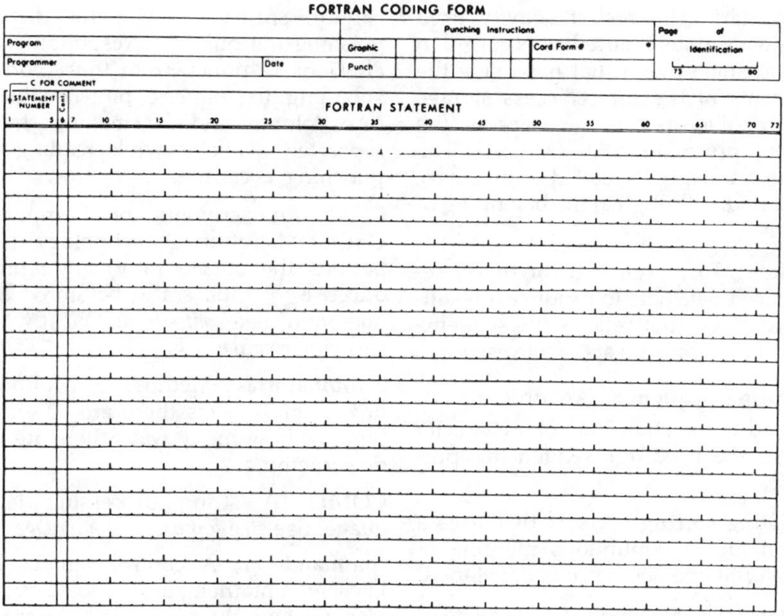
FORTRAN CODING FORM
Punching Instructions
Page of
Program
Graphic
Card Form #
Identification
Programmer
Date
Punch
73 80
C FOR COMMENT
STATEMENT NUMBER
Cont.
FORTRAN STATEMENT
1 5 6 7 10 15 20 25 30 35 40 45 50 55 60 65 70 72

coding form

code conversion A process for changing the bit groupings for characters in one code into the corresponding character bit groupings for a second code.

coded decimal number A number consisting of successive characters or a group of characters that usually represents a specific figure in an associated decimal number.

code level The number of bits used to represent a given character.

coder A person whose primary duty is to write (but not design) computer programs.

code set The complete set of representations defined by a code; for example, all of the two-letter post office identifications for the 50 states.

coding (1) The writing of a list of instructions that will cause a computer to perform specified operations. (2) An ordered list or lists of the successive instructions that will cause a computer to perform a particular process.

coding form A form on which the instructions for programming a computer are written. Also called a *coding sheet*.

coding sheet See *coding form*.

coercion In programming language expressions, an automatic conversion from one data type to another.

COGO An acronym for COordinate GeOmetry. A problem-oriented programming language used to solve geometric problems. Used primarily by civil engineers.

COLOSSUS A special purpose, electronic digital computer that was built in Great Britain. First operational in 1943, it was used for deciphering German code during World War II.

cold start The restart activity used when a serious failure has occurred in a real-time system that has made the contents of the direct access storage inaccessible so that no trace of the recent processing can be used. The system must be reloaded and activity restarted as though at the beginning of a day.

collate To merge two (or more) sequenced data sets to produce a resulting data set that reflects the sequencing of the original sets. Same as *merge*.

collating sequence An ordering assigned to the characters of a character set to be used for sequencing purposes.

collating sorting A sort that uses a technique of continuous merging of data until one sequence is developed.

collator A machine used to collate or merge sets of cards or other documents into a sequence.

collection See *data collection*.

collector On a transistor, an electrode through which a primary flow of carriers leaves the interelectrode region.

collision What happens when keys collide at the same address.

column (1) The vertical members of one line of an array. (2) One of the vertical lines of punching positions on a punched card. (3) A position of information in a computer word. Contrast with *row*.

COLUMN

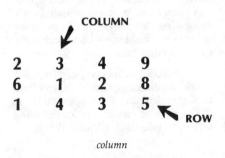

column

column split A device for distinguishing the pulses corresponding to an 11 or 12 punch from those corresponding to numeric punches in a card column and for making them separately available while reading or punching a card.

COM An acronym for Computer Output Microfilm. A technology that permits the output information produced by computers to be stored on microfilm. See *computer output (COM) microfilm recorder*.

combinatorics Methods of counting how many objects there are of some type, or how many ways there are to do something.

COMIT A string processing language. See *string processing languages*.

command (1) A control signal. (2) Loosely, a mathematical or logic operator. (3) Loosely, a computer instruction. See *operation code*.

command-chained memory A technique used in dynamic storage allocation.

command language A source language consisting primarily of commands capable of invoking a function. See *job control language*.

command processing The reading, analyzing, and performing of computer instructions.

comment cards Verbal messages inserted into a computer program that do not trigger any computer processing steps but are helpful notes for future users who may later attempt to understand or alter the program.

common carrier A government-regulated private company that provides telephone, telegraph, and other telecommunication equipment for public use.

common language A computer programming language that is sensible to two or more computers with different machine languages; for example, BASIC, Pascal, or FORTRAN.

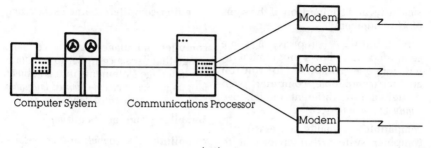

Computer System   Communications Processor

communications processor

communication (1) The flow of information from one point (the source) to another (the receiver). (2) The act of transmitting or making known. See *data communications*.

communication channel The medium of communication in an electronic telecommunication system. The path through which electrical transmission may take place. Also called communication line and communication link.

communication link See *communication channel*.

communication satellite An earth-orbiting device capable of relaying communication signals over long distances.

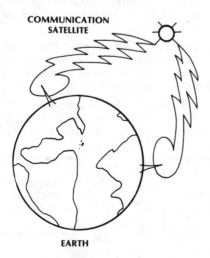

COMMUNICATION SATELLITE

EARTH

communication satellite

communications processor A computer that provides a path for data transfer between the computer system and the data communications network.

Communications Satellite Corporation A privately owned U.S. communications carrier company operating under a mandate from the Congress of the United States. It is the U.S. representative in the INTELSAT Organization and provides technical and operational services for the global communications system. Traffic on the system is coordinated through an operations center located in Washington, D.C.

compaction Packing of data structure to make room in storage.

comparative sort A sort by comparison of two or more keys.

comparator A device for checking the accuracy of transcribed data by comparing it with a second transcription, noting any variation between the two.

compare To examine the representation of a quantity to determine its relationship to zero or to examine two quantities usually for the purposes of determining identity or relative magnitude.

comparison The act of comparing. The common forms are comparison of two numbers for identity, comparison of two numbers for relative magnitude, comparison of two characters for

35

similarity, and comparison of the signs of two numbers.

compatibility A property of some computers that allows programs written for one computer to run on another (compatible) computer, even though it is a different model. See *family of computers*.

compatible A quality possessed by a computer system that enables it to handle both data and programs devised for some other type of computer system.

compilation time The time during which a source language is translated (compiled) into an object program (machine language). Contrast with *run time*.

compile To prepare a machine language program (or a program expressed in symbolic coding) from a program written in another higher-level programming language such as FORTRAN, COBOL, or Pascal.

compile-and-go An operating technique in which the loading and execution phases of a program compilation are performed in one continuous run. This technique is especially useful when a program must be compiled for a one-time application.

compiler A computer program that produces a machine language program from a source program that is usually written in a high-level language by a computer user. The compiler is capable of replacing single source program statements with a series of machine language instructions or with a subroutine.

compiler-compiler Same as *metacompiler*.

compiler language A source language that uses a compiler to translate the language statements into an object language. See *problem-oriented language* and *procedure-oriented language*.

compiler program See *compiler*.

compiling See *compile* and *cross-compiling/assembling*.

complement A number used to represent the negative of a given number. A complement is obtained by subtracting each digit of the number from the number representing its base and, in the case of two's and ten's complement, adding unity to the last significant digit.

Complementary MOS A method of making metallic oxide semiconductor (MOS) chips that uses almost no power and works faster than MOS. Abbreviated *CMOS*.

completeness check Establish that none of the fields are missing and that the entire record has been checked.

component A basic part. An *element*.

composite card A multipurpose data card, or a card that contains data needed in the processing of various applications.

compute-bound A program or computer system which is restricted or limited by the speed of the central processing unit.

computer A device capable of solving problems or manipulating data by accepting data, performing prescribed

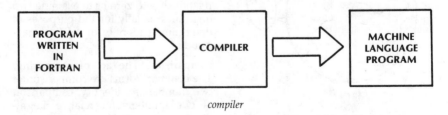

compiler

operations (mathematical or logical) on the data, and supplying the results of these operations. See *analog computer*, *computer kit*, *digital computer*, *home computer*, *microcomputer*, *microprocessor*, *minicomputer*, *personal computer*, and *small business computer*.

computer

computer-aided design A process involving direct, real-time communication between a designer and a computer, generally by the use of a cathode ray tube (CRT) display and a light pen.

computer-aided instruction See *computer-augmented learning*.

computer applications Computers are used worldwide to perform thousands of jobs and tasks. The United States is the largest user of computers; however, many other parts of the world are using computers at an ever increasing rate.

computer architecture The area of computer study that deals with the physical structure (hardware) of computer systems and the relationships among these various hardware components.

computer art Art form produced by computing equipment (usually plotters, printers, or visual display devices).

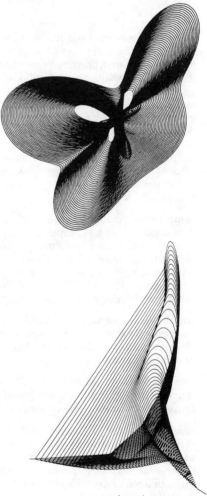

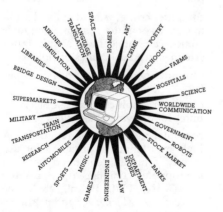

computer applications

computer art

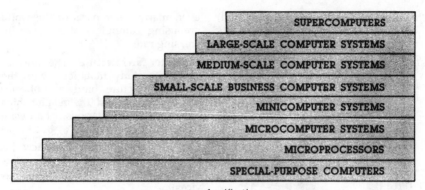

computer classifications

computer-assisted instruction (CAI)
The use of the computer to augment
individual instruction by providing
the student with programmed sequences of instruction under computer control. The manner of sequencing and progressing through the materials permits students to progress at
their own rate. CAI is responsive to
the individual needs of the individual
student. See *author language, authors,
courseware, PILOT, PLANIT, PLATO,*
and *TICCIT.*

computer-augmented learning (CAL)
A method of using a computer system
to augment, or supplement, a more
conventional instructional system. A
typical example would be using simulation programs to aid in problem
solving in a course of instruction.

computer awareness Generally, an
understanding of what a computer is,
how it works, and the role and impact
of computers in society.

computer-based learning (CBL) A
term used to embrace all the present
forms of educational computing.

computer center A facility that provides computer services to a variety of
users through the operation of computer and auxiliary hardware, and
through ancillary services provided by
its staff.

computer circuits Circuits used in
digital computers, such as gating circuits, storage circuits, triggering circuits, inverting circuits, power amplifying circuits, and others.

computer classifications Computers
fall into two major classifications: digital and analog. A third classification,
called hybrid, combines both digital and
analog computers. Digital computers
vary in size from huge supercom-
puters to minute microprocessors.

computer code A machine code for a
specific computer.

computer control console See *console.*

computer control panel See *control
panel.*

computer crime An intentional act to
misuse a computer system. Computer
crimes can range from simple fraud
schemes to actual crimes of violence.

computer family See *family of computers.*

computer graphics The use of a computer for drawing lines. *(Illus. p. 39)*

computer-independent language A
high-level language designed for use
in any computer equipped with an
appropriate compiler (i.e., BASIC,
FORTRAN, PL/I, Pascal, etc.). See
problem-oriented language and *procedure-
oriented language.*

computer graphics

computerized game playing

computer input microfilm (CIM) A technology that involves using an input device to read the contents of microfilm directly into the computer.

computer instruction See *instruction*.

computer interface unit A device used to connect peripheral devices to a computer. Abbreviated CIU.

computerized data base A set of computerized files on which an organization's activities are based and upon which high reliance is placed for availability and accuracy.

computerized game playing Computers (microcomputers, minicomputers, and larger machines) that have been programmed to play a wide variety of games such as tic-tac-toe, PAC-MAN, breakout, star raiders, space war, blackjack, hangman, backgammon, chess, and checkers, among others.

computerized numerical control See *numerical control*.

computer kit A microcomputer in kit form. The user who purchases a computer kit is expected to "build" the microcomputer as he/she would "build" a model airplane or a stereo sound system. Computer kits are popular with hobby computer users and are used in schools to help teach

computer design. See *home computer*, *microcomputer*, and *personal computer*.

computer kit

computer language See *programming language*.

computer literacy The nontechnical study of the computer and its effect upon society. This is an important area in computer education as it provides the student with some of the knowledge, tools, and understanding necessary to live in a computer-oriented society.

computer-managed instruction (CMI) An application of computers to instruction in which the computer is used as a record keeper, manager, and/or prescriber of instruction.

39

computer music Music employing computer equipment at any stage of its composition or realization as sound. See *electronic music* and *musical language*.

computer network A complex consisting of two or more interconnected computer systems, terminals, and communication facilities.

computer operator A person skilled in the operation of the computer and associated peripheral devices. A computer operator also performs other operational functions that are required in a computer center such as loading a disk drive, placing cards in the card reader, removing printouts from the line printer rack, and so forth.

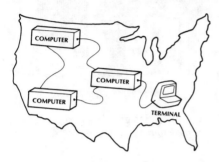

computer network

computer operator

computer-on-a-chip A complete microcomputer on an integrated circuit chip.

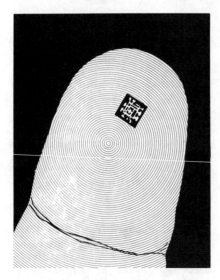

computer-on-a-chip

computer output microfilm (COM) A technology that involves recording computer output on microfilm.

computer output microfilm (COM) recorder A device that records computer output on photosensitive film in microscopic form. *(Illus. p. 41)*

computer process control system A system that uses a computer connected to sensors that monitor a process in order to control that process for handling matter or energy, and then uses its modification in order to produce a product at a profit. *(Illus. p. 41)*

computer processing cycle The steps involved in using a computer to solve a problem: write the program in a programming language such as BASIC or FORTRAN; input the program into the computer; compile and execute the program. *(Illus. p. 42)*

computer program The series of statements and instructions to cause a computer to perform a particular operation or task. See *program*. *(Illus. p. 42)*

On-line

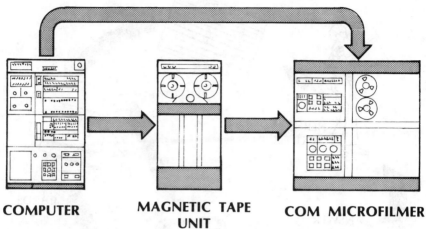

COMPUTER　　**MAGNETIC TAPE UNIT**　　**COM MICROFILMER**

computer output microfilm recorder

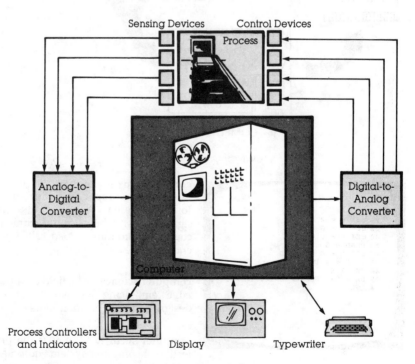

Sensing Devices　　Control Devices

Process

Analog-to-Digital Converter

Digital-to-Analog Converter

Computer

Process Controllers and Indicators　　Display　　Typewriter

computer process control system

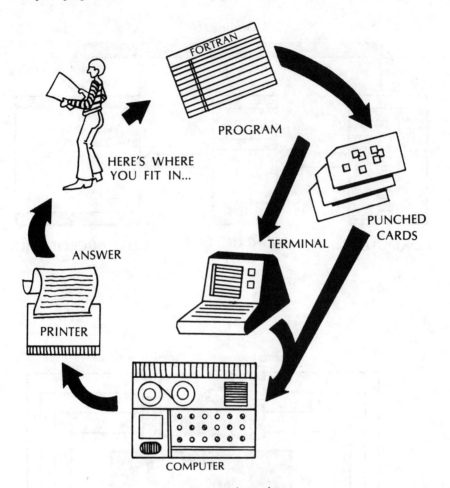

PROGRAM

HERE'S WHERE
YOU FIT IN...

PUNCHED
CARDS

ANSWER

TERMINAL

PRINTER

COMPUTER

computer processing cycle

```
20 LET C = 0
30 LET I = 0
40 LET I = I + 1
50 READ A, B
60 LET C = C + A * B
70 IF I < 4 THEN 40
80 PRINT C
90 DATA 31, 106, 14, 33, 6, 111, 19, 17
99 END
```

computer program

computer programmer A person skilled in the preparation of programs for a computer. A programmer designs, codes, debugs, and documents computer programs. Also called *programmer*. See *coder*. (Illus. p. 43)

computer science The field of knowledge embracing all aspects of the design and use of computers.

computer security Involves the protection of computer system equipment and data from unauthorized access.

computer programmer

computer store A new kind of store where you can select, from the shelf, a full computer system or just a few accessories. These stores typically sell software, books, supplies, and periodicals. In a complete computer store, you can examine and operate several types of microcomputer systems.

computer store

computer system The physical equipment and instructions, that is, hardware and software, used as a unit to process data. It includes the central processing unit (CPU), its operating system, and the peripheral equipment and programs under its control. *(Illus. p. 44)*

computer users group A group whose members share the knowledge they have gained and the programs they have developed on a computer or class of computers of a certain manufacturer. Most groups hold meetings and distribute newsletters to exchange information, trade equipment, and share computer programs.

computer utility A service that provides computational ability. A time-shared computer system. Programs, as well as data, may be made available to the user. The user also may have her or his own programs immediately available in the central processing unit, or have them on call at the computer utility, or load them by transmitting them to the computer prior to using them. Certain data and programs are shared by all users of the service; other data and programs, because of proprietary nature, have restricted access. Computer utilities are generally accessed by means of data communication subsystems. See *service bureau*.

computer utility

computer word A fixed sequence of bits, bytes, or characters treated as a unit and capable of being stored in one storage location. See *word*.

computing The act of using computing equipment for processing data; in other words, the art or science of getting the computer to do what you want.

computing system See *computer system*.

43

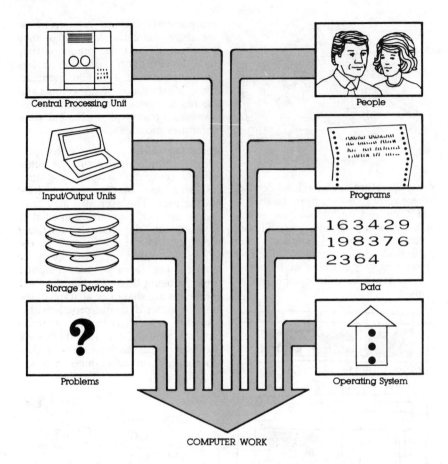

Central Processing Unit

People

Input/Output Units

Programs

Storage Devices

163429
198376
2364

Data

?

Problems

Operating System

COMPUTER WORK

computer system

COMSAT See *Communications Satellite Corporation.*

concatenate To link together or join two or more character strings into a single character string.

concatenated data set A collection of logically connected data sets.

concentrator A device which allows a number of slow-speed devices to utilize a single high-speed communication line. Also called a *multiplexer.*

concordance An alphabetic list of words and phrases appearing in a document, with an indication of the place those words and phrases appear.

concurrent processing The performance of two or more data processing tasks within a specified interval. Contrast with *simultaneous processing.*

concurrent programming The development of programs that specify the parallel execution of several tasks.

condition (1) A given set of circumstances. (2) A definite state of being.

conditional branching See *conditional transfer.*

conditional statement A statement that is executed only when a certain condition within the routine has been met.

conditional transfer An instruction that may cause a departure from the sequence of instructions being followed depending upon the result of an operation, the contents of a register, or the settings of an indicator. Contrast with *unconditional transfer*.

conditioning The improvement of the data transmission properties of a voiceband transmission line by correction of the amplitude phase characteristics of the line amplifiers.

configuration An assembly of machines that are interconnected and are programmed to operate as a system.

configuration management The task of accounting for, controlling, and reporting the planned and actual design of a product throughout its production and operational life.

connected graph Moving from a single node in a graph to any other node by traveling via a sequence of edges.

connection matrix See *incidence matrix*.

connector (1) A coupling device that provides an electrical and/or mechanical junction between two cables, or between a cable and a chassis or enclosure. (2) A device that provides rapid connection and disconnection of electrical cable and wire terminations. See *female connector* and *male connector*.

connector symbol A flowcharting symbol used to represent a junction in a line of flow; connects broken paths in the line of flow and connects several pages of the same flowchart. A small circle containing some identifier is used to represent this symbol.

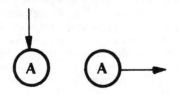

connector symbol

connect time In time-sharing, the length of time you are "on" the computer, that is, the duration of the telephone connection. Connect time is usually measured by the duration between "sign-on" and "sign-off." See *CPU time*.

consecutive Pertaining to the occurrence of two sequential events without the intervention of any other such event.

consistency check A check that ensures that specific input data fall within a predetermined set of criteria.

console The part of a computer system that enables human operators to communicate with the system. See *front panel*.

console operator Same as *computer operator*.

console printer See *console typewriter*.

console typewriter A typewriter on-line to the computer that allows communication between the machine and the *computer operator*.

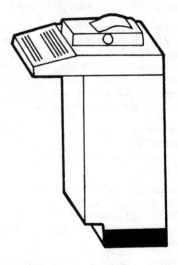

console typewriter

constant A value that does not change during the execution of the program.

constraint A condition that limits the solutions to a problem.

consultant An expert in the use of computers in specific applications environments, e.g., business data processing consultant, educational consultant, military systems consultant, health care systems consultant. Consultants often help to analyze and solve a specific problem.

content-addressable memory Same as *associative storage*.

contention A condition on a multipoint communication channel when two or more locations try to transmit at the same time.

contents directory A series of queues that indicate the routines in a given region of internal storage.

contiguous Adjacent or adjoining.

contiguous data structure See *sequential data structure*.

continuation card A punched card that contains information that was started on a previous punched card.

continuous forms Paper that is used on printers and accounting machines. Can represent checks or any type of preprinted forms as long as the small holes are on the outer edges of the form. Holes are used by equipment to advance the paper line-by-line.

continuous processing The input of transactions into a system in the order they occur and as soon after they occur as possible.

contour analysis A technique in optical character recognition that uses a spot of light to search for the outline of the character by moving around its exterior edges.

control The function of performing required operations when certain specific conditions occur or when interpreting and acting upon instructions. See *control section* and *control unit*.

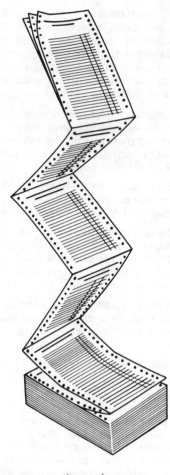

continuous forms

control block A storage area through which a particular type of information required for control of the operating system is communicated among its parts.

control cards Punched cards that contain input data required for a specific application of a general routine such as a generator or operating system; for example, one of a series of cards that directs an operating system to load and initiate the execution of a particular program. See *job control language*.

control character A character inserted into a data stream with the intent of signaling the receiving station to perform some function.

control circuits The electrical circuits within a computer that interpret the program instructions and cause the appropriate operations to be performed.

control clerk A person having responsibility for performing duties associated with the control over data processing operations.

control console That part of a computer system used for communication between the console operator or service engineer and the computer.

control data One or more items of data used as a control to identify, select, execute, or modify another routine, record, file, operation, or data value.

controlled variable One that takes on a specific set of values in an iterative structure in a programming language.

controller A device required by the computer in order to operate a peripheral component.

control panel (1) The part of a computer control console that contains manual controls. (2) A hand-wired plugboard used to control the operations of unit record devices. See *console* and *plugboard*.

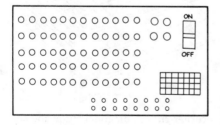

control panel

control program An operating system program responsible for the over-

all management of the computer and its resources. See *operating system*.

control punch A specific code that is punched in a card to cause the machine to perform a specific operation.

control section The part of the central processing unit responsible for directing the operation of the computer in accordance with the instructions in the program. Same as *control unit*.

control sequence The normal order of selection of instructions by a digital computer wherein it follows one instruction order at a time.

control statement An operation that terminates the sequential execution of instructions by transferring control to a statement elsewhere in the program.

control station The network station that supervises control procedures such as polling, selecting, and recovery. It is also responsible for establishing order on the line in the event of contention or any other abnormal situation.

control structures The facilities of a programming language that specify a departure from the normal sequential execution of statements.

control unit The portion of the central processing unit that directs the step-by-step operation of the entire computing system. Same as *control section*.

convention Standard and accepted procedures in computer program development and the abbreviations, symbols, and their meanings as developed for particular programs and systems.

conversational Pertaining to a program or a system that carries on a dialog with a terminal user, alternately accepting input and then responding to the input quickly enough for the user to maintain his or her train of thought. See *interactive processing*.

conversational language A programming language that uses a near-English character set that facilitates communication between the user and the computer. BASIC is an example of a conversational language.

conversational mode A mode of operation that implies a "dialog" between a computer and its user, in which the computer program examines the input supplied by the user and formulates questions or comments that are directed back and to the user. See *interactive processing* and *logging-in*.

conversational remote job entry See *CRJE*.

conversational system See *interactive system*.

conversion (1) The process of changing information from one form of representation to another, such as from the language of one type of computer to that of another or from punch cards to magnetic disk. (2) The process of changing from one data processing method to another or from one type of equipment to another. (3) The process of changing a number written in one base to changing it to the base of another numeral system.

conversion table A table comparing numerals in two different numeral systems.

convert (1) Changing data from radix to radix. Moving data from one type of record to another (i.e., floppy disk to magnetic tape).

converter (1) A device that converts information recorded on one medium to another medium (e.g., a unit that accepts information from punched cards and records the information on magnetic disks). (2) A device that converts information in one form into information in another form (e.g., analog to digital).

coordinate indexing (1) A system of indexing individual documents by descriptors of equal rank so that a library can be searched for a combination of one or more descriptors. (2) An indexing technique whereby the interrelations of terms are shown by coupling individual words.

copy To reproduce data in a new location or other destination, leaving the source data unchanged, although the physical form of the result may differ from that of the source. For example, a copy of a deck of cards onto a magnetic disk. Contrast with *duplicate*.

copy-protection A method used to prevent the copying of programs from one disk to another.

core storage A form of storage device utilizing magnetic cores usually strung through wires in the form of an array. See *magnetic core storage*.

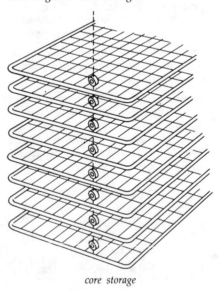

core storage

corner cut A diagonal cut at the corner of a punched card. It is used as a means of identifying groups of related cards. See *punched card. (Illus. p. 49)*

coroutine Instructions used to transfer a set of inputs to a set of outputs.

CORNER CUT

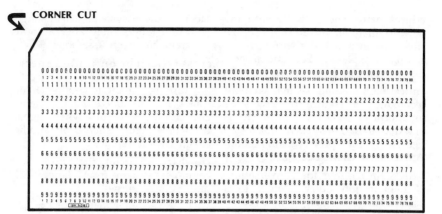

corner cut

corrective maintenance The activity of detecting, isolating, and correcting failures after occurrence. Contrast with *preventive maintenance*.

count The successive increase or decrease of a cumulative total of the number of times an event occurs.

counter A device (e.g., a register or computer storage location) used to represent the number of occurrences of an event.

coupling An interaction between systems or between properties of a system.

courseware The name given to computer programs written especially for educational applications.

cpi An abbreviation for characters per inch.

CPM An acronym for *Critical Path Method*.

CP/M An acronym for Control Program for Microprocessors. The industry standard in operating systems for small computers. A collection of programs which resides on a diskette, CP/M provides specific commands for transferring information among the devices connected to the computer system, executing programs, and manipulating files conveniently. See *MP/M*.

cps An abbreviation for characters per second.

CPS An acronym for Conversation Programming System. Refers generally to a computer system in which input and output are handled by a remote terminal; the system employs time-sharing so that the user obtains what appears to be an immediate response. Used more specifically as CPS-PL/I to mean an IBM-devised subset of the PL/I programming language used with remote terminals.

CPU An acronym for *Central Processing Unit*.

CPU time The amount of time devoted by the central processing unit to the execution of program instructions. See *connect time*.

CR An acronym for *Carriage Return*.

CRAM An acronym for Card Random Access Method. An auxiliary storage device that uses removable magnetic cards, each of which is capable of storing data in magnetic form. The storage unit is manufactured by NCR Corporation.

crash A system shutdown caused by a hardware malfunction or a software mistake.

crime, computer See *computer crime*.

critical path The path through the network that defines the shortest possible time in which the entire project can be completed. See *critical path method* and *PERT*.

critical path method A management technique for control of large-scale long-term projects involving analysis and determination of each critical step necessary for project completion. Abbreviated CPM. See *PERT*.

CRJE An acronym for Conversational Remote Job Entry. Refers to a conversational language employed by a terminal user in submitting jobs to a central site and controlling their processing from a remote terminal station.

CROM An acronym for Control ROM, an integral part of most central processing unit (CPU) chips. The CROM is the storage for the micro-instructions that the CPU assembles into a sequence to form complex "macroinstructions" (e.g., Multiply or Branch-On-Negative Accumulator) that the computer user normally uses.

cross-assembler Refers to an assembler run on one computer for the purpose of translating instructions for a different computer.

cross-check To check the computing by two different methods.

cross-compiler A compiler that runs on a machine other than the one for which it is designed to compile code.

cross-compiling/assembling A technique whereby one uses a minicomputer, large-scale computer, or time-sharing service to write and debug programs for subsequent use on microcomputers.

cross-footing check A process of cross-adding or subtracting, then zeroing-out the results.

cross-reference dictionary A printed listing that identifies all references of an assembled program to a specific

label. In many systems, this listing is provided immediately after a source program has been assembled.

cross talk The unwanted energy transferred from one circuit, called the "disturbing" circuit, to another circuit, called the "disturbed" circuit. Generally cross talk occurs when signals from one circuit emerge on another circuit as interference.

crowbar A circuit that protects a computer system from dangerously high voltage surges.

CRT An acronym for *Cathode Ray Tube*. See *display unit*.

CRT

cryogenics The study and use of devices that utilize the properties assumed by materials at temperatures near absolute zero.

cryptanalysis The operation of converting encrypted messages to the corresponding plaintext without initial knowledge of the key employed in the encryption. See *plaintext*.

cryptographic techniques Methods of concealing data by representing each character or group of characters by others.

cryptography The science of transforming messages with the purpose of making the message unintelligible to all but the intended receiver.

CT A medical application in which a computer records X rays passing through the body in changing directions and generates an image of the body's structures.

CUBE An acronym derived from Co-operating Users of Burroughs Equipment. The official organization of the users of Burroughs computers.

cue Same as *call*.

current awareness system In this process, a user is notified periodically by a central file or library when selected items of information have been acquired.

current location counter A counter kept by an assembler to determine the address that has been assigned to either an instruction or constant being assembled.

current loop A type of serial communication where the presence or absence of an electrical signal indicates the state of the bit being transmitted.

current mode logic A logic circuit that employs the characteristics of a differential amplifier circuit in its design. Abbreviated CML.

cursor (1) A moving, sliding, or blinking symbol on a video terminal that indicates where the next character will appear. (2) A position indicator used in a display on a video terminal

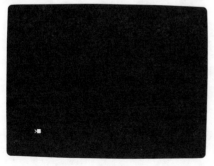

cursor

to indicate a character to be corrected or a position in which data is to be entered.

customer engineer An individual responsible for field maintenance of computer hardware and software. Abbreviated CE.

cybernetics The branch of learning that seeks to integrate the theories and studies of communication and control in machines and living organisms. See *artificial intelligence* and *Wiener, Norbert*.

cycle As related to computer storage, a periodic sequence of events occurring when information is transferred to or from the storage device of a computer. It is the time it takes to reference an address, remove the data, and be ready to select it again.

cycle stealing A technique that allows a peripheral device to temporarily disable computer control of the I/O bus, thus allowing the device to access the computer's internal memory.

cycle time (1) The minimum time interval between the starts of successive accesses to a storage location. (2) The time required to change the information in a set of registers.

cyclic code Same as *gray code*.

cyclic redundancy check An error-detection scheme (usually implemented in hardware) that is often used in disk devices. When information is stored, a cyclic redundancy check (CRC) value is computed and stored. Whenever it is reread, the CRC value is computed once again. If the two values are equal, the information is assumed to be error-free.

cyclic shift A shift in which the digits dropped off at one end of a word are returned at the other in a circular fashion; for example, if a register holds eight digits, 23456789, the result of the cyclic shift two columns to the left would be to change

51

the contents of the register to 45678923.

cylinder As related to magnetic disks, a vertical column of tracks on a magnetic disk file unit.

cypher A form of cryptography in which the plaintext is made unintelligible to anyone who intercepts it by a transformation of the information itself, based on some key.

D-A converter See *digital-to-analog converter*.

daisy chain Refers to a specific method of propagating signals along a bus. This method permits the assignment of device priorities based on the electrical position of the device along the bus.

daisy wheel printer A printer that uses a plastic disk which has printed characters along its edge. The disk rotates until the required character is brought before a hammer that strikes it against a ribbon.

data A formalized representation of facts or concepts suitable for communication, interpretation, or processing by people or by automatic means. The raw material of information.

data acquisition The retrieval of data from remote sites initiated by a central computer system.

data administrator See *data base administrator*.

data aggregate A collection of data items within a record, which is given a name and referred to as a whole.

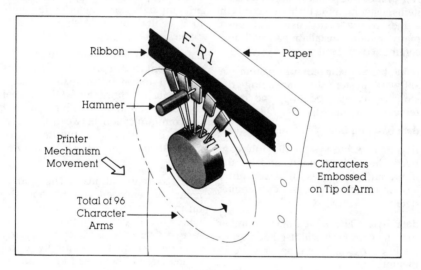

daisy wheel printer

DASD Acronym for *Direct Access Storage Device*. A device such as a magnetic disk storage unit or a magnetic drum storage unit.

DAT An acronym for *Dynamic Address Translation*.

data bank See *data base*.

data base The collection of all data used and produced by a computer program. In large systems, data base analysis is usually concerned with large quantities of data stored in disk and tape files. Smaller microcomputer systems are more frequently concerned with data base allocations of available memory locations between the program and data storage areas. Also called data bank. See *on-line data base*.

data base administrator A person who is responsible for the creation of the information system data base and, once it is established, for maintaining its security and developing procedures for its recovery from disaster.

data base environment That environment resulting from the integration of users, data, and systems by implementing the data base.

data base management A systematic approach to storing, updating, and retrieval of information stored as data items, usually in the form of records in a file, where many users, or even many remote installations, will use common data banks.

data base management system A software system for managing the storage, access, updating, and maintenance of a data base. See *DBMS*.

data base, on line See *on-line data base*.

data bus A bus system that interconnects the CPU, storage, and all the input/output devices of a computer system for the purpose of exchanging data.

data byte The 8-bit binary number that the computer will use in an arithmetic or logical operation or store in memory.

data capturing Gathering or collecting information for computer handling, the first step in job processing. Also called *data collection*.

data card A punched card that contains one or more data items.

data catalog An organized listing by full name of all data elements used by an organization.

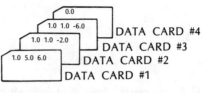

data card

data cell A magnetic storage device developed by the IBM Corporation. A direct access device that handles data recorded on magnetic strips arranged in cells.

data center A computer equipped location. The center processes data and converts the data into a desired form (e.g., reports).

data collection (1) The gathering of source data to be entered into a data processing system. (2) The act of bringing data from one or more points to a central point. Also called *data capturing*.

data communication equipment The equipment that provides the functions required to establish, maintain, and terminate a connection, the signal conversion, and the coding required for communication between data terminal devices and computers. See *input/output channel, MODEM,* and *RS-232*.

data communications The movement of encoded information by means of electrical transmission systems. Much data communication is carried over ordinary telephone lines, but often it requires specifically conditioned leased lines. See *telecommunications* and *teleprocessing. (Illus. p. 55)*

data compression A technique that saves computer storage space by eliminating empty fields, gap redundancies, or unnecessary data to reduce the size of the length of records.

data concentration Collection of data at an intermediate point from several low- and medium-speed lines for retransmission across high-speed lines.

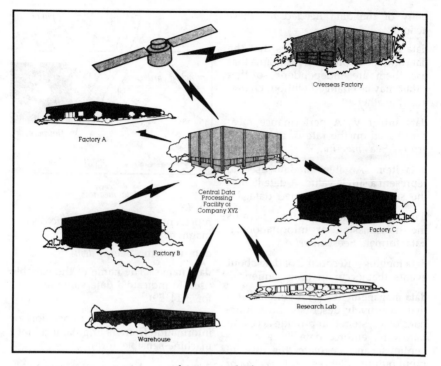

data communications

data conversion The process of changing the form of data representation as, for example, punched card to magnetic disks.

data definition language Same as *data description language*.

data description language A language that specifies the manner in which data is to be stored and managed in a data base environment by a data base management system.

data dictionary An ordered collection of data element descriptions containing specific identification attributes. It describes what the data are.

data directory An ordered collection of data element names and/or identifiers and their attributes that provides location of the elements. It describes where the data are located.

data directory/dictionary An ordered collection of data elements that combines the features of a data catalog, data dictionary, and data directory. It describes and locates each data element.

data division One of the four main components of a COBOL program.

data editing A procedure to check for irregularities in input data. See *edit*.

data element A combination of one or more data items that forms a unit or piece of information.

data entry device See *key data entry device*.

data entry operator A person who transcribes data into a form suitable for computer processing.

data file See *file*.

dataflow A generic term that pertains to algorithms or machines whose actions are determined by the availability of the data needed for these actions.

data independence Implies that the data and the application programs that use them are independent so that either may be changed without changing the other.

data integrity A performance measure based on the rate of undetected errors. See *integrity*.

data item An item of data used to represent a single value. A data item is the smallest unit of named data.

data link Equipment that permits the transmission of information in data format. See *channel*.

data logging Recording of data about events that occur in time sequence.

data management (1) A general term that collectively describes those functions of a system that provide access to hardware, enforce data storage conventions, and regulate the use of input/output devices. (2) A major function of operating systems that involves organizing, cataloging, locating, retrieving, storing, and maintaining data.

data management system (1) A system that provides the necessary procedures and programs to collect, organize, and maintain the data required by the information systems. (2) A system that assigns the responsibility for data input and integrity to establish and maintain the data bases within an organization.

data manipulating language (DML) A modified high-level language used to describe the data types in a data base and the interrelationships among these types.

data manipulation language A language for manipulating data in a data base.

data medium The material in or on which a specific physical variable may

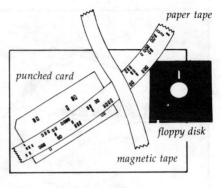

paper tape

punched card

floppy disk

magnetic tape

data medium

represent data (e.g., magnetic disk or magnetic tape).

data modem See *modem*.

data name The name of the variable used to indicate a data value (e.g., PI for 3.14159).

data origination The translation of information from its original form into machine-sensible form.

dataphone A trademark of the AT&T Company to identify the data sets manufactured and supplied by the Bell System for use in the transmission of data over the telephone network. See *data set*.

data preparation The process of organizing information and storing it in a form that can be input to the computer.

data preparation device A device that permits data capture in which the source data is collected and transformed into a medium or form capable of being read into a computer.

data processing (1) One or more operations performed on data to achieve a desired objective. (2) The functions of a computer center. (3) A term used in reference to operations performed by data processing equipment.

data processing center A computer center equipped with devices capable of receiving information, processing it according to human-made instructions, and producing the computed results.

data processing center

Data Processing Management Association See *DPMA.*

data processing manager The person who runs the information processing center, usually including the operation of the computer. The biggest part of the manager's job is concerned with developing new systems and then keeping them running.

data processing system A network of data processing hardware and software capable of accepting information, processing it according to a plan, and producing the desired results.

data processing technology The science of information handling.

data processor Any device capable of performing operations on data (e.g., a desk calculator or a digital computer).

data protection Measures to safeguard data from undesired occurrences that intentionally or unintentionally lead to destruction, modification, or disclosure of data.

data rate The rate at which a channel carries data, measured in bauds (bits per second).

data reduction The process of transforming raw data into useful, condensed, or simplified intelligence.

Often adjusting, scaling, smoothing, compacting, editing, and ordering operations are used in the process.

data security The protection of data from accidental or malicious destruction, disclosure, or modification. See *computer security, disk library,* and *tape library.*

data set (1) A device that permits the transmission of data over communication lines by changing the form of the data at one end so that it can be carried over the lines; another data set at the other end changes the data back to its original form so that it is acceptable to the machine (computer, etc.) at that end. The *dataphone* is an example. Same as *modem.* (2) A collection of related data items.

data sharing The ability of computer processes or of computer users at several nodes to access data at a single node.

data sheet A special form used to record input values in a format convenient for keypunching. See *coding form.*

data storage devices Units for storing large quantities (millions) of characters, typically, magnetic disk units, magnetic tape units, magnetic drums, and magnetic card units.

data stream The serial data that is transmitted through a channel from a single input/output operation.

data structure The relationship between data items.

data tablet A manual input device for graphic display consoles. Same as *digitizer.*

data terminal A point in a computer system or data communications network at which data can be entered or retrieved. See *terminal* and *video terminal.*

data transfer rate The speed of reading or writing data between a storage medium and the computer.

data transmission The sending of data from one part of a system to another part. See *data communications*.

data type An interpretation applied to a string of bits.

data word size Refers to the specific length of data word a particular computer is designed to handle. See *word* and *word length*.

datum A unit of information (e.g., a computer word).

DBMS An acronym for Data Base Management System. A complete collection of computer programs that organizes and processes a particular data base.

DC An acronym for (1) *Data Conversion*, (2) Design Change (3) *Digital Computer*, (4) Direct Current, (5) Direct Cycle, (6) Display Console.

DCTL An acronym for *Direct Coupled Transistor Logic*.

DDD An acronym for Direct Distance Dialing. The facility used for making long-distance telephone calls without the assistance of a telephone operator.

DDL An acronym for Data Description Language. A language for declaring data structures in a data base.

deadlock Unresolved contention for the use of a resource.

debit card A card issued by a specific bank that allows the user to deduct money directly from his/her bank account when making purchases in stores that have accounts with the same bank that issued the card.

deblocking Extracting a logical record from a block or group of logical records.

debug To detect, locate, and remove all mistakes in a computer program and any malfunctions in the computing system itself. Synonymous with troubleshoot. See *bug, debugging aids,* and *test data*.

debugging aids Computer routines that are helpful in debugging programs (e.g., tracing routine, snapshot dump, or post mortem dump).

deceleration time The time required to stop a magnetic tape after reading or recording the last piece of data from a record on that tape.

decimal A characteristic or property involving a selection, condition, or choice in which there are ten possibilities; for example, the numeration system with a radix of ten.

decimal code Describing a form of notation by which each decimal digit is expressed separately in some other number system.

decimal digit A numeral in the decimal numeral system. The radix of the decimal system is 10, and the following symbols are used: 0, 1, 2, 3, 4, 5, 6, 7, 8, and 9.

decimal number A numeral, usually of more than one digit, representing a sum, in which the quantity represented by each digit is based on the radix of ten.

decimal system Base-10 positional notation system.

decimal-to-binary conversion The process of converting a numeral written to the base ten to the equivalent numeral written to the base two.

decimal-to-hexadecimal conversion The process of converting a numeral written to the base ten to the equivalent numeral written to the base sixteen.

decimal-to-octal conversion The process of converting a numeral written to the base ten to the equivalent numeral written to the base eight.

decision The computer operation of determining if a certain relationship exists between words in storage or registers and of taking alternative courses of action.

decision instruction An instruction that affects the selection of a branch of a program (e.g., a conditional jump instruction).

decision symbol A flowcharting symbol that is used to indicate a choice or a branching in the information processing path. A diamond-shaped figure is used to represent this symbol.

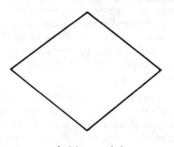

decision symbol

decision table A table listing all the contingencies to be considered in the description of a problem, together with the corresponding actions to be taken. Decision tables are sometimes used instead of flowcharts to describe the operations of a program.

decision tree A pictorial representation of the alternatives in any situation.

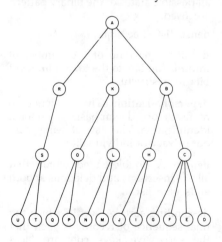

decision tree

declaration statement A part of a computer program that defines the nature of other elements of the program or reserves parts of the hardware for special use.

decode To translate or determine the meaning of coded information. Contrast with *encode*.

decoder (1) A device that decodes. (2) A matrix of switching elements that selects one or more output channels according to the combination of input signals present.

decollate To arrange copies of continuous forms in sets and remove the carbon paper from them.

decrement The amount by which a value or variable is decreased.

decryption The process of taking an encrypted message and reconstructing from it the original meaningful message.

DECUS An acronym for the Digital Equipment Computer (DEC) Users Society. A user group whose objective is the exchange and dissemination of ideas and information pertinent to DEC computers.

dedicated Programs, machines, or procedures that are designed for special use.

dedicated computer A computer whose use is reserved for a particular task.

default An assumption made by a system or language translator when no specific choice is given by the program or the user.

deferred address An indirect address. See *deferred entry, deferred exit,* and *indirect addressing.*

deferred entry An entry into a subroutine that occurs as a result of a deferred exit from the program that passed control to it.

deferred exit The passing of control to a subroutine at a time determined by an asynchronous event rather than at a predictable time.

definition of a problem The art of compiling logic in the form of algorithms, flowcharts, and program descriptions that clearly explain and define the problem.

degausser A device that is used to erase information from a magnetic device (e.g., magnetic tape). Also called bulk eraser.

degausser

delay The amount of time by which an event is retarded.

delay line storage A storage device that consists of a delay line and a means for regenerating and reinserting information into the delay line; this device was used in early computers.

delete To remove or eliminate.

deletion record A new record that will replace or remove an existing record of a master file.

delimit To fix the limits of something (e.g., to establish maximum and minimum limits of a specific variable).

delimiter A special character, often a comma or space, used to separate variable names or items in a list or to separate one string of characters from another, as in the separation of data items.

demand paging In virtual storage systems, the transfer of a page from external page storage to real storage at the time it is needed for execution.

demodulation In data communications, the process of retrieving an original signal from a modulated carrier wave. This technique is used in data sets to make communication signals compatible with computer terminal signals.

demodulator A device that receives signals transmitted over a communications link and converts them into electrical pulses, or bits, that can serve as inputs to a data processing machine. Contrast with *modulator*.

demultiplexer A circuit that applies the logic state of a single input to one of several outputs. Contrast with multiplexer.

denominator In the expression $\frac{a}{b}$, b is the denominator and a is the numerator.

dense binary code A code in which all possible states of the binary pattern are used.

dense list See *sequential list*.

density The ratio of the number of information bits to the total number of bits in a structure.

depersonalization The tendency to remove or deemphasize personal identification. The state of being without privacy or individuality.

deque A double-ended queue that allows insertions and deletions at both ends of a list.

descending sort A sort in which the final sequence of records is such that the successive keys compare "less than" or "equal to."

descriptor A significant word that helps to categorize or index information. Sometimes called a *keyword*.

design aids Computer programs or hardware elements that are intended to assist one in implementing a computer system. See *debugging aids* and *programming aids*.

design automation The use of computers in the design and production of circuit packages, new computers, and other electronic equipment.

design cycle (1) In a hardware system, the complete cycle of development for equipment, which includes breadboarding, prototyping, testing, and production. (2) In a software system, the complete plan for producing an operational system, which includes problem description, algorithm development, flowcharting, coding, program debugging, and documentation.

desk checking A manual checking process in which representative sample data items, used for detecting errors in program logic, are traced through the program before the latter is executed on the computer. Same as *dry run*.

desk checking

desk top computer A microcomputer. A small computer containing a microprocessor, input and output devices, and storage, usually in one box or package. See *home computer, microcomputer,* and *personal computer*.

destination The device or address that receives the data during a data transfer operation.

destructive read The process of destroying the information in a location by reading the contents.

detail file A file containing relatively transient information, for example, records of individual transactions that occurred during a particular period of time. Synonymous with *transaction file.* Contrast with *master file.*

detail printing An operation where a line of printing occurs for each card read by an accounting machine.

deterministic model A mathematical model for the study of data of known fixed values and direct cause-and-effect relationships.

development time The time used for debugging new programs or hardware.

device (1) A mechanical or electrical unit with a specific purpose. (2) A computer peripheral.

device code The 8-bit code for a specific input or output device.

device flag A one-bit register that records the current status of a device.

device independence The ability to command input/output operations without regard to the characteristics of the input/output devices. See *symbolic I/O assignment.*

device name The general name for a kind of device (e.g., model 3330 disk unit or Apple III microcomputer).

diagnosis The process of isolating malfunctions in computing equipment and of detecting mistakes in programs and systems.

diagnostic routine A routine designed to locate a malfunction in the central processing unit or a peripheral device.

diagnostics Messages to the user automatically printed by a computer that pinpoint improper commands and errors in logic. Sometimes called *error messages*.

diagram A schematic representation of a sequence of operations or routines. See *flowchart*.

dialect A version of a particular computer language. For example, TRS-80 BASIC, Apple II BASIC, and BASIC PLUS are all dialects of BASIC.

dial-up In data communications, the use of a dial or push-button telephone to initiate a station-to-station telephone call.

dichotomizing search See *binary search*.

dictionary (1) Words that are arranged alphabetically and usually defined. (2) A lexicon in alphabetic order.

die The tiny rectangular pieces of a circular wafer of semiconductor silicon, sawed or sliced during the fabrication of integrated circuits or transistors.

difference The amount by which one quantity or number is greater or less than another.

difference engine A machine designed by Charles Babbage in 1822 that mechanized a calculating function called the "method of differences." The machine was never built, however, because of inadequate engineering capabilities. See *Babbage, Charles* and *Scheutz, George*.

differential analyzer A machine built in 1930 that was able to calculate differential equations. It was entirely mechanical, having no electrical parts. See *Bush, Vannevar*.

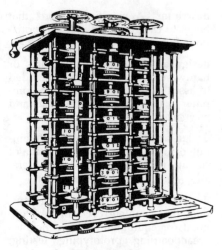

difference engine

digit One of the symbols of a numbering system that is used to designate a quantity.

digital Pertaining to data in the form of digits. Contrast with *analog*.

digital communications The transmission of information by coding it into discrete on/off electronic signals.

digital computer A device that manipulates digital data and performs arithmetic and logic operations on these data. See *computer*. Contrast with *analog computer*.

digital data Data represented in discrete, discontinuous form, as contrasted with *analog data* represented in continuous form.

digital plotter An output device that uses an ink pen (or pens) to draw graphs, line drawings, and other illustrations. *(Illus. p. 63)*

digital sorting A sort that uses a technique similar to sorting on tabulation machines. The elapsed time is directly proportional to the number of characters in the sequencing key and the volume of data. Also called *radix sorting*.

digital plotter

digital-to-analog converter Mechanical or electronic devices used to con-

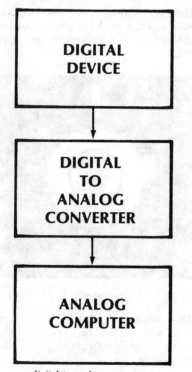

digital-to-analog converter

vert discrete digital numbers to continuous analog signals. Abbreviated D-A converter. Opposite of *analog-to-digital converter*.

digitize To convert a measurement into a digital value. In computing, this is normally done automatically and consists of converting an electrical signal into a binary number. See *analog-to-digital converter*.

digitizer An input device that converts graphic and pictorial data into binary inputs for use in a computer. Same as *data tablet*.

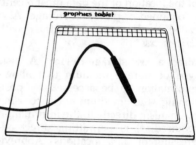

digitizer

digit place In positional notation, the site where a symbol such as a digit is located in a word representing a numeral.

digit punching position The area on a punch card reserved to represent a decimal digit (i.e., a punch in rows 1, 2, . . ., 9).

dimension The maximum size or the number and arrangement of the elements of an array.

diode An electronic device used to permit current flow in one direction and to inhibit current flow in the opposite direction.

diode transistor logic See *DTL*.

DIP An acronym for *Dual In-line Package*. A logic device on which a chip is mounted. *(Illus. p. 64)*

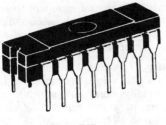

DIP

direct access Pertaining to the process of obtaining data from or placing data into storage where the time required for such access is independent of the location of the data most recently obtained or placed in storage. Also called *random access.* Contrast with *serial access.*

direct access storage device A basic type of storage medium that allows information to be accessed by positioning the medium or accessing mechanism directly to the information required, thus permitting direct addressing of data locations. Abbreviated DASD.

direct address An address that specifies the storage location of an operand. Contrast with *indirect address.*

direct coupled transistor logic A logic system that uses only transistors as active elements. Abbreviated *DCTL.*

direct distance dialing See *DDD.*

direct memory access A method by which data can be transferred between peripheral devices and internal memory without intervention by the central processing unit. Abbreviated DMA.

directory A partition by software into several distinct files; a directory of these files is maintained on a device to locate the files.

disable To remove or inhibit a normal capability. Opposite of *enable.*

disarm An interrupt level that does not allow an interrupt input signal.

disassembler A program that takes machine language code and generates the assembler language code from which the machine language was produced. See *assembly language.*

disaster dump A computer storage dump that occurs as a result of a nonrecoverable mistake in a program.

disc Alternate spelling for disk. See *magnetic disk.*

discrete Pertaining to distinct elements or to representation by means of distinct elements such as characters.

discrete component An electrical component that contains only one function, as opposed to an integrated circuit.

disk A revolving plate upon which data and programs are stored. See *floppy disk* and *magnetic disk.*

diskette A floppy disk. A low cost bulk storage medium for microcomputers and minicomputers. See *floppy disk.*

diskette

disk library A special room that houses a file of disk packs under secure, environmentally controlled conditions.

disk operating system Abbreviated DOS. See *operating system.*

disk pack A removable direct access storage device containing magnetic disks on which information is stored.

disk pack

disk unit See *magnetic disk unit.*

dispatching priority A number assigned to tasks and used to determine precedence for use of the central processing unit in a multitask situation.

dispersed data processing Same as *distributed data processing.*

displacement The difference between the base address and the actual machine language address.

display A visual representation of data (i.e., lights or indicators on computer consoles, cathode ray tube, a printed report, or a diagram produced by a plotter).

display unit A device that provides a visual representation of data. See *cathode ray tube, line printer, plasma display,* and *plotter.*

distortion An undesired change in the waveform of the original signal, resulting in unfaithful reproduction of data communication signals.

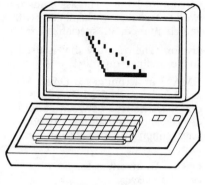

display unit

distributed data processing A concept whereby a company supplements its main computer system (often called the home office computer) with field office terminals. The field office terminals can be used to do local data processing operations without tying down the home office computer. Limited data communications can occur between the home office computer and the field office terminals, thus providing for a company-wide communication system. Contrast with *centralized data processing.*

distributed network A network configuration in which all node pairs are connected either directly or through redundant paths through intermediate nodes.

distributive sort A sort formed by separating the list into parts and then rearranging the parts in order.

disturbance An irregular phenomenon that inferferes with the interchange of intelligence during transmission of a signal.

dividend In the division operation $\frac{a}{b}$, a is the dividend and b is the divisor. The result is the quotient and remainder.

division check Multiplication check in which a zero-balancing result is compared against the original dividend.

division of labor The assignment of work to teams of workers, each with a limited number of specialized tasks.

divisor The quantity that is used to divide another quantity.

DMA An acronym for Direct Memory Access. A method by which data can be transferred between peripheral devices and internal memory without intervention by the central processing unit.

DML An acronym for *Data Manipulating Language*.

DNC An acronym for Direct Numerical Control. Computer control of automatic machine tools. Control is applied at discrete points in the process, rather than applied continuously. See *APT* and *numerical control*.

document (1) A medium and the information recorded on it for human use (e.g., a report, a book, a listing, etc.). (2) A record that has permanence and that can be read by a person or machine (e.g., a floppy disk containing report data).

documentation The preparation of documents, during systems analysis and subsequent programming, that describe such things as the system, the programs prepared, and the changes made at later dates.

documentation aids Aids that help automate the documentation process; for example, program description write-ups, flowcharts, programs, program runs, and so forth.

documentor A program designed to use data processing methods in the production and maintenance of program flowcharts, text material, and other types of tabular or graphic information.

document reader A general term referring to OCR or OMR equipment that reads a limited amount of information.

document retrieval Acquiring data from storage devices and, possibly, manipulating the data and subsequently preparing a report.

domain tip A type of storage device that uses thin films to create magnetic domains for storing digital data. See *thin film*.

dope vector A vector wherein an atom of a linked list describes the contents of the other atoms in the list.

doping The process of introducing impurity elements into the crystalline structure of pure silicon during semiconductor fabrication.

DOS An acronym for Disk Operating System. See *operating system*.

dot matrix printer A printer that forms characters as a series of impacts by a linear print head.

double-dabble The process of converting binary numbers into their decimal equivalents.

double precision Pertaining to the use of two computer words to represent a number in order to gain increased precision.

double punch More than one numeric punch in any one column of a card.

double word An entity of storage two words in length.

doubly linked list List in which each atom contains one pointer that relates to the previous atom as well as one pointer that relates to the successor atom.

download The transfer of information from a remote computer system to the user's system. Opposite of *upload*.

downtime The length of time a computer system is inoperative due to a malfunction. Contrast with *available time*.

DPMA An acronym for Data Processing Management Association. A professional data processing organization whose primary purpose is to develop and promote business methods and education in data processing and data processing management.

DPMA certificate A certificate given by the Data Processing Management Association indicating that a person has attained a certain level of competence in the field of data processing. The certificate is obtained by passing an examination that is offered yearly.

drain One of the three connecting terminals of a field effect transistor, the other two being the *source* and the *gate*. If the charge carriers are positive, the conventional current flows from the source to the drain.

driver A software driver consists of a series of instructions the computer follows to reformat data for transfer to and from a particular peripheral device. The electrical and mechanical requirements are different from one kind of device to another, and the software drivers are used to standardize the format of data between them and the central processor.

DRO An acronym for Destructive Read Out. See *destructive read*.

drop out In data transmission, a momentary loss in signal, usually due to the effect of noise or system malfunction.

drum See *magnetic drum*.

drum printer A printing device that uses a drum embossed with alphabetic and numeric characters. A type of *line printer*.

drum sorting A sort program that uses magnetic drums for auxiliary storage during sorting.

drum storage See *magnetic drum*.

dry run A program-checking technique. The process of examining the logic and coding of a program from a flowchart and written instructions and recording the results of each step of the operation before running the program on the computer. Same as *desk checking*.

DTL An acronym for Diode Transistor Logic. Microelectronic logic based on connections between semiconductor diodes and the transistor.

dual density (1) Refers to tapes, disks on which data are densely recorded. (2) A floppy disk with dual side recording capability.

dual in-line package A popular type of integrated circuit package on which a chip is mounted. Abbreviated DIP.

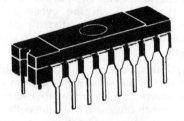

dual in-line package

dumb terminal A visual display terminal with minimal capabilities.

dummy Used as an adjective to indicate an artificial instruction, address, or record of information inserted solely to fulfill prescribed conditions.

dummy argument Variables, used as function arguments, that do not have any values.

dummy instruction (1) An artificial instruction or address inserted in a list to serve a purpose other than its execution as an instruction. (2) An instruction in a routine that, in itself, does not perform any functions. Often used to provide a point in which to terminate a program loop.

dump The data that results from a "dumping" process. See *post mortem dump* and *snapshot dump*.

dumping Copying all or part of the contents of a storage unit, usually from the computer's internal storage, into an auxiliary storage unit or onto a line printer. See *dump, post mortem dump*, and *snapshot dump*.

duplex Relates to a communications system or equipment capable of transmission in both directions. See *full duplex* and *half duplex*.

duplex channel A channel that allows simultaneous transmission in both directions. See *full duplex, half duplex*, and *simplex*.

duplexing The use of duplicate computers, peripheral equipment, or circuitry so that, in the event of a component failure, an alternate component can enable the system to continue.

duplicate To copy so that the result remains in the same physical form as the source, for example, to make a new punch card with the same pattern of holes as an original punch card. Contrast with *copy*.

duplication check A check requiring that the results of two independent performances of the same operation be identical. The check may be made concurrently on duplicate equipment or at a later time on the same equipment.

dyadic An operation that uses two operands.

dyadic operation An operation on two operands.

dynamic address translation In virtual storage systems, the change of a virtual storage address to a real storage address during execution of an instruction. Abbreviated DAT.

dynamic dump A dump taken during the execution of a program.

dynamic relocation The movement of part or all of an active (i.e., currently operating) program from one region of storage to another, with all necessary address references being adjusted to enable proper execution of the program to continue in its new location.

dynamic scheduling Job scheduling that is determined by the computer on a moment-to-moment basis, depending upon the circumstances.

dynamic storage A memory device that must be constantly recharged or "refreshed" at frequent intervals to avoid loss of data. A very volatile memory.

dynamic storage allocation Automatic storage allocation. See *storage allocation*.

EAM An acronym for *Electronic Accounting Machine*. Usually refers to unit record equipment.

EAROM An acronym for Electrically Alternable ROM. ROM memory that can be selectively altered without erasing all stored data, as is done with EPROM devices.

EBAM An acronym for Electron Beam Addressed Memory. An electronic storage device that uses electrical circuits to control a beam which reads from or writes on a metallic oxide semiconductor surface.

EBCDIC An acronym for Extended Binary Coded Decimal Interchange Code. An 8-bit code used to represent data in modern computers. EBCDIC can represent up to 256 distinct characters and is the principal code used in many of the current computers.

echo check A check upon the accuracy of a data transfer operation in which the data received is transmitted back to the source and compared with the original data.

Eckert, J. Presper Co-inventor of the ENIAC, an early electronic computer. See *ENIAC* and *Mauchly, John*.

ECL An acronym for Emitter Coupled Logic, also called *Current Mode Logic* (CML). ECL is faster than TTL, but much less popular.

edge A connection between two nodes in a graph.

edge card A circuit board (or card) with contact strips along one edge, designed to mate with an edge connector.

edge connector An electrical socket, slot-shaped, whereby a circuit card

J. Presper Eckert

may be attached to a mother board or chassis.

edge cutter/trimmer A device for removing the sprocketed margin from continuous line printer paper.

edge-punched card A card into which data may be recorded by punching holes along one edge in a pattern similar to that used for punched tape. Hole positions are arranged to form coded patterns in five, six, seven, or eight channels and usually represent data in a binary code decimal system.

edit (1) To check the correctness of data. (2) To change as necessary the form of data by adding or deleting certain characters. For example, part of program can edit data for printing, adding special symbols, spacing, deleting nonsignificant zeros, and so on.

editing Making the corrections or changes in a program or data. See *data editing.*

editing run In batch processing the editing program will check the data for ostensible validity (e.g., test to assure that dates and numbers fall within the expected ranges, compare totals with separately entered batch or hash totals, and prove check digits) and identify any errors for correction and resubmission.

editor Computer program designed to make it easy to review and alter a file or program interactively. For example, one editing command might locate and display the first occurrence of a given string of characters; a second command might delete or change those characters wherever they occur.

EDP An acronym for Electronic Data Processing, data processing performed largely by electronic digital computers.

EDS An acronym for Exchangeable Disk Store.

EDSAC An acronym for Electronic Delayed Storage Automatic Computer. The first digital computer to feature the stored program concept. It was developed in Great Britain in 1949 at Cambridge University. See *Wilkes, Maurice Vincent.*

EDVAC An acronym for Electronic Discrete Variable Automatic Computer. Developed at the Moore School of Electrical Engineering, University of Pennsylvania, in 1949. It was the first U.S. built computer that featured a stored program unit.

EEROM An acronym for Electronically Erasable Read-Only Memory.

effective address The address that is derived by performing any specified address modification operations upon a specified address.

EFT An acronym for Electronic Funds Transfer. An EFT network transfers funds from one account to another with electronic equipment rather than with paper media, such as checks.

EIA An acronym for Electronic Industries Association.

electrolysis The process of changing the chemical composition of a material by sending an electric current through it.

electromagnetic delay line A delay line whose operation is based on the time of propagation of electromagnetic waves through distributed or lumped capacitance and inductance. Used in early computers.

electromechanical A system for processing data that uses both electrical and mechanical principles.

electronic Pertaining to the flow of electricity through semiconductors, valves, and filters, by contrast with the free flow of current through simple conductors. The essence of computer technology is the selective use and combination of electronic apparatus whereby current can be allowed to flow or can be halted by electronic switches working at very high speed.

electronic accounting machine Pertaining to data processing equipment that is predominantly electromechanical, for example, keypunch, mechanical sorter, tabulator, or collator.

electronically programmable Pertains to a Programmable ROM (Read Only Memory) or any other digital device in which the data 1's and 0's in binary code can be entered electrically, usually by the user with a piece of equipment called a *PROM Programmer.*

electronic data processing Data processing performed largely by electronic equipment.

electronic data processing system The general term used to define a system for data processing by means of machines using electronic circuitry at electronic speed, as opposed to electromechanical equipment.

electronic fund transfer (EFT) A cashless approach to pay for goods and services. Electronic signals between computers are often used to adjust the accounts of the parties involved in a transaction.

electronic mail The transmission of messages by the use of computing systems and telecommunications facilities.

electronic music Music in which the sounds are produced by electronic means. See *computer music* and *synthesizer*.

electronic pen A pen-like stylus that is commonly used in conjunction with a cathode ray tube for inputting or changing information under program control. Often called a *light pen*.

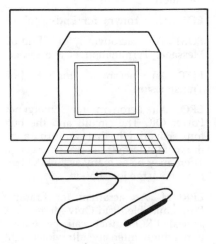

electronic pen

electronics The branch of physics concerned primarily with the natural and controlled flow of electrons through various substances.

electroplate To deposit a metal on a surface of certain materials by electrolysis.

electrosensitive paper Printer paper with a thin coating of conductive material, such as aluminum. Print becomes visible through darkening where a matrix-type print head allows electric current to flow on to the conductive surface.

electrostatic printer A high-speed line printer. Same as *electrothermal printer*.

electrothermal printer A high-speed printer that uses heated elements to create characters as matrices of small dots on heat sensitive paper.

element An item of data within an array.

elements of a microcomputer Microprocessor for the central processing unit, program memory (usually ROM), data storage (usually RAM), input/output circuitry, and clock generators.

eleven-punch A punch in the second row from the top of a Hollerith punched card. Synonymous with *X-punch*.

emitter An electrode within a transistor.

empty string A string containing no characters. Also called a *null string*.

emulate To imitate one system with another, such that the imitating system accepts the same data, executes the same programs, and achieves the same results as the imitated system.

emulator A type of program or device that allows user programs, written for one kind of computer system, to be run on another system.

emulsion laser storage See *laser storage*.

enable To switch a computer device or facility so that it can operate. The opposite of *disable*.

enclosure A housing for any electrical or electronic device.

encode To convert data into a code form that is acceptable to some piece of computer equipment.

encoder A device that produces machine-readable output, for example, paper tape, either from manual keyboard depressions or from data already recorded in some other code.

encryption The coding of information or data in such a way as to make them unintelligible without the key to its decryption.

end-around carry A carry from the most significant digit place to the least significant digit place.

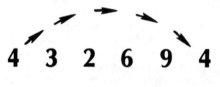

4 3 2 6 9 4

end-around carry

end-around shift See *circular shift*.

end mark A code or signal that indicates termination of a unit of data.

end-of-block Termination of a block. Abbreviated EOB.

end-of-file Termination or point of completion of a quantity of data. End-of-file marks are used to indicate this point on magnetic files. Abbreviated EOF. See *end-of-tape marker*.

end-of-message Termination of a message. Abbreviated EOM.

end-of-tape marker A marker on a magnetic tape used to indicate the end of the permissible recording area.

engineering units Units of measure as applied to a process variable (e.g., PSI, Degrees C, etc.).

ENIAC An acronym for Electronic Numerical Integrator And Calculator. An early all-electronic digital computer. It was built by J. Mauchly and J. Eckert at the Moore School of Electrical Engineering, University of Pennsylvania, in 1946. See *Eckert, J. Presper* and *Mauchly, John. (Illus. p. 73)*

entry point Any location in a routine to which control can be passed by another routine. Entry is also referred to as the transfer address.

environment In computing context, this is more likely to refer to the mode of operation (e.g., "in a time-sharing environment") than to physical conditions of temperature, humidity, and so forth. But either kind of environment may affect operational efficiency.

environment division One of the four main component parts of a COBOL program.

EOB An acronym for End-of-Block. Termination of a block.

EOF An acronym for *End-of-File*. When all the records in a file have been processed, the computer is said to have encountered an "end-of-file" condition.

EOJ An acronym for End-of-Job.

EOM An acronym for End-of-Message. Termination of a message.

EOT An acronym for End-of-Transmission.

EPO An acronym for Emergency Power Off. The circuit, and the buttons activating it, that can turn an entire computer off in an emergency. There may be as many as 20 EPO buttons in a large installation.

EPROM An acronym for Erasable Programmable Read Only Memory. A special PROM that can be erased under high intensity ultraviolet light and reprogrammed. EPROMs can be reprogrammed repeatedly.

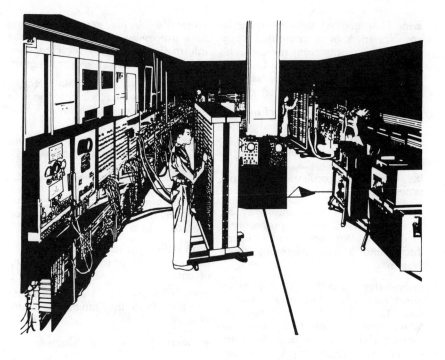

ENIAC

equality The idea expressed by the equal sign, written =. In many programming languages and program design, the = sign is also used as a "replacement symbol."

equation A mathematical sentence with an = sign between two expressions that name the same number; for example, $y = x^2 + 4x - 36$ is an equation.

equipment Part of a computer system. See *computer, hardware,* and *peripheral equipment.*

erasable programmable read only memory See *EPROM.*

erasable storage A storage medium that can be erased and reused. Magnetic disk, drum, or tape are mediums that can be erased and reused while punched cards or punched paper tape cannot.

erase To remove data from storage without replacing it.

erase head In a domestic tape recorder, the erase head is the device that cleans the tape of earlier signals immediately before new matter is recorded. In a computer storage device based on magnetization of ferric-oxide surfaces (for example, tape, card or disc, but not core), the erase head operates immediately before the write head to perform a precisely similar function.

ergonomics The study of workers and their environment; adapting machines to the convenience of operators, with the general aim of maximum efficiency. For example, adding a numeric keypad to a standard keyboard.

EROM An acronym for Erasable ROM. Same as *EPROM.*

73

error The general term referring to any deviation of a computed or a measured quantity from the theoretically correct or true value. Contrast with *fault*, *malfunction*, and *mistake*. See *intermittent error* and *round-off error*.

error analysis The branch of numerical analysis concerned with studying the error aspects of numerical analysis procedures. It includes the study of errors that arise in a computation because of the peculiarities of computer arithmetic.

error control A plan, implemented by software, hardware, or procedures, to detect and/or correct errors introduced into a data communications system.

error-correcting code (1) A code in which each acceptable expression conforms to specific rules of construction. Nonacceptable expressions are also defined. If certain types of errors occur in an acceptable expression, an equivalent will result and the error can be corrected. (2) A code in which the forbidden pulse combination produced by the gain or loss of a bit will indicate which bit is wrong. Same as *self-correcting code*.

error correction A system that detects and inherently provides correction for errors caused by transmission equipment or facilities.

error-detection code (1) A code in which each expression conforms to specific rules of construction. When expressions occur that do not conform to the rules of these constructions, an error is indicated. (2) A code in which errors produce forbidden combinations. A single error-detecting code produces a forbidden combination if a digit gains or loses a single bit. A double error-detecting code produces a forbidden combination if a digit gains or loses either one or two bits, and so on. Also called a *self-checking code*.

error file A file generated during data processing to retain erroneous information sensed by the computer, often printed out as an error report.

error guessing A test data selection technique. The selection criterion is to pick values that seem likely to cause errors.

error message A printed statement indicating the computer has detected a mistake or malfunction.

error rate In data communications, a measure of quality of circuit or equipment; the number of erroneous bits or characters in a sample.

error ratio The ratio of the number of data units in error to the total number of data units.

error transmission A change in data resulting from the transmission process.

evaluate To find the value of.

event An occurrence or happening.

exception reporting A technique for screening large amounts of computerized data in order to display or print reports containing only specific information.

excess-three code A binary coded decimal notation in which each decimal digit X is represented by the binary numeral of X plus three.

Decimal Digit	Excess 3 Code
0	0011
1	0100
2	0101
3	0110
4	0111
5	1000
6	1001
7	1010
8	1011
9	1100

excess-three code

exchangeable disk See *disk pack.*

exchange buffering A technique using data chaining for eliminating the need to move data in internal storage.

exclusive OR The Boolean operator that gives a truth table value of true if only one of the two variables it connects is true. If both variables it connects are true, this value is false. Abbreviated XOR.

executable A program statement that gives an instruction of some computational operation to be performed then (e.g., assignment statements are executable). Contrast with *nonexecutable.*

execute To run a program on the computer or to carry out an instruction. Same as *run.*

execute cycle The period of time during which a machine instruction is interpreted and the indicated operation is performed on the specified operand.

execution The process of carrying out the instructions of a computer program by a computer.

executive A master program that controls the execution of other programs. Often used synonymously with *monitor, supervisory system,* and *operating system.*

exerciser A device that enables users to create and debug programs and hardware interfaces by manual means.

expansion card A card added to a system for the purpose of mounting additional chips or circuits to expand the system capability.

exponent A symbol or number written above and to the right of another symbol or number that denotes the number of times the latter is used as a factor.

exponential smoothing A forecasting technique.

exponentiation The mathematical process of raising a number to a power of a base (e.g., 2^4).

expression A source language combination of one or more operations. A character sequence that specifies a rule for calculating a value.

Extended Binary Coded Decimal Interchange Code See *EBCDIC.*

extender board A debugging aid that allows one to monitor circuit boards more conveniently.

extensible language A concept whereby the user adds new features to a programming language by modifying existing ones.

extent A collection of physical records that are contiguous in auxiliary storage.

external data file Data that is stored separately from the program that processes it.

external label An identification label attached to the outside of a file medium holder identifying the file (e.g., a paper label or sticker attached to the cover containing a magnetic disk).

external reference A reference to a symbol defined in another routine.

external sort The second phase of a multipass sort program, wherein strings of data are continually merged until one string of sequenced data is formed.

external storage See *auxiliary storage.*

external symbol (1) A control section name, entry point name, or external reference. (2) A symbol contained in the external symbol dictionary.

external symbol dictionary Control information associated with an object program that identifies the external symbols in the program.

extract To remove specific information from a computer word as determined by a mask or filter.

F

f   An abbreviation for *frequency*.

fabricated language   Same as *symbolic language*.

FACE   An acronym for *Field Alterable Control Element*.

facilities management   The use of an independent service organization to operate and manage a data processing installation.

facility   See *channel*.

facsimile   (1) Transmission of pictures, maps, diagrams, and so on. The image is scanned at the transmitter, reconstructed at the receiving station, and duplicated on some form of paper. (2) A precise reproduction of an original document; an exact copy. (3) A hard copy reproduction. Abbreviated FAX.

factor analysis   A mathematical technique for studying the interaction of many factors to determine the most significant factors and the degree of significance.

fail-safe system   A system designed to avoid catastrophe but possibly at the expense of convenience. For example, when a fault is detected in a computer-controlled traffic light system, a fail-safe arrangement might be to set all the traffic lights to red rather than turn them off. Similarly, in a power plant operation, overheating might simply disconnect the power supply. See *fail-soft system*.

fail-soft system   A system that continues to process data despite the failure of parts of the system. Usually accompanied by a deterioration in performance. Using the two examples described under fail-safe system, the traffic lights might turn to flashing amber rather than red, and the over-heated system might maintain battery power for emergency equipment while the main source of power was turned off. See *fail-safe system*.

failure prediction   A technique that attempts to determine the failure schedule of specific parts or equipment so that they may be discarded and replaced before failure occurs.

fall-back   Back-up systems brought into use in an emergency situation, especially the reserve data base and programs that would be switched in quickly, or even automatically, in the event of a detected fault in a real-time system.

family of computers   Series of central processing units allegedly of the same logical design, but of different speeds. This philosophy is supposed to enable the user to start with a slower/less expensive CPU and grow to a faster/more expensive one as the workload builds up, without having to change the rest of the computer system.

FAMOS   An acronym for Floating gate Avalanche injection MOS, a fabrication technology for charge storage devices such as PROMs.

fan-in   The number of signal inputs to a digital logic element.

fan-out   The number of TTL unit loads a given TTL device output can supply or drive under the worst case conditions.

father file   A system of updating records that retains a copy of the original record as well as providing an amended version. When a file update program is run, the old master file is termed the "father file." The updated file is termed the "son file." The file that was used to create the father file is termed the "grandfather file." The technique is particularly applicable to files held on magnetic media such as disk or tape.

fault A condition that causes a component, a computer, or a peripheral device to not perform to its design specifications (e.g., a broken wire or a short circuit). Contrast with *error*, *malfunction*, and *mistake*.

fault tolerant computing The art of building computing systems that continue to operate satisfactorily in the presence of faults.

FAX Facsimile. An equipment configuration that facilitates the transmission of images over a common carrier network.

FCC Federal Communications Commission.

feasibility study Concerned with a definition of the data processing problem, together with alternative solutions, a recommended course of action, and a working plan for designing and installing the system.

feed The mechanical process whereby lengthy materials (e.g., paper or magnetic tape, line printer paper, printer ribbon, etc.) are moved along the required operating position.

feedback (1) A means of automatic control in which the actual state of a process is measured and used to obtain a quantity that modifies the input in order to initiate the activity of the control system. (2) In data processing, information arising from a particular stage of processing could provide a feedback to affect the processing of subsequent data; for example, the fact that an area of storage was nearly full might either delay the acceptance of more data or divert it to some other storage area.

feed holes Holes punched in a paper tape to enable it to be driven by a sprocket wheel.

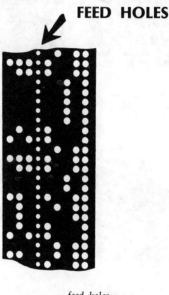

FEED HOLES

feed holes

Felt, Dorr (1862-1930) In 1885, Felt designed an experimental multiple-order key-driven calculating machine. Two years later he produced the Comptometer, a practical adding-listing machine. *(Illus. p. 78)*

female connector Pertaining to the recessed portion of a device into which another part fits. See *connector* and *male connector*.

ferrous oxide One medium used to contain encoded information on magnetic tape.

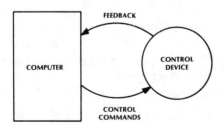

feedback

77

Dorr Felt

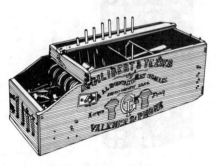

Felt's calculating machine

FET An acronym for *Field Effect Transistor*. A semiconductor device used as a storage element.

fetch To locate and load a quantity of data from storage.

FF An acronym for *Form Feed*.

fiber optic cable A data transmission medium made of tiny threads of glass or plastic that transmits huge amounts of information at the speed of light.

field A group of related characters treated as a unit, for example, a group of adjacent card columns used to represent an hourly wage rate. An item in a record.

field alterable control element A chip used in some systems to allow the user to write microprograms. Abbreviated FACE.

fieldata code The U.S. military code used in data processing as a compromise between conflicting manufacturers' codes.

field effect transistor A three-terminal semiconductor device that acts as a variable charge storage element. The most commonly used type in microcomputers is the Metallic Oxide Semiconductor (MOS) transistor. Abbreviated FET.

FIFO An acronym for First In-First Out. A method of storing and retrieving items from a list, table, or stack, such that the first element stored is the first one retrieved. Contrast with *LIFO*.

FIFO-LIFO Refers to two techniques for the collection of items to which additions and deletions are to be made. See *FIFO* and *LIFO*.

fifth generation computer plan A plan proposed by the Japan Information Processing Development Center to develop an advanced computer by the year 1990.

figure shift A keyboard key (or the code generated by the key) which signifies that the following characters are to be read as figures until a letter shift appears in the message. Same as *letter shift*.

file A collection of related records treated as a unit.

file conversion Changing the file medium or structure.

file gap See *interrecord gap*.

file label A label identifying a file.

file layout The arrangement and structure of data in a file, including the sequence and size of its components.

file librarian A person who has responsibility for the safe-keeping of all computer files, for example, programs and data files on disk packs, magnetic tapes, punched cards, microfilm, and so forth.

file librarian

file maintenance The updating of a file to reflect the effects of nonperiodic changes by adding, altering, or deleting data; for example, the addition of new programs to a program library on magnetic disks.

file name Alphanumeric characters used to identify a particular file.

file name extension Short addition to the file name that identifies the kind of data in the file.

file organization The manner in which the application programmer views the data.

file processing The periodic updating of master files to reflect the effects of current data, often transaction data contained in detail files; for example, a monthly inventory run updating the master inventory file.

file protection A technique or device used to prevent accidental erasure of data from a file, for example, a magnetic tape file protect ring or a gummed tab over the write protect notch of a floppy disk. See *file protect ring* and *write protect notch*.

file protect ring Used to protect data on magnetic tape. Accidental writing on the tape is prevented by removing the ring from the tape reel.

file size The number of records in a file.

file storage Devices that can hold a reservoir of mass data within the computer system. Magnetic disk units, magnetic tape units, and magnetic card units are examples of file storage devices.

filter See *mask*.

finite To have limits, an end, or a last number.

finite element method An approximation technique used to solve field problems in various engineering fields.

firmware A program permanently held in a ROM (Read Only Memory), as compared to a software program held outside a computer (for example, on a disk or tape). See *ROM*.

first generation The first commercially available computers, introduced with UNIVAC I in 1951, and terminated with the development of the transistor in 1959. First generation computers are characterized by their use of vacuum tubes. Now museum pieces.

first in-first out See *FIFO*.

fixed area That portion of internal storage that has been assigned to specific programs or data areas.

fixed-head disk unit A storage device consisting of one or more magnetically coded disks, on the surface of which data is stored in the form of magnetic spots arranged in a manner to represent binary data. These data are arranged in circular tracks around the disks and are accessible to reading and writing by read-write heads assigned one per track. Data from a given track are read or written sequentially as the disk rotates under the read-write head.

fixed-length record A record that always contains the same number of characters. Contrast with *variable-length record*.

fixed point Pertaining to a number system in which each number is represented by a single set of digits and the position of the radix point is implied by the manner in which the numbers are used. Contrast with *floating point*.

fixed point arithmetic (1) A method of calculation in which the operations take place in an invariant manner, and in which the computer does not consider the location of the radix point. This is illustrated by desk calculators with which the operator must keep track of the decimal point. This occurs similarly with many automatic computers, in which the location of the radix point is the computer user's responsibility. (2) A type of arithmetic in which the operands and results of all arithmetic operations must be properly scaled to have a magnitude between certain fixed values.

fixed program computer See *wired program computer*.

fixed size records File elements, each of which has the same number of words, characters, bytes, bits, fields, and so on.

fixed storage Storage whose contents are not alterable by computer instructions (e.g., *read-only storage*). See *ROM* and *PROM*.

fixed word length Pertaining to a machine word or operand that always has the same number of bits, bytes, or characters. Contrast with *variable word length*.

flag (1) An indicator used frequently to tell some later part of a program that some condition occurred earlier. (2) A symbol used to mark a record for special attention. For example, on a listing of a program, all statements that contain errors may be flagged for the attention of the program writer.

flat-bed plotter See *plotter*.

flat pack A small, low-profile (flat), integrated circuit package that can be spot-welded or soldered to a terminal or a printed circuit board. The pins extend outward, rather than pointing down as on a DIP.

flexowriter A form of typewriter accepting paper tape input. Used as an input/output device with many older computers.

flip-flop A device or circuit containing active elements, capable of assuming either one of two stable states at a given time. Synonymous with *toggle*.

floating point A form of number representation in which quantities are represented by a number called the mantissa multiplied by a power of the number base. Contrast with *fixed point*. See *characteristic* and *mantissa*.

floating point arithmetic A method of calculation that automatically accounts for the location of the radix point.

floating point BASIC A type of BASIC language that allows the use of decimal numbers.

floating point routine A set of subroutines that causes a computer to execute floating point arithmetic. These routines are used to simulate floating point operations on a computer with no built-in floating point hardware.

floppy disk A flexible disk (*diskette*) of oxide-coated mylar that is stored in paper or plastic envelopes. The entire envelope is inserted in the disk unit.

Floppy disks provide low-cost storage that is used widely with minicomputers and microcomputers. Floppy disks were originally developed for low capacity storage, low cost, and relatively low data transfer rates. Regular floppy disks have a diameter of 20.32 cm (8 inches), mini floppy disks have a diameter of 13.3 cm (5¼ inches), and micro floppy disks have a diameter of 7.6 cm (3 inches). See *magnetic disk*.

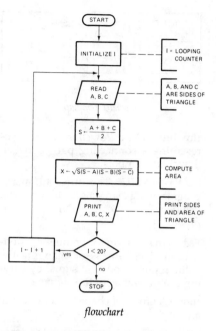

flowchart

floppy disk

floppy disk unit A peripheral storage device in which data are recorded on magnetizable floppy disks (diskettes).

floppy disk unit

flow A general term to indicate a sequence of events.

flowchart A diagram that uses symbols and interconnecting lines to show (1) the logic and sequence of specific program operations (program flowchart) or (2) a system of processing to achieve objectives (system flowchart).

flowchart symbol A symbol used to represent operations, data, flow, or equipment on a flowchart. See *annotation symbol, connector symbol, decision symbol, input/output symbol, processing symbol,* and *terminal symbol*.

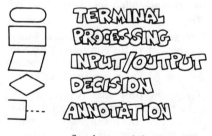

flowchart symbol

flowchart template A plastic guide containing cutouts of the flowchart symbols that is used in the preparation of a flowchart. (*Illus. p. 82*)

flowchart text The descriptive information that is associated with flowchart symbols.

flow diagram See *flowchart*.

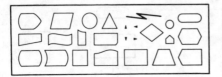

flowchart template

flowline On a flowchart, a line representing a connecting path between flowchart symbols.

FLOW-MATIC The first automatic programming language. It was developed for an early UNIVAC computer.

FM An acronym for Frequency Modulation. The process of changing the value represented by a signal by varying the frequency of the signal.

font A group of characters of one size and style.

force To intervene manually in a program and cause the computer to execute a jump instruction.

forecast An effort to describe some future events that have a reasonable probability of occurrence.

foreground job See *foreground program*.

foreground processing The automatic execution of the computer programs that have been designed to preempt the use of the computing facilities.

foreground program A program that has a high priority and therefore takes precedence over other concurrently operating programs in a computer system using multiprogramming techniques. Contrast with *background program*.

foreground task See *foreground program*.

forest A collection of trees. See *tree*.

form (1) A preprinted document requiring additional information to make it meaningful. (2) The format of the program output.

formal language Abstract mathematical objects used to model the syntax of programming languages such as COBOL or BASIC, or of natural languages such as English or French.

formal logic The study of the structure and form of valid argument without regard to the meaning of the terms in the argument.

format The specific arrangement of data.

form feed (1) The physical transport of continuous paper to the beginning of a new line or page. (2) The standard ASCII character to cause a form feed to occur. Abbreviated FF. See *line feed*.

forms control The operational procedure established by an organization to exercise direction in the utilization of documents that are used to collect and/or report information.

forms design The planning of forms that will communicate the data needed for particular transactions.

Jay Wright Forrester

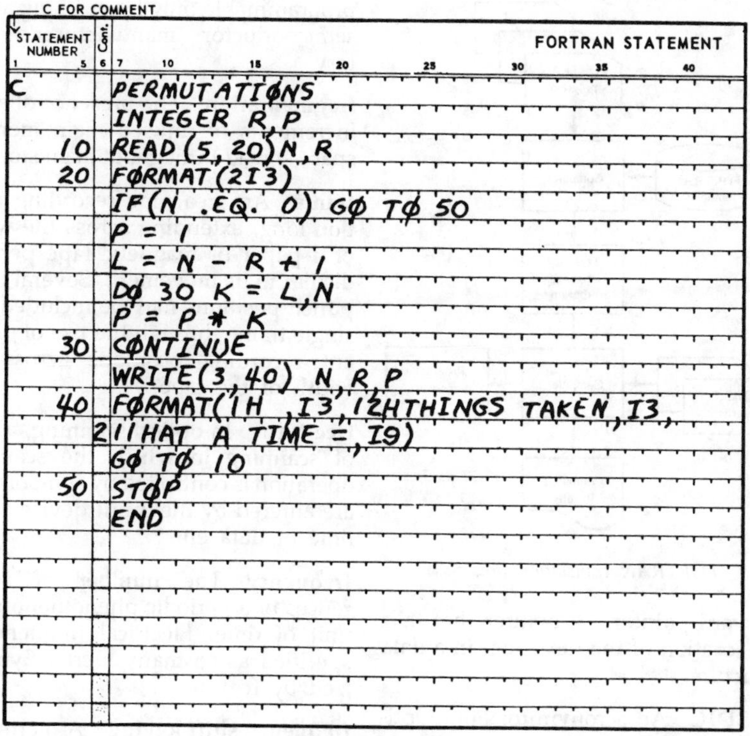

```
C FOR COMMENT

STATEMENT                                              FORTRAN STATEMENT
NUMBER  Cont.
1     5 6 7    10      15      20      25      30      35      40

C         PERMUTATIONS
          INTEGER R,P
   10     READ (5, 20) N,R
   20     FORMAT (2I3)
          IF (N .EQ. 0) GO TO 50
          P = 1
          L = N - R + 1
          DO 30 K = L,N
          P = P * K
   30     CONTINUE
          WRITE (3,40) N,R,P
   40     FORMAT (1H ,I3,12HTHINGS TAKEN,,I3,
          2 11HAT A TIME =,I9)
          GO TO 10
   50     STOP
          END
```

FORTRAN

formula A rule expressed as an equation; for example, $C = 2\pi r$ is the formula for finding the circumference of a circle. It is a way of showing the equal relationship between certain quantities.

Forrester, Jay Wright Headed the team of people at M.I.T. who built the Whirlwind computer. This machine was perhaps the most influential of the early computers in terms of today's commercial machines. Both the invention of magnetic core memory and the parallel synchronous method for handling information inside the machine were first developed by Whirlwind's designers. *(Illus. p. 82)*

FORTH A programming language for use in functional programming, with specific orientation toward productiv-

ity, reliability, and efficiency. Capabilities include structured programming, top-down development, and virtual memory.

FORTRAN An acronym for FORmula TRANslator. A high-level programming language used to perform mathematical, scientific, and engineering computations. FORTRAN has been approved as an American Standard programming language in two versions (FORTRAN and Basic FORTRAN). A widely used programming language.

FORTRAN translation process The process used to produce computed results from a program written in the FORTRAN language. Involves compiling and executing the program on the computer. *(Illus. p. 84)*

83

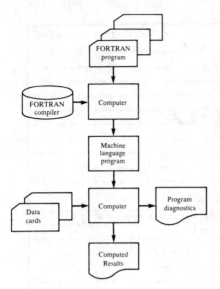

FORTRAN translation process

forward pointer A pointer that tells the location of the next item in a data structure.

FOSDIC An acronym for Film Optical Sensing Device for Input to Computers. An input device used by the Census Bureau to read completed census questionnaire data into a computer.

four-address instruction A machine instruction usually consisting of the addresses of two operands, the address for storing the result, the address of the next instruction, the command to be executed, and miscellaneous indices.

four-out-of-eight code A code for error detection.

fourth generation A modern digital computer that uses large scale integrated (LSI) or very large scale integrated (VLSI) circuitry.

FPLA An acronym for Field Programmable Logic Array. A FPLA can be programmed by the user in the field, whereas an ordinary PLA is programmable only by masking at the semiconductor manufacturer's factory.

fragmentation The presence of small increments of unused main memory space spread throughout main storage.

frame An area, one recording position long, extending across the width of a paper or magnetic tape perpendicular to its movement. Several bit or punch positions may be included in a single frame through the use of different recording positions across the width of the tape.

free form In optical scanning, a type of scanning in which the scanning operation is controlled by symbols that are entered by the input device at the time of data entry.

frequency The number of recurrences of a periodic phenomenon in a unit of time. Electrical frequency is specified as so many Hertz. Symbolized by f.

frequency shift keying A method of data transmission in which the state of the bit being transmitted is indicated by an audible tone. Abbreviated FSK.

front end processor A dedicated communications computer at the front end of a host computer. It may perform communication line assignment, data conversion, error analysis, message handling, and other data communication functions.

front panel The collection of switches and indicators whereby the computer operator may control a computer system. Same as *control panel*. *(Illus. p. 85)*

FSK An acronym for *Frequency Shift Keying*.

full adder A computer circuit capable of adding three binary bits, one of which is a "carry" from a previous addition.

front panel

full duplex Pertaining to the simultaneous, independent transmission of data in both directions over a communications link. Contrast with *half duplex* and *simplex*.

function (1) A process that is performed on a number or character string; for example, squaring is the mathematical function of multiplying a number by itself. (2) A precoded routine. (3) In business, a job.

functional design The specification of the working relations between the parts of a system in terms of their characteristic actions.

functional programming Programming that uses function application as the only control structure.

functional units of a computer The organization of digital computers into five functional units: arithmetic-logic unit, storage unit, control unit, input device, and output device.

function subprogram A subprogram that returns a single value result.

fuse A protective device, usually a short piece of wire, designed to melt and break a circuit when the current exceeds its rated capacity.

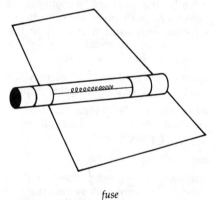

fuse

fusible link A widely used PROM programming technique. An excessive current is used to destroy a metallized connection in a storage device, creating a zero, for instance, if a conducting element is interpreted as a one.

G

gain The increase or amplification of a signal as it passes through a control system. Opposite of *attenuation*.

game playing See *computerized game playing*.

game theory A branch of mathematics concerned, among other things, with probability. The term was first used by John von Neumann in 1928 to describe the strategy of winning at poker. A mathematical process of selecting an optimum strategy in the face of an opponent who has a strategy of her or his own.

gamut The total range of colors which can be displayed on a computer display.

gang punch To punch identical or constant information into all of a group of punch cards.

gap See *interblock gap*.

garbage (1) A term often used to describe incorrect answers from a computer program, usually resulting from equipment malfunction or a mistake in a computer program. (2) Unwanted and meaningless data carried in storage. (3) Incorrect input to a computer. See *GIGO*.

garbage collection Loosely, a term for cleaning dead storage locations out of a file.

gate This term has two distinct meanings in computer technology: the controlling element of certain transistors, or a logic circuit that has two or more inputs that control one output.

gb (gigabyte) One billion bytes. One thousand megabytes (mb).

GEMISCH A programming language developed for medical record applications.

generalized routine A routine designed to process a large range of specific jobs within a given type of application.

general-purpose Being applicable to a wide variety of uses without essential modification. Contrast with *special-purpose*.

general-purpose computer A computer that is designed to solve a wide class of problems. The majority of digital computers are of this type. Contrast with *special-purpose computer*. See *digital computer*.

general-purpose register A CPU register used for indexing, addressing, and arithmetic and logical operations.

general register A storage device that holds the inputs and outputs of the various functional units of a computing system. Also used for temporary storage of intermediate results.

generate The creation of new data from some given information.

generation (of computers) A term usually applied to the progression of computers from those using vacuum tubes (*first generation*) to those using transistors (*second generation*), to those using integrated circuits (*third generation*), and to those using LSI circuits (*fourth generation*). (*Illus. p. 87*)

generator A computer program that constructs other programs to perform a particular type of operation (e.g., a report program generator, I/O generator).

generic Pertaining to the next (generally improved) type of item or device.

geocoding A method of providing a graphic display of data in relation to a geographic area.

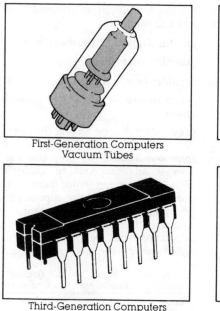

First-Generation Computers
Vacuum Tubes

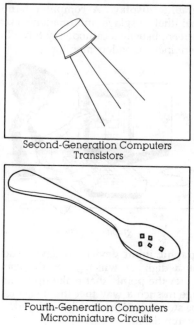

Second-Generation Computers
Transistors

Third-Generation Computers
Integrated Circuits

Fourth-Generation Computers
Microminiature Circuits

generation

get To obtain a record from an input file.

gibberish A term used to describe unnecessary data.

gigabyte One billion bytes.

GIGO An acronym for Garbage In-Garbage Out. A term used to describe the data into and out of a computer system, that is, if the input data is bad (Garbage In) then the output data will also be bad (Garbage Out).

glitch A popular term for an electrical hardware or software problem. See *bug*.

global variable A variable that has the same value regardless of where or in what program it is used.

GP An acronym for *General Purpose*.

GPSS An acronym for General Purpose Systems Simulation. A problem-oriented language used to develop simulation systems.

grabber A fixture on the end of a test equipment lead wire, with a spring actuated hook and claw designed to connect the measuring instrument to a pin of an integrated circuit, socket, transistor, and so forth.

gram A metric unit of mass weight equal to 1/1000 kilogram.

grammatical mistake A violation of the rules of use of a given programming language.

grandfather file See *father file*.

graph A set containing two elements: edges (lines) and nodes (points). It provides a mathematical model for data structures in which the nodes correspond to data items and the edges to pointer fields. Cross-referenced model for program planning.

graphic display A computer terminal that displays information on a screen, usually a cathode ray tube, TV terminal, or video monitor.

graphic display

graphic input device A device such as a digitizer which gives the computer the points that make up an image in such a way that the image can be stored, reconstructed, displayed, or manipulated.

graphic output device A device used to display or record an image. A display screen is an output device for "soft copy"; hard copy output devices produce paper, film, or transparencies of the image.

graphics A general term meaning the appearance of pictures or diagrams on

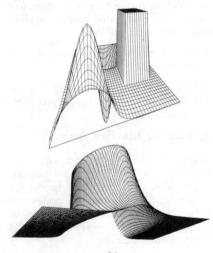

graphics

the display screen as opposed to letters and numbers.

graphic digitizer See *digitizer*.

graphic tablet See *digitizer*.

graphics terminal See *graphic display*.

graph theory The study of graphical objects.

gray code A code having the characteristic that successive integers differ from one another by only one digit. This is advantageous in analog-to-digital conversion equipment. Gray code is used only for input/output purposes. The coded values must be converted to binary before arithmetic calculations can be performed. Also called *cyclic code* and *reflected code*.

Gray Code	Binary Equivalent	Decimal Equivalent
0000	0000	0
0001	0001	1
0011	0010	2
0010	0011	3
0110	0100	4
0111	0101	5
0101	0110	6
0100	0111	7
1100	1000	8
1101	1001	9
1111	1010	10
1110	1011	11
1010	1100	12
1011	1101	13
1001	1110	14
1000	1111	15

gray code

gray code-to-binary conversion A binary equivalent of a gray code number can be obtained by applying the following rule: The most significant binary digit equals the corresponding gray code digit while the following binary digits change if the gray code digit is a 1 and remain the same if the gray code digit is a zero. For example, the gray code value 110100110 equals the binary number 100111011.

Grosch's law A law formulated by Herbert Grosch concerning the economics of scale in computers; namely, that computing power increases as the square of the cost.

grouping Arranging data into related groups, having common characteristics.

group mark Any indicator to signal the end of a word or other unit of data.

group printing An operation during which information prints from only the first card of each group passing through the accounting machine.

GUIDE An acronym for Guidance of Users of Integrated Data processing Equipment. An international association of users of large-scale IBM computers.

gulp A small group of bytes.

gun The group of electrodes constituting the electron beam emitter in a cathode ray tube.

H

hacker A computer enthusiast.

half adder A computer circuit capable of adding two binary bits.

half duplex A circuit that permits one-direction electrical communications between stations. Technical arrangements may permit operation in either direction, but not simultaneously.

halfword A contiguous sequence of bits, bytes, or characters that comprises half a computer word and is capable of being addressed as a unit. See *word*.

halt instruction A machine instruction that stops the execution of the program.

hamming code A 7-bit error-correcting data code capable of being corrected automatically.

hand calculator A small, hand-held calculator suitable for performing arithmetic operations and other more complicated calculations.

hand-held computer A portable, battery-operated, hand-held computer that can be programmed in BASIC to perform a wide variety of tasks. Also called a *pocket computer*.

| Position | 1 | 2 | 3 | 4 | 5 | 6 | 7 | |
Bit Weights	A	B	8	C	4	2	1	
	0	0	0	0	0	0	0	zero
	1	1	0	1	0	0	1	one
	0	1	0	1	0	1	0	two
	1	0	0	0	0	1	1	three
	1	0	0	1	1	0	0	four
	0	1	0	0	1	0	1	five
	1	1	0	0	1	1	0	six
	0	0	0	1	1	1	1	seven
	1	1	1	0	0	0	0	eight
	0	0	1	1	0	0	1	nine
	1	0	1	1	0	1	0	ten
	0	1	1	0	0	1	1	eleven
	0	1	1	1	1	0	0	twelve
	1	0	1	0	1	0	1	thirteen
	0	0	1	0	1	1	0	fourteen
	1	1	1	1	1	1	1	fifteen

hamming code

handler A program with the sole function of controlling a particular input, output, or storage device, a file, or the interrupt facility.

handshaking The exchange of predetermined signals when a connection

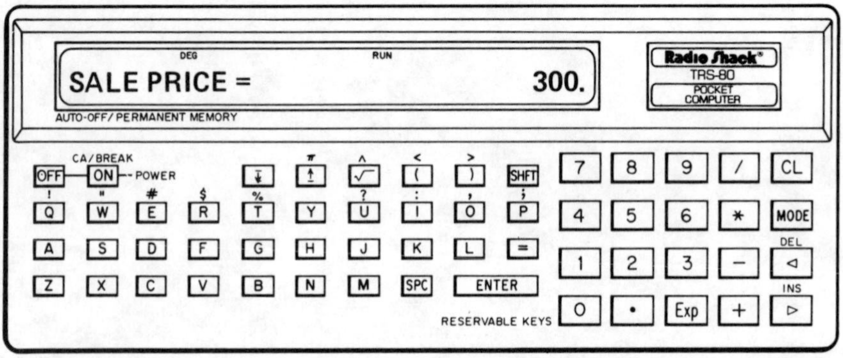

hand-held computer

is established between the central processing unit and a peripheral device.

hang-up A nonprogrammed stop in a routine. It is usually an unforeseen or unwanted halt in a machine run. It is often caused by improper coding of a problem, by equipment malfunction, or by the attempted use of a nonexistent or illegal operation code.

hard copy A printed copy of machine output in readable form, for example, reports, listings, documents, or summaries. See *soft copy*.

```
26940124
49302441
52295672
95223910
33367921
34652900
22098374
33885922
13798455
```

hard copy

hard disk Storage disk made of rigid material. Hard disk devices can generally store more information and access it faster. Cost considerations, however, usually restrict their usage to medium and large scale applications.

hard sector Magnetic floppy disk are divided into wedges called sectors that are physically marked by holes punched through the disk to indicate the various sectors. Contrast with *soft sector*.

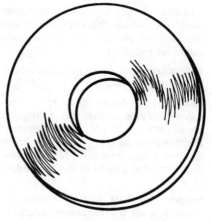

hard disk

hardware Physical equipment such as electronic, magnetic, and mechanical devices. Contrast with *software*.

hardware

hardware description languages (HDL) Languages and notations that facilitate the documentation, design, simulation, and manufacture of digital computer systems.

hardware resources CPU time, internal storage space, direct access storage space, and input/output devices, all of which are required to do the work of processing data automatically and efficiently.

hard-wired Physically connected to a computer, usually by an electronic conductor.

hashing A key-to-address transformation in which the keys determine the location of the data. Sometimes called hash coding.

hash totals The totals of the numbers of identifying fields.

head (1) A device that reads, records, or erases data on a storage medium, for example, a small electromagnet used to read, write, or erase data on a magnetic disk. (2) A special data item that points to the beginning of a list.

header The first part of a message containing all the necessary information for directing the message to its destination(s).

header card A card that contains information about the data in cards that follow.

header record A record containing constant, common, or identifying information for a group of records that follows.

heap sort See *tree sort*.

Hertz Cycles per second. Abbreviated Hz.

heuristic Descriptive of an exploratory method of attacking a problem, in which the solution is obtained by successive evaluations of the progress toward the final results (e.g., guided trial and error). Contrast with *algorithm*. See *artificial intelligence* and *machine learning*.

hex See *hexadecimal*.

hexadecimal Pertaining to a numeral system with a radix of 16. Digits greater than "9" are represented by letters of the alphabet. For example, the binary numeral 1110001011010011 can be represented as hexadecimal E2D3.

hexadecimal number A numeral, usually of more than one digit, representing a sum in which the quantity represented by each digit is based on a radix of 16. The digits used are 0, 1, 2, 3, 4, 5, 6, 7, 8, 9, A, B, C, D, E, and F.

hexadecimal point The radix point in a hexadecimal numeral system. The point that separates the integer part of a mixed hexadecimal numeral from the fractional part. In the numeral 3F.6A7 the hexadecimal point is between the digits F and 6.

hierarchial network A computer network in which processing and control functions are performed at several levels by computers specially designed for the functions performed.

hierarchy (1) Order in which the arithmetic operations, within a formula or statement, will be executed. (2) Arrangement into a graded series.

high-level language A programming language oriented toward the problem to be solved or the procedures to be used. Contrast with *machine language*. See *problem-oriented language* and *procedure-oriented language*.

high order Pertaining to the digit or digits of a number that have the greatest weight or significance; for example, in the number 7643215, the high order digit is 7. Contrast with *low order*. See *most significant digit*.

high order column The leftmost column of a punch card field.

high-punch Same as *twelve-punch* and *Y-punch*.

high-speed printer See *line printer*.

hi-res graphics Abbreviation of high-resolution graphics. A smooth and realistic picture on a display screen, produced by a large number of pixels. Contrast with *low-res graphics*.

HIS An acronym for Hospital Information System.

hit A successful comparison of two items of data. Contrast with *match*.

hobby computer See *home computer, microcomputer,* and *personal computer*.

holding time In data communications, the length of time a communication channel is in use for each transmission. Includes both message time and operating time.

Hollerith, Herman (1860–1929) As a statistician and employee of the Census Bureau, he proposed using punched cards in conjunction with electromechanical relays to accomplish simple additions and sortings needed in the 1890 census. He set up a company to manufacture his punched card tabulator, and it became one of the parents of IBM Corporation.

Hollerith card A punched card consisting of 80 columns, each of which is divided from top to bottom into 12 punching positions.

Hollerith code A particular type of code used to represent alphanumeric data on punched cards. Named after Herman Hollerith, the originator of punched card tabulating. Each card column holds one character, and each decimal digit, letter, and special character is represented by one, two, or three holes punched into designated row positions of the column.

Hollerith's tabulator This tabulating equipment was used in the eleventh census of the United States (1890) and handled the records of over 63 million people. *(Illus. p. 94)*

Herman Hollerith

holography A potentially high-capacity data storage system that uses a laser beam to create images on film.

home computer A microcomputer used in the home. It may be used to play games, to control household appliances, to aid students with school homework, to perform business computation, and for a wide variety of other tasks. See *microcomputer* and *personal computer. (Illus. p. 94)*

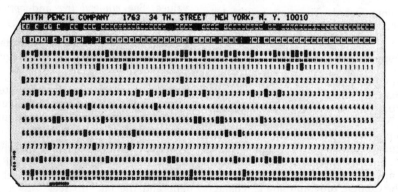

Hollerith card

Hollerith's tabulator

Grace Hopper

home computer

home record The first record in a chain of records used with the chaining method of file organization.

hopper See *card hopper*.

Hopper, Grace (born 1906) A mathematician and programmer who developed programs for the Mark 1 and early UNIVAC computers. She later became a pioneer in the field of computer languages. She wrote the first practical "compiler" program and played an important role in the development of the COBOL programming language.

host computer The primary or controlling computer in a multiple-computer network operation.

housekeeping Computer operations that do not directly contribute toward the desired results; in general, initialization, set-up, and clean-up operations. Sometimes called *bookkeeping*.

HSP An acronym for *High-Speed Printer*.

huffman tree Tree with minimum values. See *minimal tree* and *optimal merge tree*.

hybrid computer system A system that uses both analog and digital equipment. *(Illus. p. 95)*

hybrids Circuits fabricated by interconnecting smaller circuits of different technologies mounted on a single substrate.

hypertape A magnetic tape unit that uses a cartridge rather than a reel of tape. The cartridge consists of a reel of tape and the take-up reel.

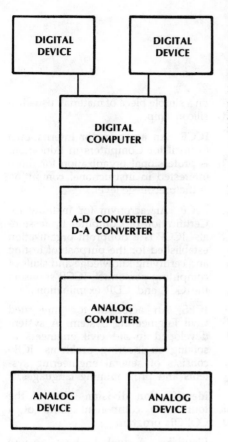

hybrid computer system

hysteresis The lagging of an effect behind the cause that is producing it; for example, the lagging of the polarization of a magnetic material behind the magnetizing force that is producing it.

Hz An abbreviation for Hertz; cycles per second.

IAMCS An acronym for International Association for Mathematics and Computers in Simulation. A professional organization to facilitate the exchange of scientific information among specialists, builders, or users interested in analog and hybrid computational methods.

IBI An acronym for Intergovernmental Bureau of Informatics. An organization consisting of members of the United Nations, UNESCO, or other UN Agencies. The goal is to promote scientific research, computer education and training, and the exchange of information between developed and developing countries. The main focus of IBI is to promote informatics, particularly in developing countries.

IBM Corporation The world's largest manufacturer of data processing equipment.

IBM Personal Computer A popular microcomputer system manufactured by IBM Corporation.

IBM System 32/34/38 Business computer systems designed by the IBM Corporation.

IBM System 32/34/38

IC An acronym for *Integrated Circuit*, a complex electronic circuit fabricated on a simple piece of material, usually a silicon chip.

ICCE An acronym for International Council for Computers in Education. A professional organization for those interested in instructional computing at the precollege level.

ICCP An acronym for Institute for Certification of Computer Professionals. ICCP is a nonprofit organization established for the purpose of testing and certifying knowledge and skills of computing personnel. ICCP sponsors the CCP and CDP examinations.

ICES An acronym for Integrated Civil Engineering System. A system developed to aid civil engineers in solving engineering problems. ICES consists of several engineering systems and programming languages.

identification division One of the four main component parts of a COBOL program.

identifier A symbol whose purpose is to identify, indicate, or name a body of data.

idle time The time that a computer system is available for use, but is not in actual operation.

IDP An acronym for *Integrated Data Processing*.

IEEE An acronym for Institute of Electrical and Electronics Engineers. A professional engineering organization with a strong interest in computer systems and their uses.

IEEE-CS The IEEE Computer Society. A group formed to advance the theory and practice of computer and information processing technology. See *IEEE*.

IFAC An acronym for International Federation of Automatic Control. A multinational organization concerned with advancing the science and technology of control.

IFIPS An acronym for International Federation of Information Processing Societies. A multinational organization representing professional and educational societies actively engaged in the field of information processing. Meets every three years.

IIR An acronym for International Institute for Robotics.

I²L An acronym for Integrated Injection Logic. I²L chips are used in electronic wristwatches and as control devices for industrial products, automobiles, and computer systems. This is a developing technology that will be used in future microprocessors and semiconductor memories.

illegal character A character or combination of bits which is not accepted as a valid or known representation by the computer.

illegal operation A process that the computer cannot perform.

image An exact logical duplicate stored in a different medium. See *card image*.

image processing Techniques for processing pictorial information by computer.

immediate access Ability of a computer to put data in (or remove it from) storage without delay.

immediate access storage See *internal storage*.

immediate address Pertaining to an instruction whose address part contains the value of an operand rather than its address. It is not an address at all, but rather an operand supplied as part of an instruction.

impact printer A data printout device that imprints by momentary pressure of raised type against paper, using ink or ribbon as a color medium. See *line printer*.

impedance The total opposition (resistance) a circuit offers to the flow of alternating current at a given frequency.

implementation (1) The process of installing a computer system. It involves choosing the equipment, installing the equipment, training the personnel, and establishing the computing center operating policies. (2) The representation of a programming language on a specific computer system. (3) The act of installing a program.

IMS An acronym for Information Management System. A data base management system software package that provides the facilities for storing and retrieving information from hierarchically structured files and data bases.

incidence matrix A two-dimensional array that describes the edges in a graph. Also called a *connection matrix*.

inclusive OR The Boolean operator that gives a truth table value of true if either or both of the two variables it connects is true. If neither is true, the value is false. Abbreviated OR.

increment An amount added to or subtracted from a value of a variable.

incremental plotter See *plotter*.

indegree The number of directed edges that point to a node.

index (1) A symbol or number used to identify a particular quantity in an array of similar quantities; for example, X(5) is the fifth item in an array of X's. (2) A table of references held in storage in some sequence, which may be addressed to obtain the addresses of other items of data; for example, items in a file. See *index register*.

indexed address An address that is modified by the content of an index register prior to or during the execution of a computer instruction.

indexed sequential access method A means of organizing data on a direct access device. A directory or index is created to show where the data records are stored. Any desired data record can thus be retrieved from the device by consulting the index(es).

indexing A programming technique whereby an instruction can be modified by a factor called an index. See *index*.

index register A register whose contents can be added to or subtracted from an address prior to or during the execution of an instruction.

indicator A device that registers a condition in the computer.

indirect addressing Using an address that specifies a storage location that contains either a direct address or another indirect address. Also called *multilevel addressing*.

induce To produce an electrical charge, current, or voltage by induction. A charge on the gate of a field effect transistor (FET) induces an equal charge in the channel.

inductance In a circuit, the property that opposes any change in the existing current.

induction The process in which a body having electric and magnetic properties produces an electric charge, a voltage, or a magnetic field in an adjacent body, without physical contact.

industrial robot A computer-controlled machine used in assembly and production work that performs certain predetermined operations.

infix notation A notation where operators are embedded within operands.

information Meaningful and useful facts that are extracted from data fed to a computer. The meaning assigned to data by known conventions.

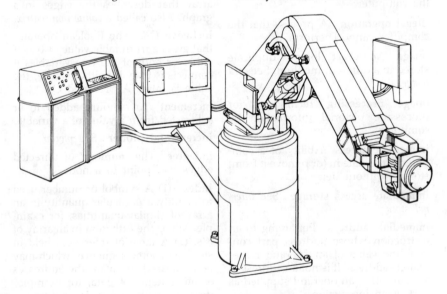

industrial robot

information bits In telecommunications, those bits that are generated by the data source and do not include error control bits.

information explosion The exponential increase in the growth and diversification of all forms of information.

information management system A system designed to organize, catalog, locate, store, retrieve, and maintain information.

information networks The interconnection of a geographically dispersed group of libraries and information centers, through telecommunications, for the purpose of sharing their total information resources among more people.

information processing The totality of operations performed by a computer; the handing of data according to rules of procedure to accomplish operations such as classifying, sorting, calculating, and recording.

information processing center See *data processing center*.

information processing machine A computer.

information providers The large businesses that supply information to a computer network, such as The Source or CompuServe, for a fee.

information retrieval (1) That branch of computer technology concerned with techniques for **storing** and searching large quantities of data and making selected data available. (2) The methods used to recover specific information from stored data.

information science The study of how people create, use, and communicate information in all forms.

information storage and retrieval See *information retrieval*.

information system A collection of people, procedures, and equipment designed, built, operated, and maintained to collect, record, process, store, retrieve, and display information.

information theory The branch of learning concerned with the likelihood of accurate transmission or communication of messages subject to transmission failure, noise, and distortion.

information utility See *computer utility*.

inhibit To prohibit from taking place.

initialize To preset a variable or counter to proper starting values before commencing a calculation. See *preset*.

in-line coding Coding that is located in the main part of a routine.

in-line processing The processing of data in random order, not subject to preliminary editing or sorting.

input The introduction of data from an external storage medium into a computer's internal storage unit. Contrast with *output*.

input area An area of internal storage reserved for input data (data transferred from an input device or an auxiliary storage device). Contrast with *output area*.

input data Data to be processed. Synonymous with *input*. Contrast with *output data*.

input device A unit that is used to get data into the central processing unit from the human user. Card read-

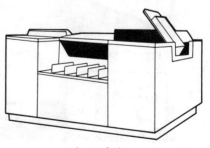

input device

ers, typewriters, MICR units, and acoustic character recognition (voice input) units are examples of input devices. Contrast with *output device*.

input job stream See *job stream*.

input media Punched cards, magnetic disks, punched tape, cassette tapes, and MICR and OCR encoded documents are typical input media.

input/output Pertaining to the techniques, media, and devices used to achieve human/machine communication. Abbreviated I/O.

input/output channel A channel that transmits input data to, or output data from, a computer. See *multiplexer channel*, *RS-232*, and *selector channel*.

input/output control system A set of routines for handling the many detailed aspects of input and output operations. Abbreviated IOCS.

input/output device A unit that is used to get data into the central processing unit from the human user, and to transfer data from the computer's internal storage to some storage or output device. See *input device*, *output device*, and *peripheral equipment*.

input/output instructions Directions for the transfer of data between peripheral devices and main storage, which enable the central processing unit to control the peripheral devices connected to it.

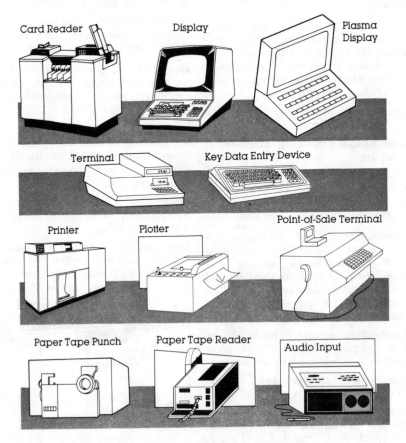

Card Reader   Display   Plasma Display

Terminal   Key Data Entry Device

Printer   Plotter   Point-of-Sale Terminal

Paper Tape Punch   Paper Tape Reader   Audio Input

input/output device

input/ouput ports The sockets on a computer where the peripherals interface. See *peripheral equipment*.

input/output symbol A flowcharting symbol used to indicate an input operation to the procedure or an output operation from the procedure. A parallelogram figure is used to represent this symbol.

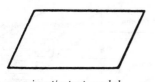

input/output symbol

input stream The sequence of control statements and data submitted to the operating system on an input unit especially activated for that purpose by the operator. Same as *job stream*.

inputting The process of entering data into a computer system.

inquiry A request for data from storage; for example, a request for the number of available airline seats in an airline reservation system.

inquiry station The device from which any inquiry is made. The inquiry station or terminal can be geographically remote from the computer or at the computer console.

insertion method See *sifting*.

installation A general term for a particular computing system in the context of the overall function it serves and the individuals who manage it, operate it, apply it to problems, service it, and use the results it produces.

installation time Time spent in installing, testing, and accepting equipment.

instruction A group of characters, bytes, or bits that defines an operation to be performed by the computer. An instruction is usually made up of an operation code and one or more operands. See *machine instruction*.

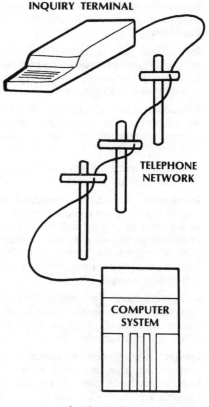

INQUIRY TERMINAL

TELEPHONE NETWORK

COMPUTER SYSTEM

inquiry station

ADD X TO R

instruction

instructional computing The educational process of teaching individuals the various phases of computer science and data processing.

instruction code Same as *operation code*.

instruction counter A counter that indicates the location of the next computer instruction to be interpreted. Same as *program counter*.

instruction format The makeup and arrangement of a computer instruction.

101

instruction register A hardware register that stores an instruction for execution.

instruction set A set of vendor-supplied operation codes for a particular computer or family of computers. Synonymous with *repertoire*.

instruction time The time it takes for an instruction to be fetched from internal storage by the control unit and interpreted.

instruction word A computer word that contains an instruction.

instrument A document designed as a form, report, questionnaire, or guide to be used in a planned systematic procedure to gather data for the purpose of providing information to the individual, group, or organization initiating the request.

instrumentation The application of devices for the measuring, recording, and/or controlling of physical properties and movements.

integer A whole number that may be positive, negative, or zero. It does not have a fractional part. Examples of integers are 26, −417, and 0.

integer BASIC A type of BASIC language that can process whole numbers (integers) only.

integrated circuit A combination of interconnected circuit elements and amplifying devices inseparably associated on or within a continuous layer of semiconductor material, called a substrate. See *large scale integration, linear IC, medium scale integration, small scale integration,* and *very large scale integration.*

integrated data processing Data processing by a system that coordinates a number of previously unconnected processes in order to improve overall efficiency by reducing or eliminating redundant data entry or processing operations. Abbreviated IDP.

integrated injection logic See I^2L.

integrity The preservation of programs or data for their intended purpose. See *data integrity.*

intelligence See *artificial intelligence.*

intelligent terminal An input/output device in which a number of computer processing characteristics are physically built into, or attached to, the terminal unit. See *point-of-scale terminal.*

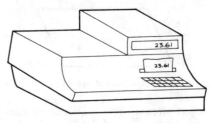

intelligent terminal

interactive An immediate response to input. The user is in direct and continual two-way communication with the computer.

interactive processing A type of real-time processing involving a continuing dialog between user and computer; the user is allowed to modify data and/or instructions. See *conversational mode.*

interactive system A system in which the human user or device serviced by the computer can communicate directly with the operating program. For human users, this is termed a conversational system.

interblock gap Same as *interrecord gap.*

interface A common boundary between two pieces of hardware or between two systems.

interference Unwanted signals that degrade the quality of wanted signals.

interlace To assign successive addresses to physically separated storage locations on a magnetic disk or drum in such a way as to reduce the access time.

interleaving A multiprogramming technique in which parts of one program are inserted into another program so that if there are processing delays in one of the programs, parts of the other program can be processed.

interlock A protective facility that prevents one device or operation from interfering with another; for example, the locking of the switches on the control console to prevent manual movement of the switches while the computer is executing a program.

intermittent error An error that occurs intermittently but not constantly and is extremely difficult to reproduce.

internal data representation Data representation in registers, storage, and other devices inside the computer.

internal memory Same as *internal storage.*

internal sort The sequencing of two or more records within the central processing unit. The first phase of a multipass sort program.

internal storage Addressable storage directly controlled by the central processing unit. The central processing unit uses internal storage to store programs while they are being executed and data while it is being processed. Also called *immediate access storage, internal memory, main storage,* and *primary storage.*

interpreter A computer program that translates each source language statement into a sequence of machine instructions and then executes these machine instructions before translating the next source language statement.

interpreting Printing on punched cards with the meaning of the holes punched in the same card.

interrecord gap The distance on a magnetic tape between the end of one record and the beginning of the next.

Such spacing facilitates tape start-stop operations. Also called file gap, interblock gap, and record gap. Abbreviated IRG.

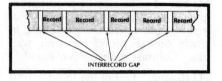

interrecord gap

interrupt A signal that, when activated, causes the hardware to transfer program control to some specific location in internal storage, thus breaking the normal flow of the program being executed. After the interrupt has been processed, program control is again returned to the interrupted program. An interrupt can be generated as the result of a program action, by an operator activating switches on the computer console, or by a peripheral device causing the interrupting signal. Often called *trapping.*

interval timer A mechanism whereby elapsed time can be monitored by a computer system.

interruption A break in the normal sequence of executing instructions.

inventory control The use of a computer system to monitor an inventory.

inventory management A term applied to the daily and periodic bookkeeping commonly associated with inventory control and with forecasting the future needs of items or groups of items.

invert To turn over; reverse.

inverted file A file organized so that it can be accessed by character rather than by record key.

inverter A circuit in which a binary one input produces a binary zero output and vice versa.

invisible refresh A scheme that refreshes dynamic memories without disturbing the rest of the system.

I/O An abbreviation for *input/output*.

I/O bound The term applied to programs that require a large number of input/output operations, resulting in much central processing unit wait time. Contrast with *compute-bound*.

I/O channel Part of the input/output system of a computer. Under the control of I/O commands the "channel" transfers blocks of data between the internal storage and peripheral equipment.

IOCS An acronym for *Input/Output Control System*. A standard set of input/output routines designed to initiate and control the input and output processes of a computer system.

I/O port A connection to a central processing unit (CPU) that provides for data paths between the CPU and peripheral devices, such as display terminals, typewriters, line printers, magnetic disk units, and so on.

IPL An acronym for Information Processing Language. See *list processing languages*.

IPL-V An acronym for Information Processing Language Five. A list

processing language primarily used for working with heuristic-type problems.

IRG An acronym for *InterRecord Gap*. See *interrecord gap*.

ISAM An acronym for *Indexed Sequential Access Method*.

ISO An acronym for International Standards Organization.

isolation In a computer security system, information is compartmentalized so that access to it is on a "need to know" basis. The state of being separated or set apart from others.

ISR An acronym for Information Storage and Retrieval. See *information retrieval*.

item A group of related characters treated as a unit. (A record is a group of related items, and a file is a group of related records.)

iterate To repeat automatically, under program control, the same series of processing steps until a predetermined stop or branch condition is reached. See *loop* and *Newton-Raphson*.

IWP An acronym for International Word Processing Association. This organization encourages the development and use of word processing systems and methods.

jack A connecting device to which a wire or wires of a circuit may be attached and which is arranged for the insertion of a plug.

Jacquard, Joseph Marie (1752–1834) Built a weaving machine (*Jacquard loom*) that used a line of punched cards to automatically control the patterns woven.

Jacquard loom

Joseph Marie Jacquard

Jacquard loom A weaving machine invented near the beginning of the 19th century by Joseph Marie Jacquard in which punched cards controlled the movements of the shuttles in order to produce tapestries of complicated design.

jargon The technical vocabulary associated with a specific trade, business, or profession.

JCL An acronym for *Job Control Language*.

jargon

job A collection of specified tasks constituting a unit of work for a computer; for example, a program or

105

related group of programs used as a unit.

job control language The language used in control cards. Cards representing job control language are interspersed with source or object card decks and data decks. These cards give information concerning who the computer user is, what charge number to use, and so on. Abbreviated JCL. See *control cards*.

job queue The set of programs and data currently making its way through the computer. In most operating systems, each job is brought into the queue and is processed (given control of the computer) when it is the "oldest" job within its own priority. An exception to this is the case of a job of higher priority that has not yet obtained sufficient resources to be processed.

job stream The input to the operating system; may consist of one or more jobs. Same as *input stream*.

job-to-job transition The process of locating a program and the files associated with the program and of preparing the computer for the execution of a particular job.

Josephson junction A potentially high capacity data storage system based upon the properties of super-cold circuits.

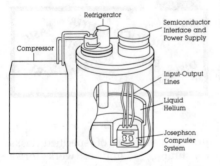

Josephson junction computer

JOVIAL An acronym for Jules' Own Version of the International Algorithmic Language. A programming language used primarily for working with scientific and command and control problems. The language has wide usage in systems implemented by the U.S. Air Force.

joystick A type of input device. It has a stick that is manipulated by the user to produce different inputs. Joysticks are often used in conjunction with graphic terminals. Also called a paddle.

joystick

JUG An acronym for Joint Users Group. An organization of digital computer user groups. See *users group*.

jump A departure from the normal sequence of executing instructions in a computer. Synonymous with *branch* and *transfer*. See *conditional transfer* and *unconditional transfer*.

justification The act of adjusting, arranging, or shifting digits to the left or right, to fit a prescribed pattern.

justify To align the characters in a field. For example, to left justify, the first character (e.g., the *most significant digit*) appears in the leftmost character position in a field. To right justify, the last character (e.g., the *least significant digit*) is written in the last or rightmost character position in the field. See *normalize*.

juxtaposition The positioning of items adjacent to each other.

K (1) An abbreviation for kilo or 1000 in decimal notation. For example, "100K ch/s" means "a reading speed of 100,000 characters per second." (2) Loosely, when referring to storage capacity, two to the tenth power; in decimal notation 1024. The expression 8K represents 8192 (8 times 1024).

Kansas City Standard A low-speed cassette storage format.

Karnaugh map A two-dimensional plot of a truth table.

kb (kilobyte) 1024 bytes.

kc One thousand characters per second. Used to express the rate of data transfer operations.

Kelvin The unit of temperature measurement of the SI metric system, for normal use expressed in degrees Celsius.

kernel The set of programs in an operating system which implement the most primitive of that system's functions. See *primitive*.

key (1) The field or fields that identify a record. (2) The field that determines the position of a record in a sorted sequence. (3) A lever on a manually operated machine such as a typewriter or visual display keyboard.

keyboard A group of marked levers operated manually for recording characters.

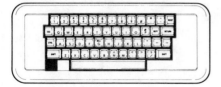

keyboard

keyboard terminal A typewriter-like keyboard that allows data to be entered into a computer system.

keyboard-to-disk system A data entry system in which data can be entered directly onto a disk by typing the data into a keyboard.

keyboard-to-tape system A system in which data can be entered directly onto a tape by typing the data at a keyboard.

key data entry device The equipment used to prepare data so that computer equipment can accept it, including keypunch machines, key-to-disk units, and key-to-tape units.

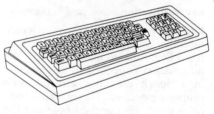

key data entry device

keypunch A keyboard operated device used to punch holes in punch cards to represent data. *(Illus. p. 108)*

keypunching The process by which original, or source data, is recorded in punch cards. The operator reads source documents and, by depressing keys on a keypunch machine, converts source document information into punched holes.

keystroke The action of pressing one of the keys on a keyboard.

key-to-address See *hashing*.

key-to-disk unit A keyboard unit used to store data directly on a magnetic disk.

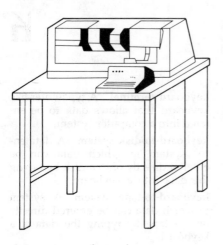

keypunch

key-to-tape unit A keyboard unit used to store data directly on magnetic tape.

key verification See *card verification*.

key-verify The use of the punch card machine known as a verifier, which has a keyboard, to make sure that the information supposed to be punched in a punch card has actually been properly punched. The machine indicates when the punched hole and the depressed key disagree. See *verifier machine*.

keyword (1) One of the significant and informative words in a title or document that describe the content of that document. (2) A primary element in a programming language statement (e.g., words such as LET, GOTO, and INPUT in the BASIC programming language).

key-word-in-context See *KWIC*.

kHz An abbreviation for *kilohertz*.

kilo Metric prefix, means 1000 times.

kilobit A thousand bits.

kilobyte A kilobyte is 2^{10} or 1024 bytes. It is commonly abbreviated to "K" and used as a suffix when describing memory size. Thus, 24K really means a $24 \times 1024 = 24,576$ byte memory system.

kilocycle One thousand cycles per second.

kilohertz One thousand hertz. Abbreviated kHz.

kilomegacycle A billion cycles per second.

kludge Makeshift. A collection of mismatched components that has been assembled into a system.

knowledge engineering The engineering discipline whereby knowledge is integrated into computer systems to solve complex problems normally requiring a high level of human expertise.

knowledge industries The industries that perform data processing and provide information products and services.

KSR An acronym for Keyboard Send/Receive. A teletypewriter unit with keyboard and printer.

KWIC An acronym for Key-Word-In-Context. A method of indexing information by preselected words or phrases that takes into consideration the context in which the words are used.

label An identifier or name that is used in a computer program to identify or describe an instruction, statement, message, data value, record, item, or file. Same as *name*.

lag The relative difference between two events, mechanisms, or states.

language A set of rules, representations, and conventions used to convey information. See *programming language*.

language statement A statement that is coded by a user of a computing system and is used to convey information to a processing program such as a language translator program, service program, or control program. A statement may signify that an operation be performed or may simply contain data that is to be passed to the processing program.

language subset A part of a language that can be used independently of the rest of the language.

language translation The process of changing information from one language to another; for example, Russian to English, English to German, BASIC to FORTRAN, or FORTRAN to Pascal.

language translator A program that transforms statements from one language to another without significantly changing their meaning (e.g., a *compiler* or *assembler*).

LARC An acronym for Livermore Automatic Research Computer. One of the first of the high-performance giant computers.

large scale integration The process of placing a large number (usually over 100) of integrated circuits on one silicon chip. Abbreviated LSI. See *very large scale integration*.

laser A tightly packed, narrow beam of light formed by the emission of high-energy molecules.

laser storage A storage system that uses a controlled laser beam to expose small sections of a photosensitive area. See *holography*.

last in-first out See *LIFO*.

latency The rotational delay in reading or writing a record to a direct access auxiliary storage device such as a disk or drum.

layout The overall design or plan such as system flowcharts, schematics, diagrams, format for printer output, format for card columns, makeup of a document (book), and so forth.

LCD An acronym for Liquid Crystal Display. A way to make letters and numbers appear by reflecting light on a special crystalline substance.

leader A blank section of tape at the beginning of a reel of paper tape or magnetic tape.

leading edge (1) The edge of a punched card that first enters the card reader. (2) In optical scanning, the edge of the document or page that enters the read position first. Contrast with *trailing edge*.

LEADING EDGE

leading edge

leaf   A terminal node of a tree.

leased line   Generally refers to a private full-period data communication line.

least significant digit   Pertaining to the digit of a number that has the least weight or significance (e.g., in the number 54321, the least significant digit is 1). Abbreviated LSD. See *justify* and *low order*.

LED   An acronym for Light Emitting Diode, a commonly used alphanumeric display unit that glows when supplied with a specified voltage.

left justify   See *justify*.

Leibniz, Gottfried (1646–1716)   A German mathematician who invented a calculating machine called a "stepped reckoner" (1672) that could add, subtract, and multiply.

Leibniz's calculator   A calculating machine designed by Baron von Leibniz. The machine performed addition and subtraction in the same manner as Pascal's calculator; however, additional gears were included in the machine that enabled it to multiply directly.

length   As related to a computer word, the number of characters, bytes, or bits in a computer word. A variable word is made up of several characters ending with a special end character. A fixed word is composed of the same number of bits, bytes, or characters in each word. See *fixed word length* and *variable word length*.

Gottfried Leibniz

letter shift   A keyboard key (or the code generated by the key) which signifies that the characters which follow are to be read as letters until a figure shift appears in the message. Same as *figure shift*.

level   The degree of subordination in a hierarchy. A measure of the distance from a node to the root of a tree.

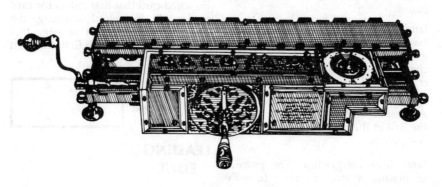

Leibniz's calculator

lexicon A language with definitions for all terms.

LF An abbreviation for *Line Feed*.

librarian (1) A person who is responsible for an organization's library of technical documentation, including manuals used by programmers, operators, and other employees. (2) A person who has responsibility for the safekeeping of all computer files, for example, disk packs, magnetic tapes, etc. Also called a *file librarian* and *tape librarian*.

librarian

library A published collection of programs, routines, and subroutines available to every user of the computer. Same as *program library*. See *disk library* and *tape library*.

library automation Application of computers and other technology to library operations and services.

library routine A tested routine that is maintained in a program library.

LIFO An acronym for Last In-First Out, the way most microprocessor program stacks operate. The last data or instruction word placed on the stack is the first to be retrieved. See *FIFO* and *push down stack*.

light emitting diode See *LED*.

light pen An electrical device that resembles a pen and can be used to write or sketch on the screen of a cathode ray tube, that is, to provide input to the computer through its use. A tool for display terminal operators.

light pen

limiting operation The capacity of a total system with no alternative routings can be no greater than the operation with the least capacity. The total system can be effectively scheduled by simply scheduling the limiting operation. Synonymous with *bottleneck*.

line See *channel*.

linear IC An analog integrated circuit, as opposed to a digital integrated circuit. See *integrated circuit*.

linear list See *sequential list*.

linear programming Technique for finding an optimum combination when there may be no single best one. For example, linear programming could be used to solve this problem: "What combination of foods would give the most calories and best nutrition for the least money?" A computer need not be used; linear programming is often used because such problems

111

would take too long to solve by hand. Abbreviated LP.

linear search A search that begins with the first element and compares until a matching key is found or the end of the list is reached.

line circuit A physical circuit path, as a data communication line.

line feed The operation that advances the paper by one line. Abbreviated LF. See *form feed.*

line number In programming languages such as BASIC, a number that begins a line of the source program for purposes of identification; a numerical label.

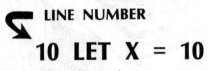

LINE NUMBER

10 LET X = 10

line number

line printer An output peripheral device that prints data one line at a time. See *electrostatic printer.*

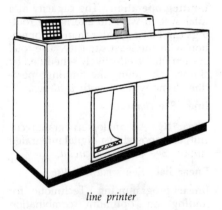

line printer

line printer controller A device that provides character print buffers and automatic control and timing for a specific printer.

line printing The printing of an entire line of characters as a unit.

line speed The maximum rate at which signals may be transmitted over

a given channel, usually in baud or bits per second.

lines per minute Usually used to describe the speed of a line printer. Abbreviated LPM.

link In data communications, a physical connection between one location and another whose function is to transmit data. See *communication channel.*

linkage Coding that connects two separately coded routines; for example, the coding that links a subroutine to the program with which it is to be used. See *calling sequence.*

linking loader An executive program that connects different program segments so they may be run in the computer as one unit. A useful piece of software that makes subtasks easily available to a main task.

liquid crystal display A visual display that is made of two glass plates sandwiched together with a nematic liquid crystal solution between them.

LISP An acronym for LISt Processing. A list processing language primarily designed to process data consisting of lists. See *list processing languages.*

list (1) Organization of data using indexes and pointers to allow for nonsequential retrieval. (2) An ordered set of items. (3) To print every relevant item of input data. (4) A system command to print program statements; for example, the LIST command in the BASIC language will cause the system to print a listing of the program. (5) An ordered collection of atoms.

listing Generally, any report produced on a printing device (line printer or typewriter). For example, a source listing is a printout of the source program processed by the compiler; an error listing is a report showing all input data found to be invalid by the processing program. See *assembly listing. (Illus. p. 113)*

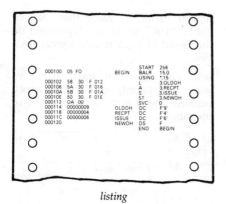

```
000100   05 FO              START  256
                      BEGIN  BALR   15,0
                            USING  *,15
000102   58  30  F 012       L     3,OLDOH
000106   5A  30  F 016       A     3,RECPT
00010A   5B  30  F 01A       S     3,ISSUE
00010E   50  30  F 01E       ST    3,NEWOH
000112   0A  00              SVC   0
000114   00000009    OLDOH   DC    F'9'
000118   00000004    RECPT   DC    F'4'
00011C   00000006    ISSUE   DC    F'6'
000120               NEWOH   DS    F
                             END   BEGIN
```

listing

list processing A method of processing data in the form of lists. Usually, chained lists are used so that the logical order of items can be changed without altering their physical locations.

list processing languages Languages designed especially to process data that is in list form. Examples include IPL, LISP, POP-2, and SAIL.

liter A metric unit of liquid capacity equal to one cubic decimeter.

literal Another name for *constant*. A symbol that defines itself.

liveware Revolting (and misleading) expression meaning computer people.

load (1) To read information into the storage of a computer. (2) To put cards into a card reader, to put a paper tape onto a paper tape reader, or to put a disk pack on a disk drive unit.

load-and-go An operating technique in which the loading and execution phases of a program are performed in one continuous run. See *compile-and-go*.

loader A service routine designed to read programs into internal storage in preparation for their execution.

load point A spot at the beginning of a tape.

load sharing The technique of using two or more computers in order to handle excess volumes during peak periods. It is desirable to have one computer handle less than peak loads with the others acting as the fall-back equipment.

local A term that refers to computer equipment at your own location. Contrast with *remote*.

local intelligence Processing power and storage capacity built into a terminal so that it does not need to be connected to a computer to perform certain tasks. A "dumb terminal" has no local intelligence. See *smart terminal*.

local store A relatively small number of high-speed storage elements that may be directly referred to by the instructions.

location A place in the computer's memory where information is to be stored.

lock code A sequence of letters and/or numbers provided by the operators of a time-sharing system to prevent unauthorized tampering with a user's program. The lock code serves as a secret "password" in that the computer will refuse any changes to the program unless the user supplies the correct lock code. Also called password.

lockout (1) Suppression of an interrupt. (2) A programming technique used to prevent access to critical data by both CPU's at the same time (in a multiprocessing environment).

log A record of the operations of data processing equipment, listing each job or run, the time it required, operator actions, and other pertinent data.

logarithm The exponent of the power to which a fixed number is to be raised to produce a given number. The fixed number is called the base and is usually 10 or e. Example: $2^3 = 8$, 3 is the logarithm of 8 to the base 2; this means that 2 must be raised to the third power to produce 8.

logging-in The process of establishing communication with and verifying the authority to use the computer during conversational programming. See *conversational mode*.

logic (1) The science dealing with the formal principles of reasoning and thought. (2) The basic principles and application of truth tables and interconnection between logical elements required for arithmetic computation in an automatic data processing system.

logical decision Generally, a decision as to which one or two possible courses of action is to be followed.

logical design The specification of the working relations between the parts of a system in terms of symbolic logic and without primary regard for hardware implementation.

logical file A collection of one or more logical records. See *logical record*.

logical instruction An instruction that executes an operation that is defined in symbolic logic such as AND, OR, or NOR.

logical multiply The AND operator.

logical operations The computer operations that are logical in nature, such as logical tests and decisions. This is in contrast with the arithmetic and data transfer operations, which involve no decision.

logical product The AND function of several terms. The product is 1 only when all of the terms are 1; otherwise it is 0.

logical record The record as defined by the program designer. One or more logical records are normally stored in a physical record. Contrast with *physical record*.

logical sum The inclusive OR function of several terms. The sum is 1 when any or all of the terms are 1; it is 0 only when all are 0.

logical unit number A number assigned to a physical peripheral device.

logical value A value that may be either "true" or "false" depending on the result of a particular logical decision.

logic card A circuit board that contains components and wiring which perform one or more logic functions or operations.

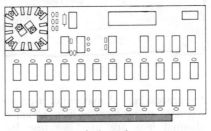

logic card

logic circuits A series of flip-flops and gates that directs electrical impulses to and from the appropriate portions of a computer system.

logic diagram A diagram that represents a logical design and sometimes the hardware implementation.

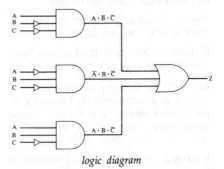

logic diagram

logic element A device that performs a logic function.

logic operator Any of the Boolean operators such as AND, OR, NAND, EXCLUSIVE OR, and NOR.

logic symbol A symbol used to represent a logic element graphically. *(Illus. p. 115)*

log in To sign in on a computer. Same as *log on*.

AND

OR

NAND

NOR

INVERTER

EXCLUSIVE OR

logic symbol

looping Executing the same instruction or series of instructions over and over again.

Lovelace, Ada Augusta (1815–1852) Ada Augusta, the Countess of Lovelace, wrote about Charles Babbage's proposed machine: "The Analytical Engine weaves algebraical patterns just as the Jacquard loom weaves flowers and leaves." She was a skilled mathematician and close friend of Charles Babbage. She developed the essential ideas of programming. See *Ada, analytical engine,* and *Babbage, Charles.*

Ada Augusta Lovelace

LOGO A higher-level, interactive programming language that assumes the user has access to some type of on-line terminal. The language was designed for school students and seems particularly suited to students in the younger age groups.

log on The action by which a user begins a terminal session. Same as *log in.*

look-up See *table look-up.*

loop A sequence of instructions in a program that can be executed repetitively until certain specified conditions are satisfied. See *closed loop.*

loop code The repetition of a sequence of instructions by using a program loop. Loop coding requires more execution time than would straight line coding but will result in a savings of storage. Contrast with *straight line code.*

loophole A mistake or omission in software or hardware which allows the system's access controls to be circumvented.

low-level language A machine-dependent programming language translated by an assembler into instructions and data formats for a given machine. Same as *assembly language.*

low order Pertaining to the digit or digits of a number that have the least weight or significance; for example, in the number 7643215, the low order digit is 5. Contrast with *high order.* See *least significant digit.*

115

low order column The rightmost (highest numbered) column of a punch card field.

low-res graphics Abbreviation of low-resolution graphics. A blocky and jagged picture on a display screen, produced by a small number of pixels. Contrast with *hi-res graphics*.

LP An acronym for *Linear Programming*.

LPM An acronym for *Lines Per Minute*.

LSC An acronym for Least Significant Character. See *Least Significant Digit*.

LSD An acronym for *Least Significant Digit*.

LSI An acronym for *Large Scale Integration*.

Lukasiewicz notation See *Polish notation*.

M Abbreviation for mega, meaning 1 million. Used to represent 1,048,576. Often used to label the capacity of storage devices (i.e., disks).

machine address Same as *absolute address*.

machine code An operation code that a machine is designed to recognize.

machine error A deviation from correctness in data resulting from an equipment failure.

machine independent (1) A term used to indicate that a program is developed in terms of the problem rather than in terms of the characteristics of the computer system. (2) The ability to run a program on the computers made by different manufacturers, or upon the various machines made by the same manufacturer.

machine instruction An instruction that a computer can directly recognize and execute. See *instruction*.

machine language The basic language of a computer. Programs written in machine language require no further interpretation by a computer.

machine learning Refers to a heuristic process where a device improves its performance based on past actions. See *artificial intelligence* and *heuristic*.

machine operator See *computer operator*.

machine-oriented language A programming language that is more like a machine language than a human language.

machine-readable information Information recorded on any medium in such a way that it can be sensed or read by a machine. Also called *machine-sensible*.

machine run See *run*.

machine-sensible See *machine-readable information*.

macro A single, symbolic programming language statement that when translated results in a series of machine language statements.

macro assembler An assembler that allows the user to create and define new computer instructions (called *macro instructions*).

macro instruction (1) A source language instruction that is equivalent to a specified number of machine language instructions. (2) A machine language instruction that is composed of several micro instructions.

macroprogramming Programming with macro instructions; for example, writing control programs for a microprocessor using macro instructions. See *macro instruction* and *micro instruction*.

magcard A magnetic card developed by IBM Corporation, coated with a magnetic substance on which information is recorded. Magcards are frequently used in word processing systems.

magnetic Of, producing, caused by, or operated by magnetism.

magnetic bubble memory A memory that uses magnetic "bubbles" that move. The bubbles are locally magnetized areas that can move about in a magnetic material, such as a plate of orthoferrite. It is possible to control the reading in and out of this "bubble" within the magnetic material and, as a result, a very high-capacity memory can be built. Magnetic bubble memory devices will likely find uses in future data-storage systems.

magnetic card   A storage device consisting of a tray or cartridge of magnetically coated cards. These cards are made of material similar to magnetic tape (although considerably thicker) and have specific areas allocated for storing information. A magnetic card may be visualized as a magnetic tape cut into strips; several strips are placed side by side on a plastic card and mounted in a cartridge. See *CRAM* and *data cell*.

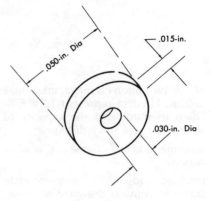

magnetic core

magnetic card

magnetic characters   A set of characters that is used for checks, insurance billings, utility bills, invoices, and so forth that permit special character-reading devices (MICR readers) to be employed to read the characters automatically. See *magnetic ink character recognition*.

magnetic core   A tiny, doughnut-shaped piece of magnetizable material that is capable of storing one binary digit.

magnetic core plane   A network of magnetic cores, each of which represents one core common to each storage location. A number of core planes are stacked together to form a magnetic core storage unit.

magnetic core storage   A system of storage in which data are represented in binary form by means of the directional flow of magnetic fields in tiny doughnut-shaped arrays of magnetic cores.

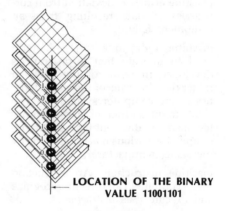

LOCATION OF THE BINARY VALUE 11001101

magnetic core storage

magnetic disk   A disk made of rigid material (hard disk) or heavy mylar (floppy disk). The disk surface is used to hold magnetized information.

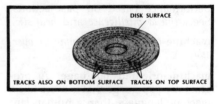

magnetic disk

magnetic disk unit   A peripheral storage device in which data is recorded on magnetizable disk surfaces.

See *direct access, disk pack, fixed-head disk unit, floppy disk,* and *moveable-head disk unit.*

devices such as magnetic tapes, disks, or drums.

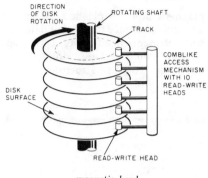

magnetic head

magnetic disk unit

magnetic drum A peripheral storage device consisting of a cylinder with a magnetizable surface on which data is recorded. See *direct access.*

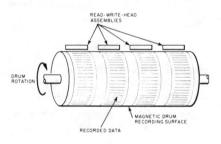

magnetic drum

magnetic film storage A storage device that uses 35mm magnetic film which is contained on a spool. The spool may be loaded onto a film handler unit.

magnetic head A device that is used for reading and writing information on

magnetic ink An ink that contains particles of a magnetic substance whose presence can be detected by magnetic sensors.

magnetic ink character recognition The recognition of characters printed with a special magnetic ink by machines. Abbreviated MICR.

magnetic ink character recognition

magnetic resonance The phenomenon in which a movement of a particle or system of particles is coupled resonantly to an external magnetic field.

magnetic storage Utilizing the magnetic properties of materials to store data on such devices and media as disks, tapes, cards, drums, cores, and films.

magnetic strip card A small card resembling a credit card to which a strip of magnetizable material is affixed. Information can be read from or written on this magnetic strip.

magnetic tape A plastic tape having a magnetic surface for storing data in a code of magnetized spots. Data may be represented on tape using a six- or eight-bit coding structure.

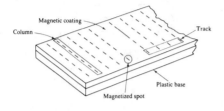

magnetic tape

magnetic tape cartridge A magnetic tape contained in a cartridge. The cartridge consists of a reel of tape and the take-up reel. Similar to a cassette, but of slightly different design.

magnetic tape cassette A magnetic tape storage device. A cassette consists of a one-eighth-inch magnetic tape housed in a plastic container.

magnetic tape cassette

magnetic tape cassette recorder An input/output and storage device that reads and writes cassette tapes. Used widely with microcomputer systems.

magnetic tape code The system of coding that is used to record magnetized patterns on magnetic tape. The magnetized patterns represent alphanumeric data. See *BCD* and *EBCDIC*.

magnetic tape deck Same as *magnetic tape unit*.

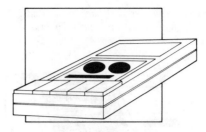

magnetic tape cassette recorder

magnetic tape density The number of characters that can be recorded on 2.54 cm (1 inch) of magnetic tape. A common recording density for magnetic tape is 630 characters per cm.

magnetic tape drive A device that moves tape past a head. Synonymous with *magnetic tape transport*.

magnetic tape reel A reel used to preserve the physical characteristics of magnetic tape. The tape is usually 1.27 cm (1/2 inch) wide and 751.52 meters (2400 feet) in length.

magnetic tape reel

magnetic tape sorting A sort program that uses magnetic tapes for auxiliary storage during a sort.

magnetic tape transport Same as *magnetic tape drive*.

magnetic tape unit A device containing a magnetic tape drive, together with reading and writing heads and associated controls. Synonymous with *magnetic tape deck*. See *magnetic tape cartridge* and *magnetic tape cassette*. (*Illus. p. 121*)

magnetic thin film See *thin film*.

magnitude (1) The absolute value of a number. (2) Size.

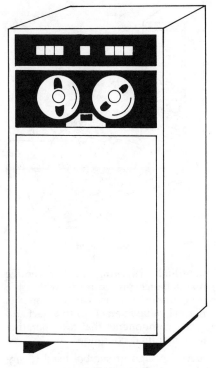

magnetic tape unit

Charles Mahon

mag tape A term sometimes used instead of magnetic tape.

Mahon, Charles (1753–1816) The Third Earl of Stanhope, who invented the Stanhope Demonstrator in 1777. This machine was the first arithmetical machine that used geared wheels.

mail box A set of locations in a RAM storage area. An area reserved for data addressed to specific peripheral devices or other microprocessors.

mainframe (1) The cabinet that houses the central processing unit and main memory of a computer system. (2) A designation of medium and large scale computers.

main memory Same as *internal storage*.

main storage The fastest general purpose storage of a computer. Same as *internal storage*.

maintainability The characteristic associated with the isolation and repair of a failure.

maintenance Tests, adjustments, repairs, or replacements that keep hardware and/or software in proper working order.

male connector A plug adapted so as to fit into a matching hollow part. See *connector* and *female connector*.

malfunction A failure in the operation of the central processing unit or peripheral device. The effect of a *fault*. Contrast with *error* and *mistake*. See *crash*.

management The individuals responsible for planning, organizing, and controlling a function or organization.

management information system An information system designed to supply organizational managers with the necessary information needed to plan, organize, staff, direct, and con-

121

trol the operations of the organization. Abbreviated MIS.

management science A mathematical or quantitative study of the management of resources of a business, usually with the aid of a computer.

mantissa That part of a floating point number that specifies the significant digits of the number. For example, in $.64321 \times 10^3$, .64321 is the mantissa.

manual input Data entered manually by the computer user to modify, continue, or resume processing of a computer program.

manual operation Processing of data in a system by direct manual techniques.

manufacturer's software A set of programming aids that the computer manufacturer supplies or makes available with a computer. See *systems programs*.

map A list that indicates the area of storage occupied by various elements of a program and its data. Also called *storage map*.

mapping A transformation from one set to another set; a correspondence.

manual input

marginal checking A preventive maintenance procedure in which the unit under test is varied from its normal value in an effort to detect and locate components that are operating in a marginal condition.

mark A sign or symbol used to signify or indicate an event in time or space.

Mark I An early electromechanical computer developed under the direc-

Mark I

tion of Howard Aiken at Harvard University. Also called *ASCC* (Automatic Sequence Controlled Calculator). See *Aiken, Howard*.

mark sensing The ability to mark cards or pages with a pencil to be read directly into the computer via a mark-sense reader. This is a very useful technique for acquiring data by hand and for avoiding the time lag and inaccuracy of keypunching. See *optical mark reader*.

MASER An acronym for Microwave Amplification by the Stimulated Emission of Radiation. A device capable of amplifying or generating radio frequency radiation. Maser amplifiers are used in satellite communication ground stations to amplify the extremely weak signals received from communication satellites.

mask A machine word containing a pattern of bits, bytes, or characters that is used to extract or select parts of other machine words by controlling an instruction that retains or eliminates selected bits, bytes, or characters. (2) A glass photographic plate that contains the circuit pattern used in the silicon-chip fabrication process.

mass storage Auxiliary storage as opposed to internal storage. Disk units and magnetic tape units are common mass storage devices. See *auxiliary storage*.

master clear A switch on some computer consoles that will clear certain operational registers and prepare for a new mode of operation.

master clock The device that controls the basic timing pulses of a computer.

master file A file containing relatively permanent information that is used as a source of reference and is generally updated periodically. Contrast with *detail file*.

master-slave computer system A computer system consisting of a master computer connected to one or more slave computers. The master computer provides the scheduling function and jobs to the slave computer(s).

match To check for identity between two or more items of data. Contrast with *hit*.

matching A data processing operation where two files are checked to determine if there is a corresponding item or group of items in each file.

mathematical functions A set of mathematical routines that are available in most programming languages. They are usually supplied as part of the language. *(Illus. p. 124)*

mathematical logic The use of mathematical symbols to represent language and its processes, in which these symbols are manipulated in

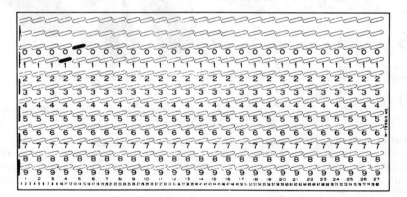

mark sensing

FUNCTION	MEANING
SQR(X) -	square root of X
SIN(X) -	trigonometric sine of X
COS(X) -	trigonometric cosine of X
TAN(X) -	trigonometric tangent of X
ATN(X) -	angle whose tangent is X
ABS(X) -	absolute value of X
INT(X) -	integer part of X
EXP(X) -	exponential of X
LOG(X) -	logarithm of X
RND(X) -	random number

mathematical functions

accord with mathematical rules to determine whether or not a statement or a series of statements is true or false. See *logic*.

mathematical model A group of mathematical expressions that represents a process, a system, or the operation of a device. See *simulation*.

mathematical software The set of computer algorithms in the area of mathematics.

mathematics The study of the relationships between objects or quantities, organized so that certain facts can be proved or derived from others by using logic. See *applied mathematics*.

matrix A group of elements (numbers, symbols, or characters) organized on a rectangular grid and treated as a unit. The numbers can be referenced by their position on the grid. See *array*.

6	4	2	5
2	8	7	3
9	3	5	7

matrix

matrix notation Introduced by the English mathematician Arthur Cayley in 1858. He used an abbreviated notation, such as $ax = b$, for expressing systems of linear equations.

matrix printer A printer that uses a matrix of dots to form an image of the character being printed. A type of *line printer*.

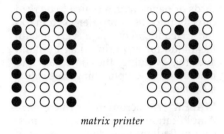

matrix printer

Mauchly, John (1907–1980) Co-inventor of the ENIAC, an early electronic computer. See *Eckert, J. Presper* and *ENIAC*.

John Mauchly

mb (megabyte) One million bytes. 1000 kb.

mechanical data processing A method of data processing that involves the use of relatively small and simple (usually nonprogrammable) mechanical machines.

mechanical translation A generic term for language translation by computers or similar equipment.

mechanization The use of machines to simplify or replace work previously accomplished by human workers.

media The plural form of medium. Media can be classified as source, input, and output. Checks are an example of source media. Punched cards and diskettes are examples of input media. Output media can be magnetic tape, paper printouts, and paper tape.

medium The physical substance upon which data is recorded, for example, magnetic disk, paper tape, floppy disk, magnetic tape, punch cards, and paper.

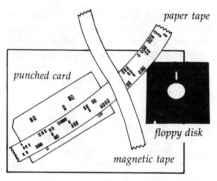

medium

medium scale integration The class of integrated circuits having a density between those of large scale integration (LSI) and small scale integration (SSI). Abbreviated MSI. See *TTL*.

mega A prefix indicating million.

megabit A million binary digits.

megabyte One million bytes.

megacycle A million cycles per second.

megahertz A million cycles per second. Abbreviated MHz.

memory The storage facilities of the computer, capable of storing vast amounts of data. See *auxiliary storage, floppy disk, internal storage, magnetic bubble memory, magnetic core storage, magnetic disk, magnetic drum, magnetic tape, PROM, RAM, ROM, semiconductor storage, storage,* and *virtual storage.*

memory allocation See *storage allocation.*

memory chip A semiconductor device that stores information in the form of electrical charges.

memory cycle See *cycle.*

memory dump See *storage dump.*

memory map See *storage map.*

memory protection See *storage protection.*

menu A list of options within a program that allows the user to choose which part to interact with. Menus allow computer users a facility for using programs without knowing any technical methods.

merge To combine items into one sequenced file from two or more similarly sequenced files without changing the order of the items. Same as *collate.*

mesh A set of branches forming a closed path in a network.

message A group of characters having meaning as a whole and always handled as a group.

message format Rules for the placement of such portions of a message as message heading, address text, and end of message.

message header The leading part of a message that contains information concerning the message, such as the source or destination code of the message, the message priority, and the type of message.

message retrieval The capability to retrieve a message some time after it has entered an information system.

message switching The switching technique of receiving a message, storing it until the proper outgoing circuit and station are available, and then retransmitting it toward its destination. Computers are often used to perform the switching function.

message switching center A center in which messages are routed according to information contained within the messages themselves.

metacharacter In programming language systems, these characters have some controlling role in respect to the other characters with which they are associated.

metacompiler A compiler for a language that is used primarily for writing compilers, usually syntax-oriented compilers. A special-purpose metacompiler language is not very useful for writing general programs.

metalanguage A language that is used to describe a language.

metallic oxide semiconductor (1) A field-effect transistor in which the gate electrode is isolated from the channel by an oxide film. (2) A capacitor in which semiconductor material forms one plate, aluminum forms the other plate, and an oxide forms the dielectric. Abbreviated MOS. See *CMOS.*

meta-metalanguage A language that is used to describe a metalanguage.

meter Base unit of length in the SI metric system, approximately equal to 1.1 yards.

method A way of doing something.

metric system Système International d'Unités or SI. The modern version of the metric system currently in wide use in the world. It is based on 7 base units: meter, kilogram, second, ampere, Kelvin (degrees Celsius), candela, and mole.

metric ton Measure of weight equal to 1000 kilograms or about 2200 pounds.

MFT An acronym for Multiprogramming with a Fixed number of Tasks, the tasks being programs. Sometimes called (jokingly, of course) Multiprogramming with a Finite amount of Trouble.

MHz An abbreviation for megahertz, million cycles per second.

MICR An acronym for *Magnetic Ink Character Recognition.*

micro (1) One millionth, used as a prefix; for example, a microsecond is a millionth of a second. (2) Computerese for quite small, for example, as in microcomputer.

micro code Software that defines the instruction set of a microprogrammable computer. See *microprogrammable computer* and *microprogramming.*

microcoding Composing computer instructions by combining basic, elementary operations to form higher-level instructions such as addition or multiplication. See *micro instruction, microprogrammable computer,* and *microprogramming.*

microcoding device Circuit board with fixed instructions for performing standard functions through miniature logic circuits, thus avoiding the need to code these instructions during programming.

microcomputer A type of small computer, consisting of a microprocessor

microcomputer

and associated storage and input/output elements. See *home computer* and *personal computer*.

microcomputer applications Microcomputers are finding applications in business, technology, industry, and the home. They are used in video game machines, traffic control systems, point-of-sale terminals, scientific instruments, blood analyzers, credit card verification, pinball machines, automotive ignition control, and inventory control systems. Industry is using microcomputers and microprocessors in microwave ovens, sewing machines, flow meters, gas station pumps, paint mixing machines, process monitoring, pollution monitoring, and as control units for hundreds of other devices.

microcomputer chip A microcomputer on a chip. Differs from a microprocessor in that it not only contains the central processing unit (CPU), but also includes on the same piece of silicon a RAM, a ROM, and input/output circuitry. Often called a "computer-on-a-chip." See *microcomputer* and *microprocessor*.

microcomputer components The major components of a microcomputer are a microprocessor, a memory (ROM, PROM, EPROM, RAM), and Input/Output circuitry.

microcomputer development system A computer system, based upon a particular microprocessor, that is utilized for developing both hardware and software. The system usually includes an assembler, text editor, monitor, system console, PROM programmer, and disk/tape system.

microcomputer kit See *computer kit*.

microcontroller A device or instrument that controls a process with high resolution, usually over a narrow region. A microprogrammed machine (microcomputer or microprocessor) used in a control operation, that is, to direct or make changes in a process or operation. For example, Singer Company uses a microcontroller and a ROM to operate sewing machines. See *microcomputer* and *microprocessor*.

microelectronics The field that deals with techniques for producing miniature circuits; for example, integrated circuits, thin film techniques, and solid logic modules.

microfiche A sheet of film about 10 cm by 15 cm (4 inches by 6 inches) upon which the images of computer output may be recorded. Up to 270 pages of output may be recorded on one sheet of microfiche. See *computer output microfilm recorder* and *ultrafiche*.

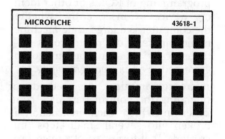

microfiche

microfilm Photographic film used for recording graphic information in a reduced size. See *computer output (COM) microfilm recorder*.

micro floppy disk A new type of soft disk memory about 7.6 cm (3 inches) in diameter. See *floppy disk*.

micrographics The use of miniature photography to condense, store, and retrieve graphic information. Involves the usage of all types of microforms and microimages such as *microfilm*, *microfiche*, and computer output microfilm.

micro instruction A low-level instruction used to obtain a macro, or machine language instruction. See *microprogramming*.

micrologic The use of a permanent stored program to interpret instructions in a microprogram.

microminiaturization A term implying very small size, one step smaller than miniaturization.

microprocessor The basic arithmetic, logic, and control elements required for processing (generally contained on one integrated circuit chip). Microprocessors are widely used as the control devices for household appliances, business machines, calculating devices, toys, video game machines, and thousands of other devices.

microprogrammable computer A term referring to any computer whose instruction set is not fixed but can be tailored to individual needs by the programming of ROMs or other memory devices. Consequently—whether the computer is a large scale machine, minicomputer, or microprocessor—theoretically it can be microprogrammed. See *microprogramming*.

microprogramming A method of operating the control part of a computer in which each instruction is broken into several small steps (microsteps) that form part of a microprogram. Some systems allow users to microprogram, and hence determine the instruction set of their own machine. See *micro code* and *microprogrammable computer*.

microsecond One millionth of a second (0.000001), abbreviated μs or μsec.

microwave An electromagnetic wave in the super-high frequency radio spectrum (890 to 300,000 megacycles per second).

milli One thousandth, used as a prefix; for example, a millisecond is a thousandth of a second.

millimicrosecond Same as *nanosecond*, one billionth of a second.

millisecond One thousandth of a second (0.001), abbreviated ms or msec.

minicomputer A digital computer that is characterized by higher performance than microcomputers, more powerful instruction sets, higher prices, and a wide selection of available programming languages and operating systems.

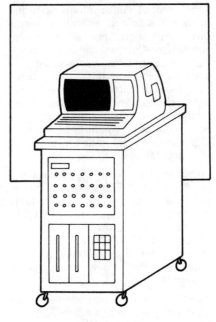

minicomputer

mini floppy disk A 13.3 cm (5¼ inch) diameter disk used in microcomputer systems. See *floppy disk, magnetic disk,* and *micro floppy disk*.

minimal tree Tree whose terminal nodes are ordered to make the tree operate at optimum.

minuend A number from which another number, called the subtrahend, is to be subtracted. In the subtraction $7 - 3 = 4$, 7 is the minuend, 3 is the subtrahend, and 4 is the difference.

mips Millions of instructions per second.

MIS An acronym for *Management Information System.*

mistake A human failing that produces an unintended result; for example, faulty arithmetic, using incorrect computer instructions, incorrect keypunching, or use of incorrect formula. Contrast with *error, fault,* and *malfunction.* See *bug.*

mixed number A number having a fractional part (e.g., 63.71, −18.006, 298.413).

ML An acronym for Manipulator Language. An IBM programming language for controlling robots.

mnemonic Pertaining to a technique used to aid human memory. A word or name that is easy to remember and identify.

ADD

mnemonic

mnemonic code An easy-to-remember assembly language code, for example, a code that uses an abbreviation such as MPY for "multiply."

mnemonic language A programming language that is based on easily remembered symbols and can be assembled into machine language by the computer.

mode (1) A method of operation. (2) The form of a number, name, or expression. (3) The most common or frequent value in a group of values.

model See *mathematical model.*

modem An acronym for *mod*ulator-*dem*odulator. A device that provides the appropriate interface between a communications link and a data processing machine or system by serving as a modulator and/or demodulator. Same as *data set.*

modify (1) To alter a portion of an instruction so that its interpretation and execution will be other than normal. The modification may permanently change the instruction or leave it unchanged and affect only the current execution. (2) To alter a program according to a defined parameter.

modular programming A technique for designing a system or program as a number of self-contained modules. See *module.*

modulation In data communications, the process by which some characteristic of a high frequency carrier signal is varied in accordance with another, lower frequency "information" signal. This technique is used in data sets to make computer terminal signals compatible with communication facilities.

modulator A device that receives electrical pulses, or bits, from a data processing machine and converts them into signals suitable for transmission over a communications link. Contrast with *demodulator.*

module (1) Specifically, one logical part of a program. A major program may be broken down into a number of logically self-contained modules. These modules may be written (and possibly tested separately) by a number of programmers. The modules can then be put together to form the complete program. This is called *modular programming.* (2) An interchangeable plug-in item containing components.

modulo A mathematical function that yields the remainder of division. A number x evaluated modulo n gives the integer remainder of $\frac{x}{n}$. For example, 100 modulo 84 equals the remainder of 100/84, or 16.

monadic An operation that uses only one operand.

monadic Boolean operator A Boolean operator with only one operand, such as the NOT operator.

129

monitor (1) A control program. (2) A video display. See *operating system* and *video monitor*.

monolithic The single silicon substrate upon which an integrated circuit is constructed.

monolithic integrated circuit A class of integrated circuits wherein the substrate is an active material such as the semiconductor silicon. See *integrated circuit*.

Monroe, Jay R. In 1911, using earlier designs of Frank Baldwin, he developed the first keyboard rotary machine to attain commercial success.

Jay R. Monroe

monte carlo A trial-and-error method of repeated calculations to discover the best solution of a problem. Often used when a great number of variables are present, with interrelationships so ex-

tremely complex as to eliminate straightforward analytical handling.

Morlund, Samuel (1625–1695) Improved on Napier's bones to invent a multiplier, and in 1666 he invented an arithmetical machine that could calculate the four processes of arithmetic. See *Napier's bones*.

Samuel Morlund

MOS An acronym for *Metallic Oxide Semiconductor*. A semiconductor structure that is used in many FETs and integrated circuits.

MOSFET An acronym for Metallic Oxide Semiconductor Field Effect Transistor. A semiconductor characterized by an extremely high input impedance, a fairly high active impedance, and low switching speeds. When a voltage (negative with respect to the substrate) is applied to the gate, then the MOSFET is a conductor; and, if a potential difference is applied between source and drain, there will be current flow.

MOS/LSI See *metallic oxide semiconductor* and *large scale integration*.

most significant digit Pertaining to the digit of a number that has the greatest weight or significance (e.g., in the number 54321, the most significant digit is 5). Abbreviated MSD. See *high order* and *justify*.

motherboard An interconnecting assembly into which printed circuit cards, boards, or modules are connected. Synonym for *backplane*.

move To transfer from one location of storage to another location.

moveable-head disk unit A storage device or system consisting of magnetically coated disks, on the surface of which data are stored in the form of magnetic spots arranged in a manner to represent binary data. These data are arranged in circular tracks around the disks and are accessible to reading and writing heads on an arm that can be moved mechanically to the desired disk and then to the desired track on that disk. Data from a given track are read or written sequentially as the disk rotates. See *magnetic disk*.

moveable-head disk unit

MP/M A multi-user operating system that allows several terminals to be used simultaneously on a computer system. MP/M provides all the facili-

ties found in CP/M plus more. See *CP/M* and *operating system*.

MPU An acronym for MicroProcessing Unit. See *microprocessor*.

MPX Multiplexer.

ms An abbreviation for millisecond.

μs, μsec See *microsecond*.

MSD An acronym for *Most Significant Digit*.

MSI An acronym for *Medium Scale Integration*.

MTBF An acronym for Mean Time Between Failure. Average length of time a system or component is expected to work without failure.

MTTF An acronym for Mean Time To Failure. The average length of time for which the system, or a component of the system, works without fault.

MTTR An acronym for Mean Time To Repair. Average time expected to be required to detect and correct a fault in a computer system.

mu The name of the Greek letter μ. The symbol is used to denote the prefix micro. For example, μs means microsecond.

MUG An acronym for MUMPS Users' Group. See *MUMPS*.

multiaddress Pertaining to an instruction format containing more than one address part.

multicomputer system A computer system consisting of two or more central processing units.

multi-drop line A communication system configuration using a single channel or line to serve multiple terminals.

multifile sorting The automatic sequencing of more than one file, based upon separate parameters for each file, without operator intervention.

multijob operation A term that describes concurrent execution of job steps from two or more jobs.

multilayer A type of printed circuit board that has several circuit layers connected by electroplated holes.

multilevel addressing See *indirect addressing.*

multilinked list List with each atom having at least two pointers.

multipass sort A sort program that is designed to sort more data than can be contained within the internal memory of a central computer. Intermediate storage, such as disk, tape, or drum, is required.

multiple access A system with a number of on-line communication channels providing concurrent access to the common system.

multiple-address instruction An instruction consisting of an operation code and two or more addresses. Usually specified as a two-address, three-address, or four-address instruction.

multiple-address message A message to be delivered to more than one destination.

multiple connector A connector to indicate the merging of several lines of flow into one line, or the dispersal of one line of flow into several lines.

multiple-job processing Controlling the performance of more than one data processing job at a time.

multiple punching The punching of two or more holes in a card column.

multiplex To interleave or simultaneously transmit two or more messages over a single channel or other communications facility.

multiplexer A device that makes it possible to transmit two or more messages simultaneously over a single channel or other transmission facility.

Abbreviated MPX or MUX. Same as *concentrator.*

multiplexer channel A special type of input/output channel that can transmit data between a computer and a number of simultaneously operating peripheral devices.

multiplexor An alternate spelling of *multiplexer.*

multiplicand The quantity that is multiplied by another quantity.

multiplication time The time required to perform a multiplication. For a binary number, it will be equal to the total of all the addition times and all the shift time involved in the multiplication.

multiplier The quantity that is used to multiply another quantity.

multiprecision arithmetic A form of arithmetic where two or more computer words are used to represent each number.

multiprocessing The simultaneous execution of two or more sequences of instructions by multiple central processing units under common control. See *multiprogramming.*

multiprocessor A computer network consisting of two or more central processors under a common control.

multiprogramming Running two or more programs at the same time in the same computer. Each program is allotted its own place in memory and its own peripherals, but all share the central processing unit. Made economical by the fact that peripherals are slower than the central processing unit, so most programs spend most of their time waiting for input or output to finish. While one program is waiting, another can use the central processing unit.

multireel sorting The automatic sequencing of a file having more than one input tape, without operator intervention.

multitask operation See *multiprogramming*.

MUMPS An acronym for Massachusetts General Hospital Utility Multi-Programming System. A programming language designed specifically for handling medical records. The language is strong in data management and text manipulation features.

μs, μsec See *microsecond*.

musical language A method in which musical notation may be represented in code suitable for computer input. See *computer music*.

musicomp A compositional programming language that provides techniques for generating original musical scores as well as for synthesizing music.

MUX An acronym for *multiplexer*. A channel used to connect low-speed devices to a computer.

MVT An acronym for Multiprogramming with a Variable number of Tasks; the tasks being programs. (Also jokingly called Multiprogramming with a Vast amount of Trouble.)

mylar A DuPont trademark for polyester film, often used as a base for magnetically coated or perforated information media.

N

name An alphanumeric term that identifies a program, a control statement, data areas, or a cataloged procedure. Same as *label*.

nand A logical operator having the property that, if P is a statement, Q is a statement, . . . then the nand of P, Q, . . . is true if at least one statement is false and false if all statements are true.

NAND gate A gate or circuit that performs the NAND operation.

nanosecond One billionth of a second (0.000000001), one thousand-millionth of a second; abbreviated as ns. Same as millimicrosecond.

Napier, John (1550–1617) A Scottish aristocrat who made many contributions to mathematics and computing. He invented logarithms and a calculating device known as Napier's bones,

and he is known for improving the abacus and for additions to the field of spherical trigonometry.

Napier's bones A set of numbering rods that are used to multiply, divide, and extract roots. The calculating rods were developed by John Napier in 1614 and were used by William Oughtred in 1630 in the invention of the slide rule.

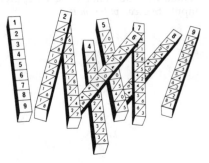

Napier's bones

narrowband Pertains to a data communications system that handles low volumes of data.

National Computer Conference An annual meeting of computer users, computer science educators, and computer equipment manufacturers. Abbreviated NCC.

native language A computer language that is peculiar to the machines of one manufacturer.

natural language A human language such as English, German, Spanish, French, and so on. Contrast with *artificial language*.

natural language processing Refers to the computer processing of natural language as language, rather than as a meaningless string of letters or sounds.

John Napier

NBS An acronym for National Bureau of Standards. A government agency.

N/C An acronym for *Numerical Control.*

NCC An acronym for *National Computer Conference.*

NCIC An acronym for the FBI's computerized National Crime Information Center, the heart of a large law enforcement network.

NDRO An acronym for Non-Destructive ReadOut. See *nondestructive read.*

negate To perform the logical operator "NOT."

NELIAC An acronym for Naval Electronices Laboratory International Algorithmic Compiler. A high-level programming language used primarily for solving scientific and real-time control problems.

nesting (1) Including a routine or block of data within a larger routine or block of data. (2) A loop of instructions that may contain another loop and so on, perhaps down through several levels. Algebraic nesting, such as (W + X* (Y − Z)), where execution proceeds from the innermost to the outermost level.

network (1) A system of interconnected computer systems and terminals. (2) A series of points connected by communication channels.

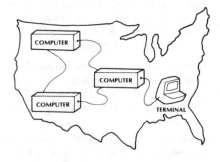

network

Neumann, John von See *von Neumann, John.*

Newton-Raphson A term applied to an iterative procedure used for solving equations. See *iterate.*

nibble One half of a byte, namely a four-bit data element. Sometimes spelled nybble.

niladic An operation for which no operands are specified.

nil pointer A pointer used to denote the end of a linked list.

nine's complement A numeral used to represent the negative of a given value. A nine's complement numeral is obtained by subtracting each digit from a numeral containing all nines; for example, 567 is the nine's complement of 432 and is obtained by subtracting 432 from 999.

ninety column card A punched card used with early UNIVAC card handling equipment.

ninety-six column card A punched card used with card handling equipment. The card physically contains 18 rows and 36 columns as three characters are punched in each column. *(Illus. p. 136)*

NMOS An acronym for N-channel MOS. Circuits that use currents made up of negative charges and produce devices at least twice as fast as PMOS. See *PMOS.*

node Any terminal, station, or communications computer in a computer network.

noise (1) Loosely, any disturbance tending to interfere with the normal operation of a device or system, including those attributable to equipment components, natural disturbance, or manual interference. (2) Spurious signals that can introduce errors. (3) An unwanted signal.

noise immunity A device's ability to accept valid signals while rejecting unwanted signals.

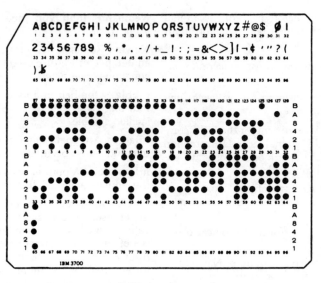

ninety-six column card

nonconductor A substance through which electricity cannot pass.

nondestructive read A read operation that does not alter the information content of the storage media.

nonerasable storage A storage device whose information cannot be erased during the course of computation; for example, punched paper tape, punched cards, and certain nondestructible readout magnetic memories.

nonexecutable A program statement that sets up a program but does not call for any specific action on the part of the program in which it appears. Contrast with *executable*.

nonprint An impulse that inhibits line printing under machine control.

nonreflective ink Any color of ink that is recognizable to an optical character reader.

nonsequential computer A computer that must be directed to the location of each instruction.

nonswitched line A communications link that is permanently installed between two points.

nonvolatile storage A storage media that retains its data in the absence of power.

no-op An abbreviation of the term no-operation, as in *no-operation instruction.*

no-operation instruction A computer instruction whose only effect is to advance the instruction counter. It accomplishes nothing more than the movement beyond itself to the next instruction in normal sequence.

NOP An acronym for No OPeration. See *no-operation instruction.*

nor The Boolean operator that gives a truth table value of true only when both of the variables connected by the logical operator are false.

NORC An acronym for Naval Ordinance Research Calculator. An early computer (1954) built by the IBM Corporation for the U.S. Navy Bureau of Ordnance.

normalize To adjust the exponent and fraction of a floating point quantity so that the fraction is within a prescribed range. Loosely, to *scale.*

NOT A logic operator having the property that, if P is a statement, then the NOT of P is true if P is false and false if P is true.

notation See *positional notation.*

NOVA A designation for computers manufactured by Data General Corporation.

ns An abbreviation for nanosecond, one billionth of a second.

nucleus That portion of the control program that must always be present in internal storage.

null Pertaining to a negligible value or a lack of information, as contrasted with a zero or a blank that conveys information, such as numerals and spaces between words.

null string String with no characters. See *empty string.*

number (1) A symbol or symbols representing a value in a specific numeral system. (2) Loosely, a *numeral.*

number base See *radix.*

number crunching A term applied to a program or computer that is designed to perform large amounts of computation and other numerical manipulations of data.

number representation The representation of numbers by agreed sets of symbols according to agreed rules.

number system An agreed set of symbols and rules for number representation. Loosely, a *numeral system.*

numeral A conventional symbol representing a number; e.g., six, 6, VI, 110 are four different numerals that represent the same number.

numeralization Representation of alphabetic data through the use of digits.

numeral system A method of representing numbers. In computing, several numeral systems are of particular interest, in addition to the common decimal system. These are the binary, hexadecimal, and octal systems. In each system the value of a numeral is the value of the digits multiplied by the numeral system radix, raised to a power indicated by the position of the digits in the numeral.

numerator In the expression $\frac{a}{b}$, a is the numerator and b is the denominator.

numeric Pertaining to numerals or to representation by means of numerals.

numerical analysis The branch of mathematics concerned with the study and development of effective procedures for computing answers to problems.

numerical control A means of controlling machine tools through servomechanisms and control circuitry so that the motions of the tool will respond to digital coded instructions on tape or to direct commands from a computer. See *APT* and *parts programmer.*

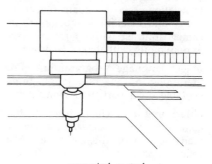

numerical control

numeric character Same as a *digit.*

numeric coding Coding that uses digits only to represent data and instructions.

numeric data Consist solely of the digits 0–9.

numeric punch A punch in any of rows 1 through 9 of a punch card.

nybble A group of four bits, or one-half of a byte. Sometimes spelled nibble.

obey   The process whereby a computer carries out an operation as specified by one or more of the instructions forming the program that is currently being executed.

object code   Output from a compiler or assembler that is itself executable machine code or is suitable for processing to produce executable machine code. Also called *object program*.

object computer   A computer used for the execution of an object program.

object deck   A set of punched cards representing the machine language equivalent of a source deck.

objective   The ends toward which an organization works.

object language   The output of a translation process. Usually object language and machine language are the same. Contrast with *source language*. Synonymous with *target language*.

object language programming   Programming in a machine language executable on a particular computer.

object program   The instructions that come out of the *compiler* or *assembler*, ready to run on the computer. Also called *object code*.

OCR   An acronym for Optical Character Recognition. Characters printed in a special type style that can be read by both machines and people. See *optical character recognition*.

octal   Pertaining to a number system with a radix of eight. Octal numbers are frequently used to represent binary numerals, with each octal digit representing a group of three binary digits (bits); for example, the binary numeral 111000010001101 can be represented as octal 70215.

OCR

octal numeral   A numeral of one or more digits, representing a sum in which the quantity represented by each figure is based on a radix of eight. The digits used in octal numerals are 0, 1, 2, 3, 4, 5, 6, and 7.

octal point   The radix point in an octal numeral system. The point that separates the integer part of a mixed octal numeral from the fractional part. In the numeral 34.17, the octal point is between the digits 4 and 1.

OEM   An acronym for Original Equipment Manufacturer. A company or organization that purchases computers and peripheral equipment for use as components in products and equipment that they subsequently sell to their customers.

office automation   The application of computers and communications technology to improve the productivity of clerical and managerial office workers.

off-line   A term describing equipment, devices, or persons not in direct communication with the central processing unit of a computer. Equipment that is not connected to the computer. Contrast with *on-line.*

off-line storage Storage not under control of the central processing unit.

offset The difference between the value or condition desired and that actually attained.

on-board regulation An arrangement where each board in a system contains its own voltage regulator.

one-address computer A computer that employs only one address in its instruction format (e.g., ADD X, where X represents the address in the instruction).

one-address instruction An instruction consisting of an operation and exactly one address. The instruction code of a single address computer may include both zero and multiaddress instructions as special cases. Most present-day computers are of the one-address instruction type. See *one-address computer.*

CLEAR X

one-address instruction

one-dimensional array An array consisting of a single row or column of elements.

one-for-one A phrase often associated with an assembler where one source language statement is converted to one machine language instruction.

one-level memory Memory in which all stored items are accessed by a uniform mechanism.

one-out-of-ten code In this code, a decimal digit is represented by ten binary digits where only one of the binary digits is permitted to be a 1.

one's complement A numeral used to represent the negative of a given value. A one's complement of a binary numeral is obtained by alternating the bit configuration of each bit in the numeral. For example, 01100101 is the one's complement of the binary numeral 10011010.

on-line A term describing equipment, devices, and persons that are in direct communication with the central processing unit of a computer. Equipment that is physically connected to the computer. Contrast with *off-line.*

on-line data base A data base that can be directly accessed by a user from a terminal, usually a visual display device.

on-line problem solving A teleprocessing application in which a number of users at remote terminals can concurrently use a computing system in solving problems on-line. Often, in this type of application, a dialogue or conversation is carried on between a user at a remote terminal and a program within the central computer system.

on-line processing Data processing involving direct entry of data into the computer or direct transmission of output from the computer.

on-line storage Storage under control of the central processing unit.

op A contraction for the term *operation.*

opacity Refers to the ease with which light passes through a sheet of paper making it more or less translucent.

op-code See *operation code.*

open-ended Having the capability by which the addition of new programs, instructions, subroutines, modifications, terms, or classifications does not disturb the original system.

open file A file is considered open when it can be accessed for reading, writing, or possibly both.

139

open shop A computer installation at which computer operation can be performed by a qualified person. Contrast with *closed shop.*

open subroutine A subroutine that is inserted into a routine at each place it is used. Contrast with *closed subroutine.*

operand The data unit or equipment item that is operated upon. An operand is usually identified by an address in an instruction. For example, in "ADD 100 TO 400," 100 and 400 are operands. See *operation code.*

operating ratio See *availability.*

operating system An organized collection of software that controls the overall operations of a computer. The operating system does many basic operations that were performed by hardware in older machines, or that are common to many programs. It is available to the computer at all times by being held either in internal storage or on an auxiliary storage device. Abbreviated OS. A disk operating system is referred to as a DOS. See *CP/M, executive, monitor, MP/M,* and *supervisory system.*

operation A defined action. The action specified by a single computer instruction or high-level language statement. Abbreviated op.

operation center A physical area containing the human and equipment resources needed to process data through a computer and produce desired output. Same as *data processing center.*

operation code The instruction code used to specify the operations a computer is to perform. For example, in "ADD 100 to 400," "ADD" is the operation code. See *operand.*

operations analysis Same as *operations research.*

operations research A mathematical science devoted to carrying out complicated operations with the maximum possible efficiency. Among the common scientific techniques in operations research are the following: linear programming, probability theory, information theory, game theory, monte carlo method, and queuing theory.

operator (1) In the description of a process, that which indicates the action to be performed on operands. (2) A person who operates a machine. See *computer operator* and *keypunching.*

operator

optical character reader An input device that accepts a printed document as input. It identifies characters by their shapes. See *OCR* and *optical character recognition.*

optical character recognition An information processing technology that converts human readable data into another medium for computer input. Light reflected from characters is recognized by optical character recognition equipment. Abbreviated OCR.

optical communications The use of light for transmitting digitally encoded information. Optical fibers and lasers make up a technology that offers the maximum transmitting capacity using devices that occupy little physical space.

optical mark reader An input device that reads graphite marks on cards or pages. See *mark sensing* and *optical mark recognition*.

optical mark recognition An information processing technology that converts data into another medium for computer input. This is accomplished by the presence of a mark in a given position, each position having a value known to the computer and which may or may not be understandable to humans. Abbreviated OCR. See *optical mark reader*.

optical printer See *electrostatic printer*.

optical reader See *optical character reader* and *optical mark reader*.

optical scanner See *optical character reader*.

optical scanning Generally defines an input method in which information is converted for machine processing by evaluating the relative reflectance of that information to the background on which it appears. See *optical character recognition*.

optimal merge tree A tree representation of the order in which strings are to be merged so that a minimum number of move operations occurs.

optimize To select storage addresses that will result in a minimization or maximization of some desired characteristic.

optimizing compiler A compiler that attempts to correct inefficiencies in a program's logic in order to improve execution times, main storage requirements, and so forth.

optimum Best and most desirable in view of established criteria.

optimum programming Programming in order to maximize efficiency

with respect to some criterion; for example, least storage usage, least usage of peripheral equipment, or least computing time.

optimum tree search A tree search whose object is to find the best of many alternatives.

OR See *exclusive OR* and *inclusive OR*.

OR circuit See *OR-gate*.

order (1) To arrange items according to any specified set of rules. (2) An arrangement of items according to any specified set of rules.

organization chart A diagram that shows the organization of a business (how responsibilities are divided up within a business). *(Illus. p. 142)*

OR-gate A computer circuit containing two switches whose output is a binary one if either or both of the inputs are binary. This electrical circuit implements the OR operator.

origin In coding, the absolute memory address of the first location of a program or program segment.

original equipment manufacturer A manufacturer who buys equipment from other suppliers and integrates it into a single system for resale. Abbreviated OEM.

orthoferrite A naturally occurring substance composed of alternate, snakelike regions of opposite magnetic polarity.

OS An acronym for *Operating System*.

oscillating sort An external tape sort that capitalizes on a tape drive's ability to read forward and backward.

oscillography The projection of a pattern of electrical signals on the face of a cathode ray tube.

oscilloscope A device for displaying on a cathode ray tube screen the value of a voltage versus time; used by computer maintenance technicians.

Oughtred, William (1575-1660) An English mathematician who invented the slide rule in 1630. See *Napier's bones* and *slide rule. (Illus. p. 143)*

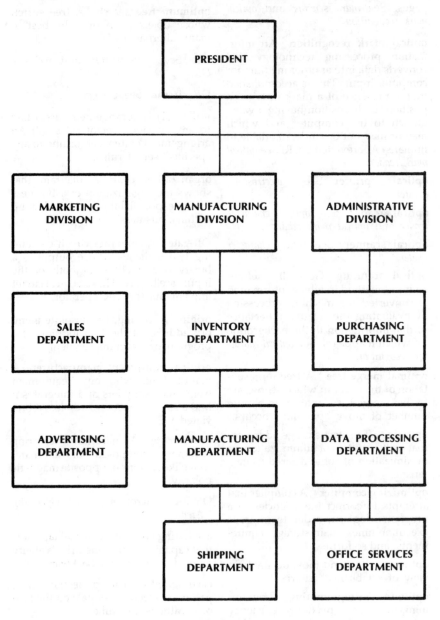

organization chart

output device

William Oughtred

outdegree The number of directed edges leaving a node.

output (1) Data transferred from a computer's internal storage unit to some storage or output device. (2) The final result of data processing; data that has been processed by the computer. Contrast with *input*.

output area An area of storage reserved for output data. Contrast with *input area*.

output data Data to be delivered from a device or program, usually after some processing. Synonymous with *output*. Contrast with *input data*.

output device A unit that is used for taking out data values from a computer and presenting them in the desired form to the user. Contrast with *input device*.

output media Documents, reports, cassette tapes, floppy disks, and punched cards are typical examples of output media.

outputting The process of producing a useful information output.

overflow In an arithmetic operation, the generation of a quantity beyond the capacity of the register or storage location that is to receive the result.

overhead (1) A collective term for the factors that cause the performance of a program or device to be lower than it would be in the ideal case. (2) Nonproductive effort, taking place when the operating system and programs are performing administrative tasks, but no production work is being done.

overlap To do something at the same time that something else is being done; for example, to perform an input operation while instructions are being executed by the central processing unit. This approach permits the computer to work on several programs at once.

overlay To transfer segments of a program from auxiliary storage into internal storage for execution, so that two or more segments occupy the same storage locations at different times. This technique is used to increase the apparent size of internal storage. This is accomplished by keeping only the programs or data that are currently being accessed within internal storage. The rest is kept on a direct storage device (magnetic disk unit) until needed.

overpunch To add holes in a card column that already contains one or more holes.

P

pack To store several short units of data into a single storage cell in such a way that the individual units can later be recovered; for example, to store two 4-bit BCD digits in one 8-bit storage location. Opposite of *unpack.*

package A program or collection of programs to be used by more than one business or organization.

packet transmission A packet-switching network, made up of high-speed switching computers, it is able to store and forward short standardized packets of messages very rapidly, typically within a fraction of a second.

packing density See *recording density.*

pad character Buffer character used to fill a blank.

padding A technique used to fill out a fixed-length block of information with dummy characters, items, words, or records.

paddle Same as *joystick.*

page A segment of a program or data, usually of fixed length, that has a fixed virtual address but can in fact reside in any region of the computer's internal storage. See *virtual storage.*

page frame A location in the rear storage of the computer that can store one page (which usually consists of either 2K or 4K words) of commands or data.

page printer A printer in which an entire page of characters is composed and determined within the device prior to printing.

page reader A piece of optical scanning equipment that scans many lines of information with the scanning pattern being determined by program control and/or control symbols intermixed with input data.

pagination The electronic manipulation of graphics and blocks of type for the purpose of setting up an entire page.

paging A technique for moving programs back and forth from real (main) storage to virtual (auxiliary) storage.

paging rate In virtual storage systems, the average number of page-ins and page-outs per unit of time.

PAM An acronym for Pulse Amplitude Modulation. Modulation in which the modulation wave is caused to amplitude-modulate a pulse carrier.

panel See *control panel* and *plugboard.*

paper tape A continuous strip of paper in which holes are punched to record numerical and alphanumerical information for computer processing. For example, 8-track paper tape is 2.54 cm (1 inch) wide, and a character is recorded by punching a code of up to eight holes across the width of the tape.

paper tape

paper tape code The system of coding that is used to relate the patterns of holes in paper tape to the alphanumeric characters they represent.

paper tape punch A code-sensitive output device that translates computer code into an external code on paper tape. *(Illus. p. 145)*

paper tape punch

paper tape reader An input device used for translating the holes in a perforated paper roll into machine processable form.

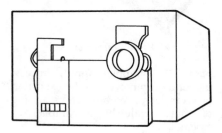

paper tape reader

paragraph A set of one or more COBOL sentences making up a logical processing entity and preceded by a paragraph header or name.

parallel Handling all the elements of a word or message simultaneously. Contrast with *serial*.

parallel access The process of obtaining information from or placing information into storage where the time required for such access is dependent on the simultaneous transfer of all elements of a word from a given storage location.

parallel adder An adder that performs its operations by bringing in all digits simultaneously from each of the quantities involved.

parallel computer A computer in which the digits or data lines are processed concurrently by separate units of the computer.

parallel conversion The system of changing to a new data processing system that involves running both the old and new systems simultaneously for a period of time.

parallel input/output Data transmission where each bit has its own wire. All of the bits are transmitted simultaneously, as opposed to being sent one at a time (serially). Contrast with *serial input/output*.

parallel operation The performance of several actions, usually of a similar nature, simultaneously through provision of individual, similar, or identical devices for each such action. Contrast with *serial operation*.

parallel printing An entire row is printed at one time.

parallel processing Pertaining to the concurrent or simultaneous execution of two or more processes in multiple devices such as processing units or channels. Contrast with *serial processing*.

parallel reading Row-by-row reading of a data card.

parallel transmission In data communications, a method of data transfer in which all bits of a character are set simultaneously. Contrast with *serial transmission*.

parameter An arbitrary constant. A variable in an algebraic expression that temporarily assumes the properties of a constant. For example, in $y = mx + b$, m and b are parameters if either is treated as a constant in a family of lines.

parentheses A grouping symbol ( ).

parity bit An extra bit added to a byte, character, or word, to ensure that there is always either an even number or an odd number of bits, according to the logic of the system. If, through a hardware failure, a bit should be lost, its loss can be detected by checking the parity. The same bit pattern remains as long as the contents of the byte, character, or word remain unchanged. See *parity checking*.

parity checking Automatic error detection by using checking bits along with the numerical bits. See *parity bit*.

parsing (1) The process of separating statements into syntactic units. (2) Analyzing a character string and breaking it down into a group of more easily processed components.

partitioning Subdividing computer storage area into smaller units which are allocated to specific jobs or tasks.

parts programmer A programmer who translates the physical explanation for machining a part into a series of mathematical steps, and then codes the computer instructions for those steps. See *APT* and *numerical control*.

Pascal A popular high-level programming language that facilitates the use of structured programming techniques. Named after Blaise Pascal.

Pascal, Blaise (1623–1662) A French mathematician who built the first desk calculator-type of adding machine in 1642. See *Pascal's calculator*.

Blaise Pascal

Pascal's calculator The first adding machine. Designed by Blaise Pascal in the 17th century. This device represented the numbers from 0 to 9 with teeth on gears and could perform addition and subtraction. See *Pascal, Blaise*.

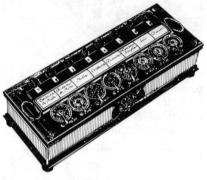

Pascal's calculator

pass (1) A complete input, processing, and output cycle in the execution of a computer program. (2) A scanning of source code by a compiler or assembler.

password See *lock code*.

patch (1) A section of coding that is inserted into a program to correct a mistake or to alter the program. (2) A temporary electrical connection.

patching (1) A makeshift technique for modifying a program or correcting programming errors by changing the object code of the program, usually to avoid recompiling or reassembling the program. (2) Making temporary patches to hardware.

path See *channel*.

patron A customer or client.

pattern recognition The recognition of forms, shapes, or configurations by automatic means.

PC An acronym for *Program Counter* and *Printed Circuit*.

PCB An acronym for Printed Circuit Board. The plastic board into which the computer's various electronic components are soldered. These are linked by thin interconnecting wires printed on its surfaces.

PCM An acronym for Punched Card Machines.

PDM An acronym for Pulse Duration Modulation. Pulse time modulation in which the duration of a pulse is varied.

PDP A designation for computers manufactured by Digital Equipment Corporation (e.g., PDP-8, PDP-10, PDP-11, and so forth).

PEEK A computer language instruction that allows the programmer to look at (peek at) any location in the computers' programmable memory. See *POLK*.

peek-a-boo system A method of checking the presence or absence of punched holes in identical locations on cards by placing one card on top of another card. See *Batten system*.

perforator A keyboard device for punching paper tape.

performance A major factor in determining the total productivity of a system. Performance is largely determined by a combination of the following factors: availability, throughput, and response time.

peripheral equipment The input/output units and auxiliary storage units of a computer system. The units are attached by cables to the central processing unit. Used to get data in

and data out, and to act as a reservoir for large amounts of data that cannot be held in the central processing unit at one time. The card reader, typewriter, and disk storage unit are examples of peripherals.

peripheral equipment operator In a busy computer room, the computer operator is assigned to the console and rarely leaves it. Additional people assist by mounting and demounting disk packs and tapes, placing cards in the card reader, labeling outputs, and operating the various input/output devices as directed. These people are usually called peripheral equipment operators.

peripheral equipment operator

persistence The length of time an image produced on a display device by activated phosphorus remains clear, bright, and sharp.

personal computer A microcomputer used in the home or office to perform a wide variety of tasks, including game playing, control functions, and business calculations. See *microcomputer. (Illus. p. 148)*

peripheral equipment

147

personal computer

personal computing The use of a personal computer (usually a microcomputer) by individuals for applications such as entertainment, home management, and education.

personal identification number A security number computer systems sometimes require before a user can access the system or before a point-of-sale terminal user can enter or receive information. Abbreviated PIN.

PERT An acronym for Program Evaluation and Review Technique. A management technique for control of large-scale, long-term projects, involving analysis of the time frame required for each step in a process and the relationships of the completion of each step to activity in succeeding steps. See *critical path method*.

PET A popular microcomputer system developed by Commodore Business Machines, Inc. See *microcomputer*.

petri nets A popular and useful model for the representation of systems with concurrency or parallelism.

photocomposition The application of electronic processing to the preparation of print. This involves the specification and setting of type, and its production by a photographic process.

photo-optic memory A memory that uses an optical medium for storage. For example, a laser might be used to record on photographic film.

physical record The unit of data for input or output; for example, a punched card, a tape block, or a record on a disk. One or more logical records may be contained in one physical record. Contrast with *logical record*.

physical security Guards, badges, locks, and other measures to control access to the equipment in a computer center.

pi The name of the Greek letter π. The symbol denotes the ratio of the circumference of a circle to its diameter,

$$\pi = 3.141,592,653,589,793,238 \ldots$$

The notation π was introduced in the eighteenth century by English mathematicians.

picosecond One trillionth of a second (0.000000000001), one thousandth of a nanosecond; abbreviated *psec*.

picture processing See *image processing*.

PILOT A textually based computer language originally designed as an author language for computer-assisted instruction (CAI); however, it is also used for teaching beginners computer programming. The language is composed of powerful and nearly syntax-free, conversation-processing statements.

PIN An acronym for Personal Identification Number. A security number computer systems sometimes require before a user can access the system or before a point-of-sale terminal user can enter or receive information.

pingpong To alternate two or more storage devices so that processing can take place on a virtually endless set of files.

pipeline An overlapping operating cycle function that is used to increase the speed of computers.

pixel A picture cell. The visual display screen is divided into rows and columns of tiny dots, squares, or cells. Each of these is a pixel. A pixel is the smallest unit on the display screen grid that can be stored, displayed, or addressed.

PLA An acronym for Programmable Logic Array. An alternative to ROM (Read Only Memory) that uses a standard logic network programmed to perform a specific function. PLAs are implemented in either MOS or bipolar circuits.

plaintext A term used by encryption experts to denote an ordinary message in its original meaningful form.

PLANIT An acronym for Programming LANguage for Interactive Teaching. A programming language designed for use with computer-assisted instruction (CAI) systems.

planning Deciding what to do.

plasma display A peripheral device with a screen upon which information may be displayed. See *PLATO*.

plasma display

platem A backing, commonly cylindrical, against which printing mechanisms strike to produce an impression.

PLATO An acronym for Programmed Logic for Automatic Teaching Operations. A computer-based instructional system that uses large computers and plasma display terminals. The system contains thousands of lessons representing 65 fields of study for all levels from kindergarten through graduate school. See *computer-assisted instruction* and *plasma display*.

PL/C A version of the PL/I programming language, designed to be used in an educational environment.

PL/I A higher level programming language designed to process both scientific and business applications. The PL/I language contains many of the best features of FORTRAN, COBOL, ALGOL, and other languages, as well as a number of facilities not available in previous languages.

```
WEATHER PROCEDURE;
    DECLARE MAXDAY(7), MINDAY(7), AVERAGE(7);
    READ LIST ((MAXDAY(I), MINDAY(I)) I = 1 TO 7);
    AVERAGE = (MAXDAY + MINDAY) / 2;
    WRITE ((MAXDAY(I), MINDAY(I), AVERAGE(I))
    I = 1 TO 7) (2F(5), F(8, 1), SPACE);
END WEATHER;
```

PL/I

PL/M A programming language used to program microcomputers. The language, developed by Intel Corporation, is a high-level language that can fully command the microcomputer to produce efficient run-time object code. PL/M was designed as a tool to help microcomputer programmers concentrate more on their problem or application and less on the actual task of programming. PL/M is derived from PL/I, a general purpose programming language. Usually implemented as a cross-compiler.

PL/M Plus An extended version of PL/M developed by National Semiconductor to simplify programming of their microprocessors.

plot To diagram, draw, or map with a *plotter*.

plotter An output unit that graphs data by an automatically controlled pen. Data is normally plotted as a series of incremental steps. Primary types of plotters are the drum plotter and the flat-bed plotter. Also called *digital plotter, incremental plotter,* and *X-Y plotter.*

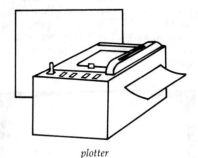

plotter

plugboard A perforated board used to control the operations of unit record devices. Also called a *control panel.*

plug compatible A peripheral device that requires no interface modification in order to be linked directly to another manufacturer's computer system.

PMOS An acronym for P-channel MOS. Refers to the oldest type of MOS circuit where the electrical current consists of a flow of positive charges. See *NMOS.*

PN An acronym for *Polish Notation.*

pocket computer A portable, battery-operated, hand-held computer that can be programmed (in BASIC) to perform a wide number of applications. Also called a *hand-held computer.*

pointer An address or other indication of location.

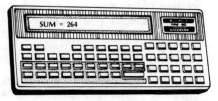

pocket computer

point-of-sale terminal A device used in retail establishments to record sales information in a form that can be input directly into a computer. This intelligent terminal is used to capture data in retail stores (i.e., supermarkets or department stores). Abbreviated POS. See *intelligent terminal* and *source data automation.*

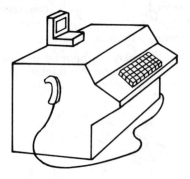

point-of-sale terminal

POL An acronym for *Procedure-Oriented Language* or *Problem-Oriented Language.*

polar A situation in which a binary 1 is represented by current flow in one direction and binary 0 by current flow in the opposite direction.

Polish notation A logical notation for a series of arithmetic operations in which no grouping symbol is used. This notation was developed by a Polish logician, Jan Lukasiewicz in 1929. For example, the expression $z = a (b + c)$ is represented in Polish notation as $bc + a \times z =$, where this expression is read from left to right.

Note that the operator follows the operands. Abbreviated PN.

POLK A computer language instruction that is used to place a value (poke) into any location in the computer's programmable memory. See *PEEK*.

polling In data communications, scanning the networks of terminals or sensors by the computer, asking one after the other if it has any data to submit.

polyphase sort External tape sort used for six or less tapes.

pop Pulling or retrieving data from the top of a program push down stack. The stack pointer is decremented to address the last word pushed on the stack. The contents of this location are moved to one of the accumulators or to another register. Also called *pull*. See *push*.

pop instruction A computer instruction that executes the *pop* operation.

POP-2 A list processing language developed at the University of Edinburgh. See *list processing languages*.

populated board A circuit board that contains all of its electronic components. Contrast with *unpopulated board*.

port That portion of a computer through which a peripheral device may communicate. See *input/output channel*.

portable (1) A computer is portable if it can be hand carried from one physical location to another. See *microcomputer*. (2) A program is portable if it can be easily executed on several different computers.

portable computer A small microcomputer that can be carried from place to place.

POS An acronym for *Point-of-Sale terminal*.

POS systems Department stores and supermarkets are currently using POS

portable computer

systems, in which the cash register is actually a special purpose computer terminal that can monitor and record transactions directly in the store's data files for inventory control, perform checks on credit card validity, and perform other data handling functions. See *point-of-sale terminal*.

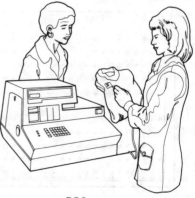

POS systems

positional notation A method for expressing a quantity using two or more figures, wherein the successive right-to-left figures are to be interpreted as coefficients of ascending integer powers of the radix.

post To enter a unit of information on a record.

post edit To edit output data from a previous computation.

postfix notation A notation in which operators follow the operands that they operate on.

post mortem Pertaining to the analysis of an operation after its completion.

post mortem dump A storage dump taken at the end of the execution of a program. See *storage dump*.

power A symbolic representation of the number of times a number is multiplied by itself. The process is called *exponentiation*.

power fail/restart A facility that enables a computer to return to normal operation after a power failure.

power surge A sudden, brief increase in the flow of current that can cause problems in the proper operation of computer equipment.

Powers card A ninety-column punch card that was used with early UNIVAC card handling equipment.

Powers code A punch card code designed by James Powers for the 1910 census.

power supply Converts AC voltage to low-voltage DC. The output of a power supply is tightly regulated to keep noise pulses and voltage variations from upsetting the computer's circuits.

PPM An acronym for Pulse Position Modulation. Pulse time modulation in which the value of each instantaneous sample of the wave modulates the position in time of a pulse.

pragmatics An investigation of the relationship between symbols and the use of those symbols.

precanned routines See *canned routines*.

precedence Rules that state which operators get executed first in an expression. See *hierarchy*.

precision The degree of exactness with which a quantity is stated. The result of calculation may have more precision than it has accuracy; for example, the true value of π to 6 significant digits is 3.14159; the value 3.14162 is precise to 6 digits given 6 digits, but is accurate only to about 5. See *accuracy*.

predefined process (1) A process that is identified only by name and

Powers card

that is defined elsewhere. (2) A *closed subroutine.*

predefined process symbol A flow-charting symbol that is used to represent a subroutine.

pre-edit See *edit.*

prefix notation A method of forming mathematical expressions in which each operator precedes its operands; for example, in prefix notation, the expression "*x* plus *y* multiplied by *z*" would be represented by "+ *xy* × *z*."

prehistoric calculations In prehistoric times, people drew symbols on the walls of caves using a charred stick or clays of different colors. Some of these symbols apparently stood for numbers. Human's first conscious calculations probably involved only simple counting: the number of spears a cave man owned, the number of hairy mammoths a cave man saw during a hunt, or the number of animals in the herd.

prehistoric calculations

preset To establish an initial condition, such as the control values of a loop or the initial values in index registers. See *initialize.*

preventive maintenance The process used in a computer system that attempts to keep equipment in continuous operating condition by detecting, isolating, and correcting failures before occurrence. It involves cleaning and adjusting the equipment as well as testing the equipment under both normal and marginal conditions. Contrast with *corrective maintenance.*

primary cluster A buildup of table entries around a single table location.

primary colors The set of colors from which all others can be derived, but which cannot be produced from each other. The additive primaries (light) are blue, green, and red. The subtractive primaries (colorant) are cyan, magenta, and yellow. The psychological primaries are the pairs red/green, yellow/blue, and black/white.

primary storage See *internal storage.*

prime shift A working shift that coincides with the normal business hours of an organization.

primitive A basic or fundamental unit, often referring to the lowest level of a machine instruction or the lowest unit of language translation.

primitive element A graphic element, such as a line segment or point, which can be readily called-up and extrapolated or combined with other primitive elements to form more complex objects or images.

print control character A control character for operations on a line printer (e.g., carriage return, page ejection, or line spacing).

printed circuit An electronic circuit printed, vacuum deposited, or electroplated on a flat insulating sheet. Abbreviated PC. *(Illus. p. 154)*

printed circuit board A circuit board whose electrical connections are made through conductive material that is

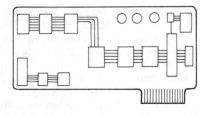

printed circuit

contained on the board itself, rather than with individual wires. Abbreviated PCB.

printer An output device that produces hard copy output. See *electrostatic printer* and *line printer*.

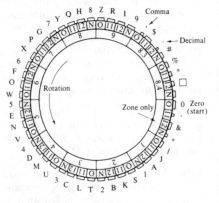

printer

printout A form of computer system output. It is printed on a page by a printer.

print wheel A single element providing the character set at one printing position of a wheel printer.

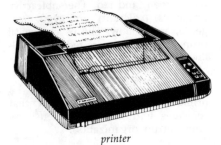

print wheel

priority interrupt An interrupt that is given preference over other interrupts within the system.

priority processing The processing of a sequence of jobs on the basis of assigned priorities. See *job queue*.

privacy Those personal aspects a person chooses to shield from public scrutiny. The right of individuals to select the time and circumstances when information about them is to be made public.

privately leased line A communication line intended for the use of a single customer.

privileged instruction A computer instruction that is not available for use in ordinary programs written by users; its use is restricted to the routines of the operating system. See *storage key* and *storage protection*.

probabilistic model A model that makes use of the mathematics of probability, used to analyze data whose individual values are unknown but whose long-range behavior can be predicted.

probability theory A measure of likelihood of occurrence of a chance event, used to predict behavior of a group.

problem analysis The use of a plan to solve a problem.

problem definition The formulation of the logic used to define a problem. A description of a task to be performed.

problem-oriented language A programming language designed for the convenient expression of a given class of problems. Abbreviated POL. Contrast with *assembly language, machine language*, and *procedure-oriented language*. See *APT, COGO, GPSS*, and *RPG*.

problem program A program that is executed when the central processing unit is in the "problem state," that is, any program that does not contain privileged instructions.

procedure (1) The course of action taken for the solution of a problem. (2) A portion of a high-level language program that performs a specific task necessary for that program.

procedure division One of the four main component parts of a COBOL program.

procedure manual A manual that describes the job functions required in a certain organization or department.

procedure-oriented language A high-level, machine-independent, programming language designed for the convenient expression of procedures used in the solution of a wide class of problems. Examples include FORTRAN, COBOL, AND PL/I. Abbreviated POL. Contrast with *assembly language, machine language, and problem-oriented language.* See *Ada, ALGOL, APL, BASIC, C, COBOL, FORTH, FORTRAN, JO-VIAL, NELIAC, Pascal, PILOT, PLANIT, PL/I, SIMSCRIPT, SNOBOL,* and *WATFOR.*

process A systematic sequence of operations to produce a specified result.

process bound Term applied to those programs that generate little input or output, are seldom waiting for data, and therefore result in little central processing unit wait time.

process control The use of the computer to control industrial processes

process control

such as oil refining and steel production.

process control computer A digital computer used in a process control system. Process control computers are generally limited in instruction capacity, word length, and accuracy. They are designed for continuous operation in nonairconditioned facilities.

process conversion Changing the method of running the computer system.

processing The computer manipulation of data in solving a problem. See *data processing.*

processing symbol A flowcharting symbol used to indicate a processing operation (e.g., a calculation). A rectangular shaped figure is used to represent this symbol.

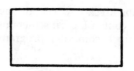

processing symbol

processor A device or system capable of performing operations upon data; for example, central processing unit (hardware) or compiler (software). A compiler is sometimes referred to as a language processor.

product The quantity that results from multiplying two quantities.

production run The execution of a debugged program that routinely accomplishes the purpose of the program. For example, running a payroll program to produce weekly paychecks is a production run.

productivity A measure of the work performed by a software/hardware system. Productivity largely depends on a combination of two factors: the facility (ease of use) of the system and the performance (throughput, response time, and availability) of the system.

program (1) A sequence of instructions that permits a computer to perform a particular task. (2) A plan to achieve a problem solution. (3) To design, write, and test one or more routines. (4) Loosely, a routine.

program card A card that is punched with specific coding and used to control the automatic operations of keypunch and verifier machines.

program control Descriptive of a system in which a computer is used to direct the operation of the system.

program correctness See *program testing*.

program counter A counter that indicates the location of the next program instruction to be executed by the computer. Same as *instruction counter*.

program deck A set of punched cards containing instructions that make up a computer program.

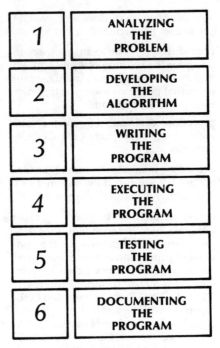

1	ANALYZING THE PROBLEM
2	DEVELOPING THE ALGORITHM
3	WRITING THE PROGRAM
4	EXECUTING THE PROGRAM
5	TESTING THE PROGRAM
6	DOCUMENTING THE PROGRAM

program development cycle

program library A collection of available computer programs and routines. Same as *library*. See *disk library* and *tape library*.

program listing See *listing*.

programmable logic array A device that provides the sum of a partial product with outputs for a given set of inputs.

programmable memory A content-changeable memory, usually where most computer programs and data are stored. It is usually RAM or magnetic core memory. Contrast with *ROM*. See *storage*.

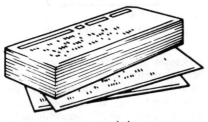

program deck

program development cycle The steps involved in the solution of a problem with a computer: problem analysis, flowcharting, coding, program testing, and documentation.

program flowchart See *flowchart*.

program generator See *generator*.

program graph A graphical representation of a program.

program language See *programming language*.

programmed check A check consisting of tests inserted into the programmed statement of a problem and performed by the use of computer instructions.

programmer A person whose job it is to design, write, and test programs and the instructions that get the computer to do a specific job. Also called *computer programmer*. See *coder* and *parts programmer*.

programmer

programmer board A board that allows a user to program PROM or EPROM memories for use in his or her computer system. See *PROM programmer*.

programming The process of translating a problem from its physical environment to a language that a computer can understand and obey. The process of planning the procedure for solving a problem. This may involve, among other things, the analysis of the problem, preparation of an algorithm, coding of the problem, establishing input/output formats, establishing testing and checkout procedures, allocation of storage, preparation of documentation, and supervision of the running of the program on a computer.

programming aids Computer programs that aid computer users (e.g., compilers, debugging packages, linkage editors, and mathematical subroutines).

programming analyst A person skilled in the definition of and the development of techniques and computer programs for the solution of a problem. See *programmer* and *systems analyst*.

programming instruction Refers to a sequence of specific instructions (not to be confused with computer programming) for teaching a human being a specific subject. However, several computer programming training courses have developed using programmed instruction techniques.

programming language A language used to express computer programs. See *Ada, ALGOL, APL, APT, BASIC, C, COBOL, COGO, DL/1, FLOW-MATIC, FORTH, FORTRAN, GPSS, ICES, JOVIAL, LOGO, NELIAC, Pascal, PILOT, PLANIT, PL/C, PL/I, PL/M, problem-oriented language, procedure-oriented language, SIMSCRIPT, SNOBOL,* and *WATFOR*.

programming linguistics Languages for communication between any two systems, be they mechanical, electrical, or human, can be described by the three interconnected concepts of syntax, semantics, and pragmatics.

program specifications A document that identifies the data requirements of a system, the files required, the input/output specifications, and the processing details.

program stack An area of computer memory set aside for temporary storage of data and instructions, particularly during an interrupt. See *pop, push, push down list, push down stack,* and *stack*.

program stop A stop instruction built into the program that will automatically stop the machine under certain conditions, or upon reaching the end of the processing, or upon completing the solution of a problem.

program storage A portion of the internal storage reserved for the storage of programs, routines, and subroutines. In many systems, protection devices are used to prevent inadvertent alteration of the contents of the program storage.

program switch A point in a programming routine at which two courses of action are possible, the correct one being determined by a condition prevailing elsewhere in the program or by a physical disposition of the system.

program testing Executing a program with test data to ascertain that it functions as expected.

projection An extension of past trends into the future.

project manager A person who takes responsibility for the enforcement of a project's goals.

PROM An acronym for Programmable Read Only Memory. A memory that can be programmed by electrical pulses. Once programmed, it is read only. The PROM chips can be purchased blank and then programmed by using a special machine (*PROM programmer*).

PROM burner See *PROM programmer.*

PROM programmer A device used to program PROMs (Programmable Read Only Memories) and reprogram EPROMs (Erasable PROMs) by electrical pulses. Sometimes called a PROM burner.

prompt A character or message provided by the computer to indicate that it is ready to accept keyboard input.

propagated error An error or mistake occurring in one operation and affecting data required for subsequent operations, so that the error or mistake is spread through much of the processed data.

protected storage Storage locations reserved for special purposes in which data cannot be stored without undergoing a screening procedure to establish suitability for storage therein.

protocol A set of procedures or conventions used routinely between equipment such as terminals and computers.

prototype A circuit board used in development systems to evaluate new system concepts. See *breadboard.*

psec An abbreviation for *picosecond;* one trillionth of a second.

pseudocode An arbitrary system of symbols used to represent operators, operands, operations, index registers, and so forth.

pseudolanguage A language, not directly understandable by a computer, that is used to write computer programs. Before a pseudoprogram can be used, it must be translated into a language that the computer understands (machine language). Same as *symbolic language.*

pseudo-operation An operation that is not part of the computer's operation repertoire as realized by hardware; hence, an extension of the set of machine operations.

pseudorandom number A number generated by a computer in a deterministic manner. These numbers have been subjected to many statistical tests of randomness and, for most practical purposes, can be used as *random numbers.*

publication language A well-defined form of a programming language suitable for use in publications. A language such as this is necessary because some languages use special characters that are not available in common type fonts.

pull See *pop.*

pull instruction An instruction that pulls or retrieves data from the top of the program push down stack. Same as *pop instruction.*

pulse An abrupt change in voltage, either positive or negative, that conveys information to a circuit.

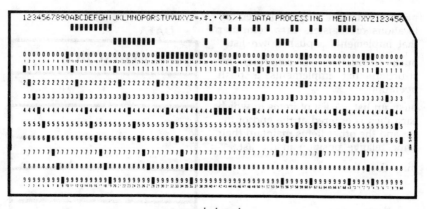

punched card

pulse modulation Use of a series of pulses that are modulated or characterized to convey information. Types of pulse modulation include amplitude (PAM), position (PPM), and duration (PDM) systems.

punched card A cardboard card used in data processing operations in which tiny rectangular holes at hundreds of individual locations denote numerical values and alphanumeric codes. See *Hollerith card* and *ninety-six column card*.

punched card code A code used to represent data on cards. See *Hollerith code*.

punched paper tape See *paper tape*.

punched tape code See *paper tape code*.

punching position One of the divisions of a card column into which a hole may be punched.

punching station The area on the keypunch and card punch machine where a card is aligned for the punching process.

pure procedure A procedure that never modifies any part of itself during execution.

push Putting data into the top location of a program stack. The stack

pointer is automatically incremented to point to the next location, which becomes the top of the stack. Also called put. See *pop*.

push down list A list written from the bottom up, with each new entry placed on the top of the list like a stack of trays in a cafeteria. The item to be processed first is the one on the top of the list. See *LIFO* (Last In–First Out).

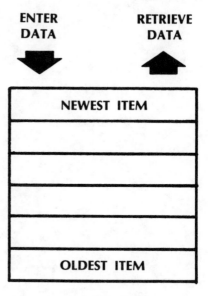

push down list

159

push down stack A set of memory locations or registers in a computer that implements a push down list.

push instruction A computer instruction that implements a push operation.

push up list A list of items in which each item is entered at the end of the list and the other items maintain their same relative position in the list.

put See *push*.

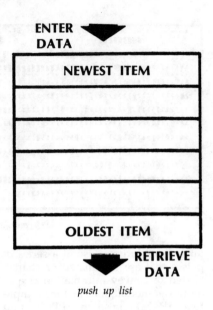

push up list

quad density Refers to tapes or disks on which data are very densely recorded.

quadratic quotient search A hashing algorithm that uses a quadratic offset when probing subsequent table locations.

quality control A technique for evaluating the quality of a product being processed by checking it against a predetermined standard and taking the proper corrective action if the quality falls below the standard.

quantity A positive or negative real number in the mathematical sense.

quantum The smallest unit of measure employed in a system.

quasi language Same as *pseudolanguage.*

QUBE An information utility which is part of an advanced cable-TV system that provides viewers everything from first-run movies to special programs for doctors and lawyers. It is an interactive Viewdata-type service.

query To ask for information.

query language A set of commands used to extract from a data base the data that meets specific criteria.

queue (1) A group of items waiting to be acted upon by the computer. The arrangement of items determines the processing priority. (2) Queues are nothing more than the waiting lines that have become an accepted and often frustrating fact of modern life.

queued access method Any access method that automatically synchronizes the transfer of data between the program using the access method and the input/output devices, thereby eliminating delays for input/output operations.

queuing A method of controlling the information processing sequence.

queuing theory A form of probability theory useful in studying delays or lineups at servicing points. Research technique concerned with the correct sequential orders of moving units. May include sequence assignments for bits of information, whole messages, assembly line products, or automobiles in traffic.

quibinary code A binary-coded decimal code that is used to represent decimal numbers in which each decimal digit is represented by seven binary digits.

Decimal Digit	Quibinary Code						
	8	6	4	2	0	1	0
0	0	0	0	0	1	0	1
1	0	0	0	0	1	1	0
2	0	0	0	1	0	0	1
3	0	0	0	1	0	1	0
4	0	0	1	0	0	0	1
5	0	0	1	0	0	1	0
6	0	1	0	0	0	0	1
7	0	1	0	0	0	1	0
8	1	0	0	0	0	0	1
9	1	0	0	0	0	1	0

quibinary code

quiescent state The time during which a circuit element is not performing its active function in the circuit.

quotient A result obtained by division.

R

rack A metal frame or chassis on which panels of electrical, electronic or other equipment such as amplifiers, power supply units, and so on may be mounted.

radix The base number in a number system (e.g., the radix in the decimal system is 10). Synonymous with *base*.

radix complement See *complement*.

radix point In a number system, the character (a dot) or implied character that separates the integral part of a numeral from the fractional part; for example, *binary point*, *hexadecimal point*, and *octal point*.

467.32

DECIMAL POINT

radix point

radix sorting Same as *digital sorting*.

RAM An acronym for Random Access Memory. A memory into which the user can call up data (read) or enter information and instructions (write). RAM is the "working memory" of the computer into which applications programs can be loaded from outside and then executed.

RAMAC An acronym for Random Access Method of Accounting and Control. The IBM 305 RAMAC was the first data processing system to employ a magnetic disk file permitting direct accessing of data records.

random access See *direct access*.

random access memory A memory whose contents can be read or written on directly without regard to any other memory location. See *RAM*.

random files Files not organized in any sequence. Data are retrieved based on the address of the record on the direct access device.

random number A patternless sequence of digits. An unpredictable number produced by chance that satisfies one or more of the tests for randomness. See *pseudorandom number*.

random number generator A computer program or hardware designed to produce a pseudorandom number or series of pseudorandom numbers according to specified limitations.

range check A range check is usually applied to a code in order to verify that it falls within a given set of characters or numbers.

rank (1) To arrange in an ascending or descending series according to importance. (2) A measure of the relative position in a group, series, array, or classification.

raster A grid. A device that stores and displays data as horizontal rows of uniform grid or picture cells (pixels).

raw data Data that has not been processed.

read To get information from any input or file storage media. For example, reading punched cards by detecting the pattern of holes, or reading a magnetic disk by sensing the patterns of magnetism.

reader Any device capable of transcribing data from an input medium.

read head A magnetic head that is designed and used to read data from the media. Contrast with *write head*.

reading station The part of a card punch and keypunch where a data card is aligned for reading by a sensing mechanism.

read ink See *nonreflective ink.*

read-only memory A special type of computer memory. It is permanently programmed with one group of frequently used instructions. Read-only memory does not lose its program when the computer's power is turned off, but the program cannot be changed by the user. In many microcomputers, the BASIC language interpreter and operating systems are contained in read-only memory. Several of the newer microcomputers use plug-in read-only memory modules that contain special programs, i.e., game programs, educational programs, business programs, and so on. Abbreviated ROM. See *EPROM, firmware, PROM, ROM,* and *solid state cartridge.*

read-only storage See *read-only memory.*

readout The manner in which a computer presents the processed information; (e.g., visual display, line printer, digital plotter, etc.).

read/write head A small electromagnet used to read, write, or erase data on a magnetic storage device (i.e., disk, tape, drum, magnetic card). See *read head* and *write head.*

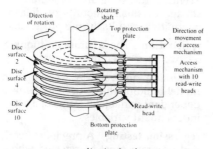

read/write head

real memory Same as *real storage.*

real storage The internal storage in a virtual memory system.

real time Descriptive of on-line computer processing systems that receive and process data quickly enough to produce output to control, direct, or affect the outcome of an ongoing activity or process. For example, in an airline reservation system, a customer booking inquiry is entered into the computer to see if space is available. If a seat is booked, the file of available seats is updated immediately, thus giving an up-to-date record of seats reserved and seats available.

real time clock A piece of hardware that interrupts the processor at fixed time intervals to synchronize the operations of the computer with events occurring in the outside world, often involving human/computer interaction.

real time input Input data inserted into a system at the time of generation by another system.

real time output Output data removed from a system at a time of need by another system.

reasonableness check A technique whereby tests are made of processed data to indicate whether a gross error exists. Programming instructions would check if the data lies within preset upper and lower limits and initiate some action if the data is not reasonable.

receive only A designation used to indicate the read-only capabilities of equipment lacking keyboards and input equipment.

record A collection of related items of data treated as a unit. See *item.*

record gap Same as *interrecord gap.*

recording density The number of useful storage cells per unit of length or area; for example, the number of characters per inch on a magnetic tape or the number of bits per inch on a single track of a disk. Also called packing density.

record layout The arrangement and structure of data in a record, including the size and sequence of its components.

record length A measure of the size of a record, usually specified in units such as words, bytes, or characters.

recoverable error An error condition that can be sensed and corrected, thereby allowing continued operation of a program.

rectifier An electrical device that changes alternating current into direct current.

recursion A set of operations or program statements in which one of the operations or statements is specified in terms of the entire set. The continued repetition of the same operation(s).

recursive Pertaining to a process that is inherently repetitive. The result of each repetition is usually dependent upon the result of the previous repetition.

recursive procedure A procedure (A) that, while being executed, either calls itself or calls another procedure (B), which in turn calls procedure (A).

recursive subroutine A subroutine capable of calling itself, or a subroutine that invokes another subroutine, which, in turn, invokes the original subroutine.

redundancy check A check based on the transfer of more bits or characters than the minimum number required to express the message itself, the added bits or characters having been inserted systematically for checking purposes. See *parity bit* and *parity checking*.

redundant code A binary coded decimal value with an added check bit.

redundant information A message expressed in such a way that the essence of the information occurs in several ways.

reel A mounting for a roll of tape.

reentrant Pertaining to a routine that can be used by two or more independent programs at the same time.

reentrant subroutine In a multiprogramming system, a subroutine of which only one copy resides in internal storage. This copy is shared by several programs.

reference edge See *aligning edge*.

reflectance In optical scanning, a relative value assigned to a character or color of ink when compared with the background.

reflectance ink In optical scanning, ink that has a reflectance level which very nearly approximates the acceptable paper reflectance level for a particular optical character reader.

reflected code Same as *gray code*.

refresh (1) A signal sent to dynamic RAM every few milliseconds to help it remember data. (2) To re-record an image on a cathode ray tube screen when it begins to fade. Typically, the image must be regenerated at a rate of 30 to 60 hertz (cycles per second) to avoid flicker.

regenerate The process of renewing some quantity. Used in storage devices to write back information that has been read in a destructive manner.

register A high-speed device used in a central processing unit for temporary storage of small amounts of data or intermittent results during processing.

registration The accurate positioning relative to a reference.

regression analysis A technique in model-building that is used to define a dependent variable in terms of a set of independent variables.

regression testing A previously verified program must be retested whenever it is extended or corrected.

relation The equality, inequality, or any property that can be said to hold (or not hold) for two objects in a specified order.

relational expression An expression that contains one or more relational operators.

relational operator A symbol used to compare two values; the operator specifies a condition that may be either true or false, such as = (equal to), < (less than), > (greater than), and so on.

relative address An address to which a base address must be added in order to form the absolute address of a particular storage location.

relative coding Coding that uses machine instructions with relative addresses.

relay A magnetically operated switch used in pre-electronic computers.

reliability A measure of the ability of a system or individual hardware device to function without failure.

relocatable addresses The addresses used in a program that can be positioned at almost any place in internal storage.

relocatable program A program existing in a form that permits it to be loaded and executed in any available region of a computer's internal storage.

relocate To move a program from one area of internal storage to another and also, to adjust the address references so that the program can be executed in its new location.

remainder The dividend minus the product of the quotient and divisor.

remote Physically distant from a local computer, terminal, etc.

remote access Relating to the communication with a computer facility by a station (or stations) that are distant from the computer.

remote batch processing The processing of data in batches at a remote

location by using a small computer system. See *batch processing*.

remote job entry Refers to the computer programs used to submit processing jobs from remote terminals. Abbreviated RJE.

remote processing The processing of computer programs through an input/output device that is remotely connected to a computer system. See *remote batch processing*.

remote station See *remote terminal*.

remote terminal A device for communicating with computers from sites that are physically separated from the computer, often distant enough so that communications facilities such as telephone lines are used rather than direct cables. See *terminal*.

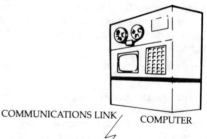

COMMUNICATIONS LINK / COMPUTER

REMOTE TERMINAL

remote terminal

repeating decimal number A nonterminating decimal number such as .3333333 . . . or .31282828 . . . .

reperforator A paper tape punch.

repertoire A complete set of instructions that belongs to a specific computer or family of computers.

repetition instruction An instruction that causes one or more instructions to be executed an indicated number of times.

repetitive Being done over and over.

replacement theory The mathematics of deterioration and failure, used to estimate replacement costs and determine optimum replacement policies.

report Usually associated with output data; involves the grouping of related facts so as to be easily understood by the reader.

report file File generated during data processing, usually used to print out or display desired output.

report generator A program that converts machine-readable data into a printed report organized for a specific purpose. See *RPG*.

report program generator See *RPG*.

reproduce To copy information on a similar media; for example, to obtain a duplicate disk pack from a specific disk pack.

reproducer Same as *reproducing punch*.

reproducing punch A device for duplicating decks of cards. The reproducing punch is capable of giving an exact copy of a master deck, or a copy of the deck may be punched in a different format.

reprogramming Changing a program written for one computer so that it will run on another.

rerun To repeat all or part of a program on a computer, usually because of a correction, a false start, or an interrupt.

reserve accumulator An auxiliary storage register allied to the main accumulator in a central processing unit. See *accumulator*.

reserved words Certain words that, because they are reserved by operating systems, language translators, and so on for their own use, cannot be used in an application program.

reset (1) To return computer components to a specified static state. (2) To place a binary cell into the zero state.

resident program A program that occupies a dedicated area of internal storage.

resistor A device connected into an electrical circuit to introduce a specified resistance.

resolution The density and overall quality of a video display. The number of pixels on the picture screen. A high-resolution picture looks smooth and realistic. It is produced by a large number of pixels. A low-resolution picture is blocky and jagged. It is produced by a small number of pixels.

resource Any component of a computer configuration. Memory, printers, visual displays, disk storage units, software, and operating personnel are all considered resources.

resource allocation The sharing of computer resources among competing tasks.

resource sharing The sharing of one central processor by both several users and several peripheral devices.

response position In optical scanning, the area designated for marking information on an OMR (mark read) form.

response time The time it takes the computer system to react to a given input. It is the interval between an event and the system's response to the event.

restart To resume the execution of a program.

retrieval See *information retrieval*.

retrieving Searching for, locating, and removing data.

return (1) A set of instructions at the end of a subroutine that permits control to return to the proper point in the main program. (2) A key on an input device that returns the carriage to its leftmost position. See *carriage return*.

reusable The attribute of a routine that permits the same copy of the routine to be used by two or more tasks.

reverse Polish notation See *Polish notation*.

rewind To return a magnetic tape to its starting position on the tape.

right justify See *justify*.

ring A cyclic arrangement of data elements. See *circular list*.

ring network A computer network where each computer is connected to adjacent computers.

ripple sort See *bubble sort*.

RI/SME An acronym for Robotics International of the Society of Manufacturing Engineers. This professional organization directs itself toward engineers interested in the design and use of robots.

RJE An acronym meaning Remote Job Entry. Refers to the programs used to submit processing jobs from terminals.

RO An acronym for Receive Only. A designation used to indicate the read-only capabilities of teletypewriters and other equipment lacking keyboards and of paper tape input equipment.

robot A computer-controlled device equipped with sensing instruments for detecting input signals or environmental conditions, with a calculating mechanism for making decisions, and with a guidance mechanism for providing control.

robot control languages Languages for programs that are designed to control robots. VAL, AL, ML, and ROBOTLAN are examples of these languages.

robotics An area of artificial intelligence related to robots. The science of robot design and use.

robot

ROBOTLAN A programming language used to control robots.

rod memory A computer storage consisting of wires, coated with a nickel-iron alloy, and cut in such a way as to form stacks of rods. See *thin film*.

rollback A system that will restart the running program after a system failure. Snapshots of data and programs are stored at periodic intervals, and the system rolls back to restart at the last recorded snapshot.

roll out To record the contents of internal storage in auxiliary storage.

rollover A property of some keyboards. Keys may be depressed in more rapid succession on a keyboard with rollover.

ROM An acronym for Read-Only Memory. Generally, a solid state storage chip that is programmed at the time of its manufacture and cannot be reprogrammed by the computer user. Also called firmware, since this implies software which is permanent, or firmly in place on a chip.

ROM cartridge A read-only memory module that contains a preprogrammed function (i.e., a game, an educational program, a business system, etc.). The module is plugged into the computer. See *firmware. Read-only memory*, and *TI-99/4*.

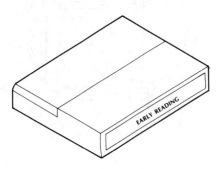

ROM cartridge

ROM simulator A general purpose device that is used to replace ROMs or PROMs in a system during program checkout. Because it offers real time in-circuit simulation, it can be used in the engineering prototype or reproduction model to find and correct program errors or in the production model to add new features.

round See *round off.*

round off To truncate the rightmost digit of a number, and to increase by one the now remaining rightmost digit if the truncated digit is greater than or equal to half of the number base. For example, the base 10 number 463.1076 would be rounded to 463.108, while the number 23.602 would be rounded to 23.60.

round-off error The error resulting from rounding off a quantity by deleting the less significant digits and applying the same rule of correction to the part retained; for example, 0.2751 can be rounded to 0.275 with a round-

off error of .0001. Contrast with *truncation error.*

routine A set of machine instructions for carrying out a specific processing operation. Sometimes used as a synonym for *program.*

routing The assignment of a path for the delivery of a message.

row (1) The horizontal members of one line of an array. (2) One of the horizontal lines of punching positions on a punched card. Contrast with *column.*

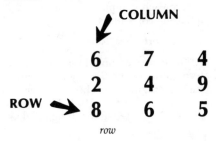

row

RPG An acronym for Report Program Generator. A popular business-oriented programming language. The language will allow a user to program many business operations as well as to generate reports. A fairly simple RPG program can perform a rather sophisticated business task. The language is relatively easy to learn.

RPROM An acronym for Reprogrammable PROM. See *EPROM.*

RS-232 A data communication industry standard for the serial transmission of data to a peripheral device, such as a printer, a video monitor, a plotter, and so forth. Most microcomputers provide for an RS-232 interface.

run The single and continuous execution of a program by a computer on a given set of data. Also called *execute.*

run manual A manual or book documenting the processing system, program logic, controls, program changes, and operating instructions associated with a computer run.

OPERATING INSTRUCTIONS

PROGRAM

FLOWCHART

DESCRIPTION

RUN MANUAL

run manual

run time The time during which the data are fetched by the control unit and the actual processing is performed in the arithmetic-logic unit. Also called *execution time*. Contrast with *compilation time*.

S

sales representative A person who sells the products of a computer equipment manufacturer, software company, or computer store.

SAM An acronym for Sequential Access Method. A method for storing and retrieving data on a disk file.

sample data A set of hypothetical data used to see if a flowchart is logical and if a program works. See *test data*.

sampling Obtaining a value of a variable at regular or intermittent intervals.

sapphire A material used as a substrate for some types of integrated circuit chips.

satellite See *communication satellite*.

satellite communications The use of orbiting transponders or microwave relays to transmit information around the world.

satellite computer (1) An additional computer, usually smaller, that sup-

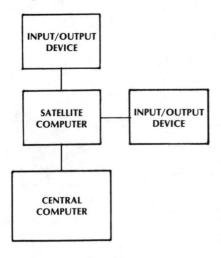

satellite computer

ports a larger computer system. An economy of processing can be effected if the satellite computer handles lower-level functions such as remote terminal coordination, data validity checking, code conversion, and input/output functions. (2) An off-line auxiliary computer.

save To store a program somewhere other than in the computer's internal memory, for example, on a cassette tape or diskette.

scale A technique used to alter or change the measure of units so that all variables are expressed within a certain range of magnitude.

scale factor One or more factors used to multiply or divide quantities occurring in a problem and to convert them into a desired range, such as the range from plus one to minus one.

scan (1) To examine point-by-point in logical sequence. (2) An algorithmic procedure for visiting or listing each node of a data structure. (3) The operation required to produce an image on a television screen.

scan area That area of a form or document which contains information to be scanned by an optical character reader.

scanner Any optical device which can recognize a specific set of visual symbols.

scanner channel A device that polls individual channels to see if they have data ready to be transmitted.

scanning The rapid examination of every item in a computer's list of data to see if a specific condition is met.

scan path In optical scanning, a predetermined area within the clear area where data to be read must be located. The position of the scan path and the amount of data that can be read will generally depend upon the machine involved.

scatter read-gather write Scatter read refers to placing information from an input record into nonadjacent storage areas. Gather write refers to placing information from nonadjacent storage areas into a single physical record.

SCDP An acronym for the Society of Certified Data Processors. An organization formed to represent exclusively the interest and wishes of the holder of the Certificate in Data Processing (CDP).

schedule A list of events in the order they should occur.

scheduler A program which schedules jobs for processing.

scheduling The task of determining what the succession of programs should be in a multiprogramming computer system.

Scheutz, George (1785–1873) In 1834, he started the construction of a machine similar to Charles Babbage's difference engine. The machine was completed and used for printing mathematical tables. See *Babbage, Charles* and *difference engine*.

Schickhardt, Wilhelm (1592–1635) A German professor of mathematics who invented a calculating machine in 1624.

scientific notation A notation in which numbers are written as a "significant digits" part times an appropriate power of 10; for example, 0.32619×10^7 or $0.32619E + 07$ to mean 3,261,900.

SCM An acronym for Society for Computer Medicine. This organization brings together physicians and computer scientists. It emphasizes the use of automation for medical applications.

George Scheutz

Wilhelm Schickhardt

SCR An acronym for Silicon Controlled Rectifier, a semiconductor device useful in controlling large amounts of DC current or voltage.

171

Basically, it is a diode turned on or off by a signal voltage applied to a control electrode called the gate. Its characteristics are similar to the old vacuum tube thyratron, which is why it is sometimes called a thyristor.

scratch file During the processing of substantial files of data, it often becomes necessary to create temporary files for later use by copying all or part of a data set to an auxiliary storage device.

scratchpad A small, fast storage that is used in some computers in place of registers. See *cache memory*.

screen A surface on which information is displayed, such as a video display screen. See *cathode ray tube, display,* and *video terminal*.

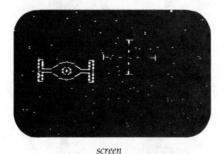

screen

scrolling The vertical movement of lines on a video display, so that the top line disappears and a new line is displayed at the bottom of the screen.

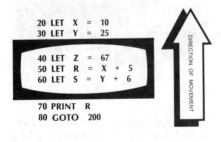

```
20 LET  X  =  10
30 LET  Y  =  25

40 LET  Z  =  67
50 LET  R  =  X  +  5
60 LET  S  =  Y  +  6

70 PRINT  R
80 GOTO  200
```

DIRECTION OF MOVEMENT

scrolling

SCS An acronym for Society for Computer Simulation. A professional computer science organization that is devoted primarily to the advancement of simulation and allied technology.

SEAC An acronym for Standards Eastern Automatic Computer. The first stored program computer to run in the United States (1950).

search To examine a set of items for those that have a desired property.

search key Data to be compared to specified parts of each item for the purpose of conducting a search.

search memory See *associative storage*.

second Base unit of time in the SI metric system; also used in our customary English system.

secondary storage See *auxiliary storage*.

second generation Computers belonging to the second era of technological development of computers when the transistor replaced the vacuum tube. These were prominent from 1959 to 1964, when they were displaced by computers using integrated circuitry.

second source A manufacturer who produces a product that is interchangeable with the product of another manufacturer.

sector One of the peripheral elements into which each track of a disk surface is divided.

security See *computer security* and *data security*.

seed A constant used to initiate a pseudorandom number generator. The seed is used to generate the first number, and all subsequent numbers are based on previous results.

seek To position the access mechanism of a direct access device at a specified location.

seek time The time required to position the access mechanism of a direct access storage device at a specified position. See *access time* and *transfer rate*.

segment (1) To divide a program into parts such that some segments may reside in internal storage and other segments may reside in auxiliary storage. Each segment will contain the necessary instructions to jump to another segment or to call another segment into internal storage. (2) The smallest functional unit that can be loaded as one logical entity during execution of an overlay program. (3) As applied to the field of telecommunications, a portion of a message that can be contained in a buffer of specified size.

selecting Extracting certain cards from a deck for a specific purpose without disturbing the sequence in which they were originally filed.

selection Choosing between alternative choices.

selection sort A sort that selects the extreme value (smallest or largest) in a list, exchanges it with the last value in the list, and repeats with a shorter list.

selector channel A term used in certain computer systems for an input/output channel that can transfer data to or from only one peripheral device at a time. Contrast with *multiplexer channel*.

self-adapting Pertaining to the ability of a system to change its performance characteristics in response to its environment.

self-checking code Same as *error-detection code*.

self-compiling compiler A compiler that is written in its own source language and is capable of compiling itself.

self-complementing code A code that has the property that the binary one's complement of the weighted binary number is also the number nine's complement in decimal notation.

self-correcting code A numerical coding system in which transmission errors are automatically detected and corrected. Same as *error-correcting code*.

self-validating code A code that makes an explicit attempt to determine its own correctness and proceed accordingly.

semantics The study or science of meaning in language forms.

semaphores Synchronization primitives used to coordinate the activities of two or more programs or processes that are running at the same time and sharing information.

semiconductor A solid material, usually germanium or silicon, with an electrical conductivity that lies between the high conductivity of metals and the low conductivity of insulators. Depending on the temperature and pressure, a semiconductor can control a flow of electricity. It is the material from which integrated circuits are made.

semiconductor device An electronic element fabricated from crystalline materials such as silicon or germanium that, in the pure state, are neither good conductors nor good insulators and are unusable for electronic purposes. When certain impurity atoms such as phosphorus or arsenic are diffused into the crystal structure of the pure metal, the electrical neutrality is upset, introducing positive or negative charge carriers. Diodes and transistors can then be implemented.

semiconductor storage A memory device whose storage elements are formed as solid state electronic components on an integrated circuit chip.

semirandom access The method of locating data in storage that combines in the search for the desired item some form of direct access, usually followed by a limited sequential search.

sense (1) To examine, particularly relative to a criterion. (2) To determine the present arrangement of some element of hardware. (3) To read holes punched on a card or tape.

sense switch A computer console switch that may be interrogated by a program. Sense switches are very useful when debugging a large, complex program.

sensitivity The degree of response of a control unit to a change in the incoming signal.

sensors Devices to detect and measure physical phenomena such as temperature, stress, heartbeat, wind direction, and fire.

sequence (1) An arrangement of items according to a specified set of rules. (2) In numeric sequence, normally in ascending order.

sequence check A check used to prove that a set of data is arranged in ascending or descending order.

sequential Pertaining to the occurrence of events in time sequence, with little or no simultaneity or overlap of events.

sequential access A term used to describe files such as magnetic tape which must be searched serially from the beginning to find any desired record.

sequential computer A computer in which events occur in time sequence with little or no simultaneity or overlap of events.

sequential data set A data set whose records are organized on the basis of their successive physical positions, such as on magnetic tape.

sequential data structure A data structure in which each atom is immediately adjacent to the next atom. Also called contiguous data structure.

sequential device A peripheral device from which data are read, or into which data are written in order; nothing can be omitted.

sequential file organization The organization of records in a specific sequence, based on a key such as part number or employee ID. The records in sequential files must be processed one after another.

sequential list A list stored in contiguous locations. Also called dense list and linear list.

sequential machine A mathematical model of a certain type of sequential switching circuit.

sequential storage Auxiliary storage where data are arranged in ascending or descending order, usually by item number.

serial (1) Pertaining to the sequential occurrence of two or more related activities in a single device. (2) The handling of data in a sequential fashion. Contrast with *parallel*.

serial access Descriptive of a storage device or medium where there is a sequential relationship between access time and data location in storage, that is, the access time is dependent upon the location of the data. Contrast with *direct access*. See *serial processing*.

serial adder An adder that performs its operations by bringing in one digit at a time from each of the quantities involved.

serial computer A computer in which each digit or data word bit is processed serially by the computer.

serial input/output Data transmission in which the bits are sent one by one over a single wire. Contrast with *parallel input/output*.

serial operation Computer operation in which all digits of a word are handled sequentially, rather than simultaneously. Contrast with *parallel operation*.

serial processing Reading, and/or writing, records of file, one by one, in the physical sequence in which they are stored. Contrast with *parallel processing*. See *serial access*.

serial reading Column-by-column reading of a punch card.

serial transmission A method of information transfer in which the bits composing a character are sent sequentially. Contrast with *parallel transmission*.

service bureau An organization that provides data processing services for other individuals or organizations. See *computer utility*.

service programs See *systems programs*.

servomechanism A feedback control system.

set (1) To place a binary cell into the one state. (2) To place a storage device into a specified state, usually other than denoting zero or blank. (3) A collection.

SETL A high-level language designed to facilitate the programming of algorithms involving sets and related structures.

setup An arrangement of data or devices to solve a particular problem.

setup time The time between computer runs or other machine operations that is devoted to such tasks as changing disk packs and moving cards, forms, and other supplies to and from the equipment.

Shannon, Claude E. Made outstanding contributions to Boolean algebra, cryptography, and computing circuits, and to communications with his mathematical theory of information.

Claude E. Shannon

SHARE An organization of users of medium and large scale IBM data processing systems.

shared file A direct access device that may be used by two systems at the same time. A shared file may link two computer systems.

shielding Protection against electrical or magnetic noise.

shift To move the characters of a unit of information column-wise right or left. For a number, this is equivalent to multiplying or dividing by a power of the base of notation.

Shockley, William Bradford (born 1910) A Bell Laboratories scientist who along with Walter Brattain and John Bardeen invented the transistor. See *transistor*.

SI Standard abbreviation of the worldwide International Metric System. (From French, Système International d'Unités—International System of Units.)

side effect A consistent result of a procedure that is in addition to the basic result.

sifting A method of internal sorting where records are moved to permit the insertion of records. Also called *insertion method*.

sign Used in the arithmetic sense to describe whether a number is positive or negative.

signal In communication theory, an intentional disturbance in a communication system. Contrast with *noise*.

signal-to-noise ratio In data communications, the ratio of the (wanted) signal to the (unwanted) noise.

sign digit The digit in the sign position of a word.

sign extension The duplication of the sign bit in the higher-order positions of a register. This extension is usually performed on one's or two's complement binary values.

sign flag A flip-flop that goes to logic 1 if the most significant bit of the result of an operation has the value, logic 1.

significant digits If the digits of a number are ranked according to their ascending higher-powers of the base, then the significant digits are those ranging from the highest-power digit (different from zero) and ending with the lowest-power digit.

sign position The position at which the sign of a number is located.

silicon A nonmetallic chemical element used in the manufacture of transistors, integrated circuits, solar cells, and so forth.

silicon controlled rectifier A semiconductor device that, when in its normal state, blocks a voltage applied in either direction. Abbreviated *SCR*.

Simon, Herbert A. (born 1916) Best known for his work in artificial intelligence and cognitive psychology. Working with other scientists, he helped develop the first heuristic programs and the IPL list processing language.

simplex Pertaining to a communications link that is capable of transmitting data in only one direction. Contrast with *full duplex* and *half duplex*.

SIMSCRIPT A high-level language specifically designed for programming simulation applications.

simulation To represent the functioning of one system by another; that is, to represent a physical system by the execution of a computer program, or to represent a biological system by a mathematical model. See *mathematical model*.

simulator A device, computer program, or system that represents certain features of the behavior of a physical or abstract system.

simultaneous processing The performance of two or more data processing tasks at the same instant of time. Contrast with *concurrent processing*.

single address See *one-address instruction*.

single step The operation of a computer in such a manner that only one instruction is executed each time that the computer is started.

skew In optical scanning, refers to a condition where a character, line, or preprinted symbol is neither parallel with nor at right angles to the leading edge.

skip To ignore one or more instructions in a sequence of instructions.

SLA An acronym for Special Library Association. This international organization of libraries and information specialists promotes the establishment of resource centers for interest groups such as banks, museums, law firms, and other businesses.

slice A special type of chip architecture that permits the cascading of devices to increase word bit size.

slide rule A device for approximate calculation using the principle of the logarithm.

small business computer

small scale integration The class of integrated circuits that have the fewest number of functions per chip. Abbreviated SSI.

smart machines Machines that use microprocessors as their control elements.

smart terminal A terminal that contains some capacity to process information being transmitted or received. See *local intelligence.*

SMIS An acronym for Society for Management Information Systems. A professional organization for fostering improved management performance and information exchange.

smooth To apply procedures that decrease or eliminate rapid fluctuations in data.

snapshot dump A dynamic dump of the contents of specified storage locations and/or registers that is performed at specified points or times during the running of a program.

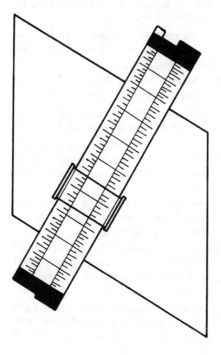

slide rule

slot A single-board position in a backplane.

SLT An acronym for Solid Logic Technique. A term coined by IBM to refer to a microelectronic packaging technique for producing a circuit module.

small business computer A standalone data processing system built around a digital computer system that is dedicated to the processing of standard business applications such as payroll, accounts receivable and payable, order entry, inventory, and general ledger.

SNOBOL A string manipulation programming language used primarily in language translation, program compilation, and combinatorial problems. The language stresses the ability to manipulate symbolic rather than numeric data. The language was developed by Bell Laboratories.

SO An acronym for Send Only. A designation used to indicate the send-only capabilities of equipment.

soft copy Data presented as a video image, in audio format, or in any other form that is not hard copy. See *hard copy. (Illus. p. 178)*

soft copy

soft sector A method of marking sectors or sections on a disk using information written on the disk. Soft sectoring is a method of determining positioning of data on the disk by software calculations rather than by physical monitoring of the disk. See *hard sector*.

software A set of programs, procedures, routines, and documents associated with the operation of a computer system. Software is the name given to the programs that cause a computer to carry out particular operations. The software for a computer system may be classified as *applications programs* and *systems programs*. Contrast with *hardware*. See *firmware*.

software documents The written or printed material associated with computer equipment and software systems.

software encryption The encoding or decoding of computerized data using programming techniques rather than hardware devices such as scramblers.

software engineering A field concerned with the efficient development of reliable and error-free software.

software flexibility A property of software that enables it to change easily in response to different user and system requirements.

software house A company that offers software support services to computer users.

software license A contract signed by the purchaser of a software product in which he/she is usually made to agree not to make copies of the software for resale.

software maintenance The ongoing process of detecting and removing errors from existing programs.

software management The management of those who build, fix, and enhance software.

software monitor A program used for performance measurement purposes.

software package A collection or set of related computer programs.

software resources The program and data resources that represent the software associated with a computing system.

software science A discipline concerned with measurable properties of computer programs.

software system The entire set of computer programs and their documentation used in a computer system.

software transportability The ability to take a program written for one computer and run it without modification on another computer.

solid state Descriptive of electronic components whose operation depends on the control of electric or magnetic phenomena in solids such as integrated circuits and transistors.

solid state cartridge A preprogrammed plug-in module that is used with several microcomputer systems. See *firmware* and *ROM*. (*Illus. p. 179*)

solid state device A device built primarily from solid state electronic circuit elements.

S-100 bus A standard means of interconnection between a microcomputer and peripheral equipment.

son file See *father file*.

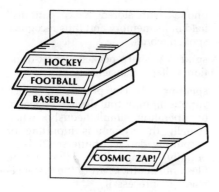

solid state cartridge

SOP An acronym for Standard Operating Procedure. The status quo.

sort (1) To arrange records according to a logical system. Nowadays, most sorting is done on the computer using magnetic disks, drums, or tapes. (2) A utility program that sorts records held on disk, drum, or tape.

sort effort The number of steps needed to order an unordered list.

sorter A device that arranges a set of card records in a preselected sequence.

sort generator A program that generates a sort program for production running.

sort/merge program A generalized processing program that can be used to sort or merge records in a prescribed sequence.

SOS An acronym for Silicon On Sapphire. The process of fabricating integrated chips on layers of silicon and sapphire.

source One of three terminals or electrodes of a field effect transistor (FET). The source is the origin of the charge carriers.

source code Symbolic code in its original form before being processed by a computer.

source computer A computer used to translate a source program into an object program.

source data automation The data that is created while an event is taking place is entered directly into the system in a machine-processable form. See *point-of-sale terminal*.

source deck A card deck comprising a computer program, in source language.

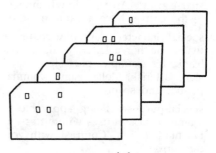

source deck

source document An original document from which basic data is extracted (e.g., invoice, sales slip, inventory tag).

source language The original form in which a program is prepared prior to processing by the computer; for example, a program written in FORTRAN or assembly language. Contrast with *object language*.

source program A computer program written in a source language such as BASIC, FORTRAN, COBOL, PL/I, or assembly language. It is converted to the machine code object program by a special processing program such as a compiler or assembler.

source register The register that contains a data word that is being transferred.

SPA An acronym for Systems and Procedures Association. A professional organization whose purpose is to promote advanced management systems and procedures through seminars, professional education, and research.

space (1) One or more blank characters. (2) The state of a communication channel corresponding to a binary zero.

spanning tree A subgraph of a graph with two properties: (a) it is a tree; and (b) it contains all the nodes of the original graph.

sparse array An array in which most of the entries have a value of zero.

special character A graphic character that is neither a letter, a digit, or a blank; for example, plus sign, equal sign, asterisk, dollar sign, comma, period, and so on.

special-purpose Being applicable to a limited class of uses without essential modification. Contrast with *general-purpose*.

special-purpose computer A computer capable of solving only a few selected types of numerical or logical problems.

specification A detailed description of the required characteristics of a device, process, or product.

specification sheet A form used for coding RPG statements.

speech recognition The ability of a computer to match the pattern of signals coming into it from a "micro-

phone" with stored "voice patterns" held in its memory and thus recognize spoken words.

spike A sharp-peaked, short-duration voltage transient.

spooling (1) The process by which various input/output devices appear to be operating simultaneously, when actually the system is inputting or outputting data via buffers. (2) Temporarily storing data on disk or tape files until another part of the system is ready to process it.

squeezer The person who lays out the LSI circuit in its original "large" form.

SSI An acronym for *Small Scale Integration*.

stack A sequential data list stored in internal storage. Rather than addressing the stack elements by their memory locations, the computer retrieves information from the stack by "popping" elements from the top (LIFO) or from the bottom (FIFO). See *program stack* and *stack pointer*.

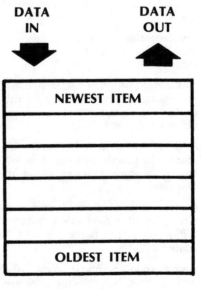

stack

speech recognition

stacked job processing A technique that permits multiple jobs to be stacked for presentation to the system and automatically processes the jobs, one after the other. A series of jobs to be executed is placed in a card reader. The computer system executes the jobs automatically in accordance with the job control cards for each job.

stacker See *card stacker*.

stack pointer A register that is used to point to locations in the stack. A stack pointer is incremented by one before each new data item is "pulled" or "popped" from the stack, and decremented by one after a word is "pushed" onto the stack. See *stack*.

staffing To make people available for organizations.

stand-alone system A self-contained computer system that is not connected to another computer or peripheral devices.

stand-alone system

standard (1) A guide used to establish uniform practices and common techniques. (2) A yardstick (meterstick!) used to measure performance of the computer system function. See *ANSI*.

standard interface A standard physical means by which all peripheral devices are connected to the central processing unit (e.g., a standard form of plug and socket).

standardize To establish standards or to cause conformity with established standards.

standby equipment A duplicate set of equipment to be used if the primary unit becomes unusable because of malfunction.

standby time (1) The period between placing an inquiry into the equipment and the availability of the reply. (2) The period after the setup of the equipment for use and its actual use. (3) The period during which the equipment is available for use.

start bit A bit used in asynchronous transmission to precede the first bit of a character transmitted serially, signaling the start of the character.

state Used most often to refer to the condition of bistable devices, which are used to represent binary digits. By definition, such devices can have only two states. The state of a switch describes whether it is on or off.

statement An expression or instruction in a computer language.

static (1) In storage, information that is fixed at all times. (2) Not moving or progressing, stationary, at rest.

static analysis Analysis of a program that is performed without executing the program.

static dump A storage dump that is performed at a particular point in time with respect to a machine run, often at the termination of a run.

static storage A specific type of semiconductor memory that does not require periodic refresh cycles. Data is held by changing the position of an electronic "switch," a transistor flip-flop, contained in integrated circuits.

station One of the input or output points on a data communications system. See *terminal*.

statistics The branch of mathematics that collects information and tabulates and analyzes it.

statizing The process of transferring an instruction from computer storage to the instruction registers and holding it there, ready to be executed.

step (1) To cause a computer to execute one instruction. (2) One instruction in a computer routine.

Stibitz, George In the design of his "analytical engine," Charles Babbage listed four elements a machine had to include to perform the functions of a human computer: an arithmetic unit; a memory; automatic "choice" of computing sequence; and input and output. In 1946, George Stibitz, then a research mathematician with Bell Telephone Laboratories, designed several relay calculators that incorporated the ideas of Babbage. See *Babbage, Charles*.

stochastic procedures Trial and error, as opposed to algorithmic procedures.

stochastic process Dealing with events that develop in time or space and which cannot be described precisely, except in terms of probability theory.

Stonehenge (B.C. 1600) One of the most fascinating calculating devices was built by Stone Age people. The ancient British stone monument is called Stonehenge. Stonehenge may have been built as an astronomical observatory, possibly used to predict the changes of the seasons. Stonehenge also could have been used to predict the eclipses of the sun and moon.

Stonehenge

stop bit A bit used in asynchronous transmission to signal the end of a character transmitted serially and representing the quiescent state in which the line will remain until the next character begins.

stop code A control character.

storage Descriptive of a device or medium that can accept data, hold them, and deliver them on demand at a later time. The term is preferred over memory. Synonymous with *memory*. See *auxiliary storage, internal storage, PROM, protected storage, RAM,* and *ROM*.

storage allocation The assignment of specific programs, program segments,

George Stibitz

and/or blocks of data to specific portions of a computer's storage. Sometimes called *memory allocation.* See *program storage.*

storage block A contiguous area of internal storage.

storage capacity The number of items of data that a storage device is capable of containing. Frequently defined in terms of computer words, bytes, or characters.

storage device A device used for storing data within a computer system (e.g., integrated circuit storage, magnetic disk unit, magnetic tape unit, magnetic drum unit, floppy disk, tape cassette, and so on).

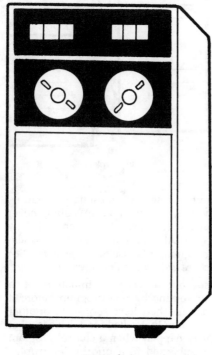

storage device

storage dump A printout of all or part of the contents of the internal storage of a computer. The printout is often used to diagnose errors. Also

called *memory dump.* See *post mortem dump* and *snapshot dump.*

storage key An indicator associated with a storage block or blocks; it requires that tasks have a matching protection key to use the blocks. See *privileged instruction* and *storage protection.*

storage location A position in storage where a character, byte, or word may be stored. Same as *cell.*

storage map A diagram that shows where programs and data are stored in the storage units of the computer system.

storage protection Protection against unauthorized writing in and/or reading from all or part of a storage device. Storage protection is usually implemented automatically by hardware facilities, usually in connection with an operating system. Sometimes called *memory protection.* See *storage key.*

storage unit See *storage device.*

store (1)The British term for storage. (2) To place in storage.

store-and-forward In data communications, the process of handling messages used in a message-switching system.

stored program computer A computer capable of performing sequences of internally stored instructions and usually capable of modifying those instructions as directed by the instructions. Same as *digital computer.*

stored program concept Instructions to a computer as well as data values are stored within the internal storage of a computer. The instructions can, thus, be accessed more quickly and may be more easily modified. This concept was introduced by John von Neumann in 1945. It is the most important characteristic of the digital computer. See *von Neumann, John.*

straight line code The repetition of a sequence of instructions by explicitly writing the instructions for each re-petition. Generally, straight line cod-ing will require less execution time and more space than equivalent loop coding. The feasibility of straight line coding is limited by the space required as well as by the difficulty of coding a variable number of repetitions. Con-trast with *loop code.*

STRESS An acronym for STRuctural Engineering System Solver. A prob-lem-oriented language used for solv-ing structural engineering problems.

STRETCH The first major solid state computer developed by the IBM Cor-poration. Formally called the IBM 7030.

string A connected sequence of char-acters or bits that is treated as a single data item.

string manipulation A technique for manipulating strings of characters.

string processing languages Pro-gramming languages designed to facil-itate the processing of strings of char-acters. COMIT, SNOBOL, AMBIT, CONVERT, AXLE, PANON, and EOL are examples of string processing lan-guages. See *string.*

structure The organization or ar-rangement of the parts of an entity. The manner in which a program is organized.

structured programming A program-ming technique used in the design and coding of computer programs. The ap-proach assumes the disciplined use of a few basic coding structures and the use of top-down concepts to decom-pose main functions into lower-level components for modular coding pur-poses. The technique is concerned with improving the programming process through better organization of pro-grams and better programming nota-tion to facilitate correct and clear descriptions of data and control structures.

stub card A card containing a de-tachable stub to serve as a receipt for future reference.

subprogram A segment of a program that can perform a specific function. Subprograms can reduce program-ming time when a specific function is required at more than one point in a program. If the required function is handled as a subprogram, the state-ments for that function can be coded once and executed at the different points in the program. Subroutines and functions may be used to provide subprograms. See *function* and *sub-routine.*

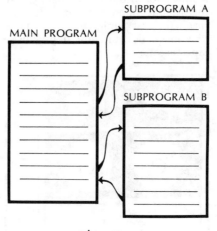

subprogram

subroutine A subsidiary routine, within which initial execution never starts. It is executed when called by some other program, usually the main program. Also called *subprogram.* See *closed subroutine* and *open subroutine.*

subroutine reentry Initiation of a subroutine by one program before it has finished its response to another program that called for it. This is what may happen when a control program is subjected to a priority interrupt.

subscript A programming notation that is used to identify an element in an array.

subscripted variable A symbol whose numeric value can change. It is denoted by an array name followed by a subscript; for example, CHESS (2,4) or A(7). See *subscript* and *variable*.

subset A set contained within a set.

substrate In microelectronics, the physical material on which a circuit is fabricated.

substring A portion of a character string.

subsystem A system subordinate to the main system.

subtrahend The quantity that is subtracted from another quantity. In the subtraction $a - b$, b is the subtrahend, and a is the minuend.

sum The quantity that results from adding two quantities.

summarize To condense a mass of data into a concise and meaningful form.

supercomputer The largest, fastest, and most expensive computer available. Used by businesses and organizations that require extraordinary amounts of computing power. Sometimes called "number crunchers" because they perform hundreds of millions of operations per second.

superscript A letter or digit written above a symbol to denote a power or to identify a particular element of a set (e.g., x^3).

supervisory system See *operating system*.

suppress To eliminate zeros or other insignificant characters from a computer printout.

SWAC An acronym for Standards Western Automatic Computer. In 1950, it was the fastest computer in existence.

swapping (1) In virtual storage, occurs when a new page is brought into internal storage from auxiliary storage and swapped for an existing page. (2) In a time-sharing system, bringing the program into internal storage or storing it on a storage device.

switch See *program switch*.

switched line Typically, a telephone line that is connected to the switched telephone network.

switching algebra The name given to Boolean algebra when it is applied to switching theory.

switching theory The theory applied to circuits that have two or more discrete states.

symbol (1) A letter, numeral, or mark that represents a numeral, operation, or relation. (2) An element of the computer's character set.

symbol

symbolic address An address, expressed in symbols convenient to the program writer, that must be translated into an absolute address (usually by an assembler) before it can be interpreted by a computer.

symbolic coding Coding in which the instructions are written in nonmachine language; that is, coding using symbolic notation for operation codes and operands.

symbolic device A name used to indicate an input/output file; for example, SYSDSK used to specify the magnetic disk unit.

symbolic editor A system program that helps computer users in the preparation and modification of source language programs by adding, changing, or deleting lines of text.

185

symbolic I/O assignment A name used to indicate an input/output unit; for example, RDR used to specify the card reader.

symbolic language A pseudolanguage made up of letters, characters, and numbers that are not the internal language of the computer system. See *assembly language, fabricated language,* and *high-level language.*

symbolic logic The discipline that treats formal logic by means of a formalized artificial language whose purpose is to avoid the ambiguities and logical inadequacies of natural language.

symbolic name See *name.*

symbolic programming Using a symbolic language to prepare computer programs.

symbolic table A mapping for a set of symbols to another set of symbols or numbers; for example, in an assembler, the symbol table contains the symbolic label addresses of an assembled object program.

symbol string A string consisting solely of symbols.

sync character A character transmitted to establish character synchronization in synchronous communication.

synchronization Adjustment of the chronological relationships between events either to cause them to coincide or to maintain a fixed time difference between them.

synchronization check A check that determines whether a particular event or condition occurs at the proper moment.

synchronous communication See *synchronous transmission.*

synchronous computer A computer in which each operation starts as a result of a signal generated by a clock. Contrast with *asynchronous computer.*

synchronous operation The operation of a system under the control of clocked pulses.

synchronous transmission Data transmission in which the bits are transmitted at a fixed rate. The transmitter and receiver both use the same clock signals for synchronization.

synonym Two or more keys that produce the same table address when hashed.

syntax The grammatical and structural rules of a language. All assembly and high-level programming languages possess a formal syntax.

syntax error The breaking of a rule governing the structure of the programming language being used.

synthesizer A machine that generates and processes sound automatically. Some synthesizers include microprocessors, which are used as controlling devices. A voice synthesizer produces sounds that closely resemble a person speaking. A music synthesizer produces music.

SYSGEN An acronym for SYStems GENeration. The process of modifying the generalized operating system received from the vendor into a tailored system meeting the unique needs of the individual user.

system A composite of equipment, skills, techniques, and information capable of performing and/or supporting an operational role in attaining specified management objectives. A complete system includes related facilities, equipment, material, services, personnel, and information required for its operation to the degree that it can be considered a self-sufficient unit in its intended operational and/or support environment. *(Illus. p. 187)*

system analyzer A portable device that can be used as a troubleshooting unit for field service of complex equipment and systems.

system

system chart A type of flowchart. See *flowchart*.

system commands Special instructions given to the computer when one operates in the conversational time-sharing mode. System commands direct the computer to execute (RUN) programs, list them (LIST), save them (SAVE), and to do other operations of a similar nature.

system design The specification of the working relations between all the parts of a system in terms of their characteristic actions.

system diagnostics A program used to detect overall system malfunctions.

system flowchart See *flowchart*.

system generation The process of initiating a basic system at a specific installation.

system interrupt A break in the normal execution of a program or routine that is accomplished in such a way that the usual sequence can be resumed from that point later on.

system loader A supervisory program used to locate programs in the system library and load them into the internal storage of the computer.

system programmer (1) A programmer who plans, generates, maintains, and controls the use of an operating system with the aim of improving the overall productivity of an installation. (2) A programmer who designs programming systems.

systems analysis The examination of an activity, procedure, method, technique, or business to determine what must be accomplished and how the necessary operations may best be accomplished by using data processing equipment.

systems analyst One who studies the activities, methods, procedures, and techniques of organizational systems in order to determine what actions need to be taken and how these actions can best be accomplished.

systems analyst

systems house A company that develops hardware and/or software systems to meet user requirements.

systems manual A document containing information on the operation of a system. Sufficient detail is provided so that management can determine the data flow, forms used, reports generated, and controls exercised. Job descriptions are generally provided.

systems programming The development of programs that form operating systems for computers. Such programs include assemblers, compilers, control programs, input/output handlers,and so forth.

systems programs Computer programs that provide a particular service to the user; for example, compilers, assemblers, operating systems, sort/merge programs, emulators, linkage editor programs, graphic support programs, and mathematical programs. See *manufacturer's software* and *utility routines*.

systems software The software used as development tools during the design of application programs.

systems study An investigation made to determine the feasibility of installing or replacing a business system. See *feasibility study*.

systems synthesis The planning of the procedures for solving a problem.

systems testing Involves the testing of a series of programs in succession to make sure that all of the programs, including input and output, are related in the way the systems analyst intended.

table A collection of data in a form suitable for ready reference, frequently as stored in consecutive storage locations or written in the form of an array of rows and columns for easy entry, and in which an intersection of labeled rows and columns serves to locate a specific piece of data or information.

table look-up A procedure for using a known value to locate an unknown value in a table.

tabulate (1) To print totals. (2) To form data into a table.

tabulating equipment Unit record machines that use punched cards and are predominately electromechanical, such as sorters, collators, interpreters, reproducing punches, and tabulators.

tabulator A machine that reads information from one medium (e.g., cards or magnetic tape) and produces lists, tables, and totals on separate forms or continuous paper.

tag A portion of an instruction. The tag carries the number of the index register that affects the address in the instruction.

tail A special data item that locates the end of a list.

tape A strip of material that may be punched or coated with a magnetic sensitive substance and used for data input, storage, or output. The data are usually stored serially in several channels across the tape transversely to the reading or writing motion.

tape cartridge See *magnetic tape cartridge*.

tape cassette See *magnetic tape cassette*.

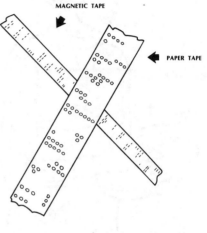

MAGNETIC TAPE

PAPER TAPE

tape

tape code See *magnetic tape code* and *paper tape code*.

tape deck Same as *magnetic tape unit*.

tape drive Same as *magnetic tape drive*.

tape handler See *magnetic tape unit*.

tape label Usually the first record on a magnetic tape reel, containing such information as the date the tape was written, identification name or number, and the number of records on the tape.

tape librarian A person who has responsibility for the safe-keeping of all computer files, for example, programs and data files on magnetic tapes, disk packs, microfilm, punched cards, and so on. *(Illus. p. 190)*

tape library A special room that houses a file of magnetic tapes under secure, environmentally controlled conditions. *(Illus. p. 190)*

tape librarian

tape library

tape-to-card converter A device that converts information directly from paper tape or magnetic tape to punch cards, usually off-line.

tape unit See *magnetic tape unit, paper tape punch,* and *paper tape reader.*

target language The language into which some other language is to be properly translated. Usually has the same meaning as *object language.*

target program Same as *object program.*

tariff In data communications, the published rate for a specific unit of equipment, facility, or type of service provided by a communication common carrier.

task A unit of work for the computer.

tb (terabyte) One trillion bytes. One thousand gb.

technology The knowledge and methods used to create a product.

telecommunications The transfer of data from one place to another over communication lines. See *data communications* and *teleprocessing.*

teleconference An "electronic meeting" conducted among people at distant locations through the use of telecommunications. Considered an alternative to travel and face-to-face meetings, a teleconference is conducted with two-way video, audio, and, as required, data and facsimile transmission.

telemedicine The use of telecommunications, particularly television, for transmitting medical data, such as x rays or live images of a patient, to a distantly located specialist for consultation.

telemetry Transmission of data from remote measuring instruments by electrical or radio means; for example, data can be telemetered from a spacecraft circling the moon and recorded at a ground station located on earth.

teleprinter An automatic printing device.

teleprocessing The use of telephone lines to transmit data and commands between remote locations and a data processing center or between two computer systems. Data processing combined with data communications. See *data communications* and *telecommunications*.

telesoftware Computer programs sent by telephone line or television as part of the teletext signal.

teletext The generic name for a television system that flashes printed text on a TV screen while the regular broadcast continues.

teletypewriter A teletype unit. A generic term referring to teleprinter equipment and to the basic equipment made by the Teletype Corporation. A device used widely as an input/output unit in computer systems. Abbreviated TTY.

teletypewriter

telex A telegraph service provided by Western Union.

telpak A service offered by communications common carriers for the

leasing of wide band channels between two or more points.

template A plastic guide used in drawing flowcharting symbols.

temporary storage In programming, storage locations reserved for intermediate results. Synonymous with *working storage*.

ten's complement A number used to represent the negative of a given value. A ten's complement number is obtained by subtracting each digit from a number containing all nines and adding one; for example, 654 is the ten's complement of 346 and is obtained by performing the computation $999 - 346 + 1$.

terminal (1) An input/output peripheral device that is on-line to the computer, but that is in a remote location: another room, another city, or another country. (2) A point at which information can enter or leave a communication network.

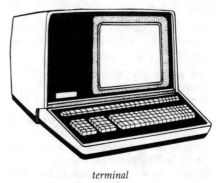

terminal

terminal emulation A situation in which special software makes a computer behave as though it were a terminal connected to another computer.

terminal symbol A flowcharting symbol used to indicate the starting point and termination point or points in a procedure. An oval-shaped figure is used to represent this symbol. (*Illus. p. 192*)

191

terminal symbol

ternary (1) Pertaining to a characteristic or property involving a selection, choice, or condition in which there are three possibilities. (2) Pertaining to the numeration system with a radix of three.

test data Data especially created to test the operation of a given program. Usually, one or more hand-calculated results, or otherwise known results, will be associated with test data so the program under test may be validated.

test driver A program that directs the execution of another program against a collection of test data sets.

testing Examination of a program's behavior by executing the program on sample data sets. See *debug* and *systems testing*.

text That part of the message that contains the information to be conveyed.

text editor A program that facilitates changes to computer-stored information; assists in the preparation of text.

theorem proving Two approaches to automated theorem proving are proof-finding and consequence-finding. A proof-finding program attempts to find a proof for a certain given theorem. A consequence-finding program is given specific axioms for which to deduce consequences. Then, "interesting" consequences are selected.

theory of numbers A branch of pure mathematics concerned generally with the properties and relationships of integers.

thermal printer A hard copy device that produces output on heat-sensitive paper.

thesaurus (1) A lexicon, more specifically where words are grouped by ideas or sets of concepts. (2) A grouping or classification of synonyms or near synonyms. (3) A set of equivalent classes of terminology.

thin film A computer storage made by placing thin spots of magnetic materials on an insulated base (usually a flat plate or wire); electric current in wires attached to the base is used to magnetize the spot. See *rod memory*.

third generation Computers that use integrated circuitry and miniaturization of components to replace transistors, reduce costs, work faster, and increase reliability. The third generation of computers began in 1964.

Thomas, Charles Xavier (Colmar, Thomas) Made a calculating machine in 1820 that is credited with being the first that ever did work practically and usefully.

Charles Xavier Thomas

thrashing Overhead associated with memory swapping in a virtual memory system. Also called *churning*.

threaded tree A tree containing additional pointers to assist in the scan of the tree.

three-address computer A computer that employs three addresses in its instruction format. For example, in the instruction ADD A B C, the values represented by A and B are added, and the result is assigned to C.

three-dimensional array An array that provides a threefold classification: row, column, and layer.

throughput The total amount of useful processing carried out by a computer system in a given time period.

thyratron See *SCR*.

thyristor A bistable device comprising three or more junctions. See *SCR*.

TICCIT An acronym for Time-shared, Interactive, Computer-Controlled, Instructional Television. A computer-aided instruction system that uses minicomputers and modified color television sets as terminals to provide individual instruction to many students simultaneously. See *computer-assisted instruction* and *PLATO*.

tie-breaker Refers to circuitry that resolves the conflict when two central processing units try to use a peripheral device at the same time.

tie line A leased communication channel.

time division multiplexing The merging of several bit streams of lower bit rates into a composite signal for transmission over a communication channel of higher bit-rate capacity.

time-sharing

193

time quantum In a time-sharing system, a unit of time allotted to each user.

timer The computer's internal clock.

time-sharing A method of operation in which a computer facility is shared by several users for different purposes at (apparently) the same time. Although the computer actually services each user in sequence, the high speed of the computer makes it appear that the users are all handled simultaneously. *(Illus. p. 193)*

time-slicing The allotment of a portion of processing time to each program in a multiprogramming system to prevent the monopolization of the central processing unit by any one program.

TI-99/4 and TI-99/4A A popular microcomputer system developed by Texas Instruments Incorporated. The system uses preprogrammed ROM cartridges as well as other forms of input. See *microcumputer* and *solid state cartridge*.

TI 99/4A

T²L Same as *TTL*.

toggle Pertaining to any device having two stable states. Synonymous with *flip-flop*.

token A symbol representing a name or entity in a programming language.

top-down A technique for designing a program or system according to its major functions and breaking these down into even smaller subfunctions. See *modular programming* and *structured programming*.

Touch-tone A service mark of the AT & T Company that identifies its push-button dialing service.

trace The scanning path of the beam in a raster display.

tracing routine A routine that provides a time history of the contents of the computer operational registers during the execution of the program. A complete tracing routine would reveal the status of all registers and locations affected by each instruction each time the instruction is executed.

track A path along which data is recorded on a continuous or rotational medium, such as paper tape, magnetic tape, or magnetic disk or drum.

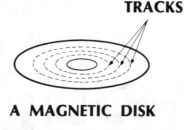

TRACKS

A MAGNETIC DISK

track

track ball Similar to a joystick, but uses a ball moved by the palm of the hand, instead of a lever held by the fingers.

traffic intensity The ratio of the insertion rate to the deletion rate of a queue.

trailer record A record that follows a group of records and contains pertinent data related to the group of records.

trailing edge The edge of a punched card that is opposite the leading edge relative to the direction of motion of the card as it passes along the card track preceding, during, or after reading or punching. Contrast with *leading edge*.

transaction code One or more characters that form part of a record and signify the type of transaction represented by the record.

transaction file Same as *detail file*.

transactions Business or other activities such as sales, expenditures, shipments, reservations, and inquiries.

transcribe To copy from one external storage medium to another. The process may involve translation.

transducer A device for converting information from one form to another.

transfer (1) To copy or read, transmit, and store an item or block of information. (2) To change control. See *branch, conditional transfer, jump,* and *unconditional transfer*.

transfer address See *entry point*.

transfer rate The speed at which accessed data can be moved from one device to another. See *access time* and *seek time*.

transformer An alternating current device used in computer power supplies to reduce 115 volts 60 Hertz to a lower, more suitable level for conversion to direct current voltage.

transient (1) A phenomenon caused in a system by a sudden change in conditions, and which persists for a relatively short time after the change. (2) A momentary surge on a signal or power line. It may produce false signals and cause component failures.

transistor A semiconductor device for controlling the flow of current between two terminals, the emitter and the collector, by means of variations in the current flow between a third terminal, the base, and one of the other two. It was developed at Bell Laboratories by William Shockley, Walter Brattain, and John Bardeen.

transistor (developed by Shockley, Brattain, and Bardeen)

transistor-transistor logic A family of integrated circuits characterized by relatively high speed and low power consumption. Abbreviated TTL.

transit error A type of error that occurs only once and cannot be made to repeat itself.

translate To change data from one form of representation to another without significantly affecting the meaning. See *language translation*.

translator A computer program that performs translations from one language or code to another; for example, a compiler. See *assembler, compiler,* and *interpreter*.

transmission The sending of data from one location and the receiving of data in another location, usually leav-

195

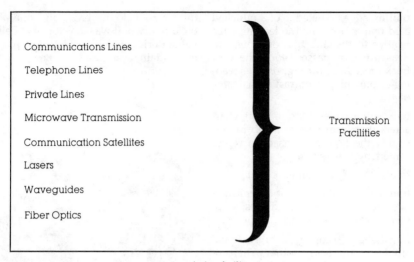

transmission facility

ing the source data unchanged. See *data transmission*.

transmission facility The communications link between remote terminals and computers.

transmit To send data from one location and to receive the data at another location.

transparent A process that is not visible to the user or to other devices. Transparent memory refresh is an example.

trap A programmed conditional jump to a known location, automatically executed when program execution reaches the location where the trap is set. Same as *interrupt*.

trapping A hardware provision for interrupting the normal flow of control of a program while transfer to a known location is made. See *interrupt*.

tree A connected graph with no cycles.

tree sort A sort that exchanges items treated as nodes of a tree. When an item reaches the root node, it is exchanged with the lowest leaf node. Also called heap sort.

trichromatic Literally, "three colored." In computer graphics, trichromatic generally refers to the three primary colors combined to create all others: blue, green, and red.

trigonometry The branch of mathematics that deals with the sides and angles of triangles and their measurements and relations.

triple precision The retention of three times as many digits of a quantity as the computer normally uses.

troubleshoot A term applied to the task of finding a malfunction in a hardware unit or a mistake in a computer program. Synonymous with debug. See *bug*, *debugging aids*, and *test data*.

TRS-80 The trade name of several microcomputer systems manufactured by Radio Shack, a division of Tandy Corporation. See *home computer, microcomputer*, and *personal computer*. *(Illus. p. 197)*

true complement Synonymous with ten's complement and two's complement.

truncate To drop digits of a number of terms of a series, thus lessening

TRS-80 microcomputer

Alan M. Turing

precision; for example, 3.14159 truncates the series for π, which could conceivably be extended indefinitely.

truncation error An error due to truncation. Contrast with *round-off error*.

trunk The direct line between two telephone switching centers.

truth table A systematic tabulation of all the possible input/output combinations produced by a binary circuit.

TTL An acronym for *Transistor-Transistor Logic*.

TTY An abbreviation for *teletypewriter*.

tunnel diode An electronic device with switching speeds of fractional billionths of seconds. Used in high-speed computer circuitry and memories.

Turing, Alan M. (1912–1954) A famous English mathematician and logician who, shortly before his death, completed the design of one of the world's first modern high-speed digital computers. See *Turing machine*.

Turing machine A mathematical model of a device that changes its internal state and reads from, writes on, and moves a potentially infinite tape, all in accordance with its present state, thereby constituting a model for computer-like behavior. See *Turing, Alan M.*

Turing's test Developed by British mathematician Alan Turing, this is a game to determine whether a computer might be considered to possess intelligence. Participants in the game include two respondents (a computer and a human) and a human examiner who tries to determine which of the unseen respondents is the human. According to this test, intelligence and the ability to think would be demonstrated by the computer's success in fooling the examiner.

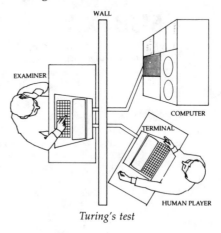

Turing's test

197

turnaround form In optical scanning, a document on which the variable information is imprinted by EDP equipment and is then used to gather information for future re-entry (via OCR) to update data in the computer.

turnaround time The time it takes for a job to get from the user to the computing center, for it to be run on the computer, and for the program results to be returned back to the user.

turnkey system A computer system containing all the hardware and software needed to perform a given application.

TVT An acronym for TeleVision Typewriter. A keyboard and electronics specially designed to convert a television into a computer terminal. A video terminal.

TV terminal A common television set used as a computer output device. See *video terminal*.

twelve-punch A punch in the top row of a Hollerith punched card. Synonymous with *Y-punch*.

two-address computer A computer that employs two addresses in its instruction format. For example, in the instruction ADD A B, the values represented by A and B are added, and the result replaces the old value of B.

SUB X,Y

two-address computer

two-dimensional array An arrangement consisting of rows and columns. See *matrix*.

two's complement A method of representing negative numbers. A positive or negative number is changed to the opposite sign by changing all 1's to 0's and all 0's to 1's, then binarily adding 1. Synonymous with *true complement*.

TWX An acronym for TeletypeWriter eXchange service. An American Telephone and Telegraph service that connects user's teleprinter equipment with the common telephone network.

type font A type face of a given size. See *font*.

typewriter An input/output device that is capable of being connected to a computer and used for communication purposes.

typewriter

UART An acronym for *Universal Asynchronous Receiver/Transmitter.*

μC An abbreviation for *microcomputer* (μ is the Greek letter mu).

ultrafiche Microfiche holding images reduced 100X or more.

ultrasonic Above the human audio range; that is, above 20 kilohertz.

ultrasonic memory The main memory of several early computers, including EDSAC, SEAC, EDVAC, UNIVAC I, and Pilot ACE.

ultraviolet light Used to erase data or instructions stored in an Erasable PROM (EPROM). Once the EPROM has been "erased," it can be reprogrammed by using a PROM programmer. See *EPROM* and *PROM programmer.*

unary See *monadic.*

unattended operation Data transmission and/or reception without an operator.

unbundled The services, programs, training, and so on sold independently of the computer hardware by the computer hardware manufacturer. Contrast with *bundled.*

unconditional transfer An instruction that always causes a branch in program control away from the normal sequence of executing instructions. Contrast with *conditional transfer.*

underflow (1) The condition that arises when a computer computation yields a result that is smaller than the smallest possible quantity the computer is capable of storing. (2) A condition in which the exponent plus the excess become negative in a floating point arithmetic operation.

underpunch A second hole, in a punched card column, that is immediately under the original standard code hole punched in the column.

union The joining or combining of two or more things.

unipolar Refers to having one pole. See *bipolar.*

unit A device having a special function (e.g., arithmetic unit, central processing unit, or magnetic tape unit).

unit position The extreme right position of a field.

unit record system A data processing system that uses electromechanical processing machines (sorters, collators, etc.) operated by technicians, as contrasted with a more automated computerized system. Today, most unit record installations have been replaced with modern computer equipment.

UNIVAC I The first commercial electronic digital computer. It was used by the Census Bureau for processing some of the data from the 1950 census. Forty-eight of these computers were built.

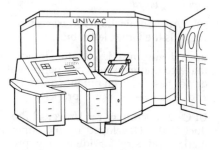

UNIVAC I

universal asynchronous receiver/ transmitter An integrated circuit that converts serial data into parallel form, and parallel data into serial form.

universal identifier A standard multidigit number assigned to an individual to be used in verifying her or his identity.

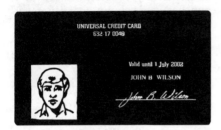

universal identifier

UPC

universal language A programming language that is available on many computers, such as FORTRAN, COBOL, and BASIC. Same as *common language*.

universal product code See *UPC*.

UNIX A general purpose time-sharing system developed at Bell Laboratories.

unpack To separate short units of data that have previously been packed. Opposite of *pack*.

unpopulated board A circuit board where the components must be supplied by the purchaser. Contrast with *populated board*.

μP An abbreviation for *microprocessor*. (μ is the Greek letter mu).

up-and-running Used to indicate that a computer system or a peripheral device has just been put into operation and that it is working properly.

UPC An acronym for Universal Product Code. Developed by the supermarket industry for identifying products and manufacturers on product tags. A variety of manufacturers produce printers to print the 10-digit bar symbols and optical scanning devices to read the codes during supermarket checkout.

update To make information more current by adding, changing, or deleting data in a computer file.

upload To transfer information from a user's system to a remote computer system. Opposite of *download*.

uptime See *available time*.

upward compatible A term used to indicate that a computer system or peripheral device can do everything that the previous model could do, plus some additional functions. See *compatibility*.

μs An abbreviation for *microsecond*; one millionth of a second (μ is the Greek letter mu). Same as μsec.

usability The worth of a system as evaluated by the person who must use it.

user (1) Anyone who utilizes a computer for problem solving or data manipulation. (2) Anyone who requires the services of a computer system.

user-oriented language See *problem-oriented language* and *procedure-oriented language*.

users group A group of computer users who share the knowledge they have gained and the programs they have developed on a computer or class of computers of a specific manufacturer. They usually meet to exchange information, share programs, and trade equipment.

user terminal See *terminal.*

utility See *computer utility.*

utility routines Software used to perform some frequently required process in the operation of a computer system (e.g., sorting, trigonometric functions, etc.). See *systems programs.*

users group

VAB An acronym for Voice Answer Back. An audio response device that can link a computer system to a telephone network to provide voice responses to inquiries made from telephone-tape terminals.

vacuum tube The dominant electronic element found in computers prior to the advent of the transistor. Those computers using vacuum tubes are referred to as *first generation computers*.

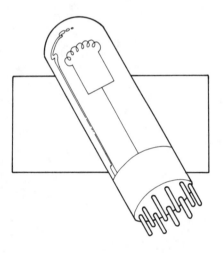

vacuum tube

VAL An acronym for Vicarm Arm Language. A computer language for controlling robots.

validation The examination of data for correctness against certain criteria such as format (patterns of numbers, spaces, and letters), ranges (upper and lower value limits), check digits, equivalent entries on a master file, and so on.

variable A quantity that can assume any of a given set of values. See *subscripted variable*.

variable-length record Pertaining to a file in which the records are not uniform in length. Contrast with *fixed-length record*.

variable word length Pertaining to a machine word or operand that may consist of a variable number of bits, bytes, or characters. Contrast with *fixed word length*.

VDL An acronym for Vienna Definition Language. A language for defining the syntax and semantics of programming languages.

VDU An acronym for Visual Display Unit. A peripheral device on which data is displayed on some type of screen.

vector (1) A list or table of numbers, all of which are expressed on the same line. (2) A quantity having magnitude and direction. (3) In computer science, a data structure that permits the location of any item by the use of a single index or subscript. Contrast with a *table, two-dimensional array,* or *matrix* that requires two subscripts to uniquely locate an item.

vendor (1) A company that sells computers, peripheral devices, time-sharing service or computer services. (2) A supplier.

Venn diagram A diagram to picture sets and the relationships between sets. *(Illus. p. 203)*

verifier machine A device used to detect keypunching mistakes by rekeying.

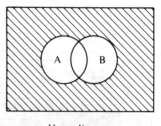

Venn diagram

video terminal

verify (1) To determine whether a data processing operation has been accomplished accurately; for example, to check the results of keypunching. (2) To check data validity.

very large scale integration The process of placing a large number (usually over 1000) of integrated circuits on one chip. Abbreviated VLSI.

videodisk A plastic platter resembling a phonograph record which uses low-intensity laser beams to store visual materials that will appear on a display screen.

video generator A device that generates the signals that control a television display.

video monitor A device that is functionally identical to a television set, except that it has no channel selector. It receives its picture signal from an external source such as a video terminal board.

video terminal A device for entering information into a computer system and displaying it on a screen. A typewriter-like keyboard is used to enter information. See *cathode ray tube, display,* and *screen.*

videotext Same as *viewdata.*

viewdata An interactive information network that is transmitted through the telephone lines but displays its inputs and outputs on a television screen. First developed in the United Kingdom by the British Post Office.

virtual Appearing to be rather than actually being.

virtual address In virtual storage systems, an address that refers to virtual storage and must, therefore, be translated into a real storage address when it is used.

virtual memory See *virtual storage.*

virtual storage A technique for managing a limited amount of internal storage and a (generally) much larger amount of lower-speed storage in such a way that the distinction is largely transparent to a computer user. The technique entails some means of swapping segments of the program and data from the lower-speed storage (which would commonly be a drum or disk) into the internal storage, where it would be interpreted as instructions or operated upon as data. The unit of program or data swapped back and forth is called a page. The high-speed storage from which instructions are executed is called real storage, while the lower-speed storage (drums or disks) is called virtual storage.

VisiCalc A business computer program that translates simple commands typed on a keyboard into computer language that the machine then uses to solve problems.

visual display A visual representation of data, that is, a picture or diagram drawn on a display screen, a diagram produced by a plotter, or a printed report.

visual display

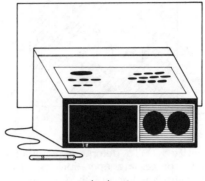

voice input

visual scanner See *optical character reader*.

VLDB An acronym for Very Large Data Base. A data base that is distributed among multiple computers with different data base management systems.

VLSI An acronym for *Very Large Scale Integration*.

vocabulary Codes or instructions that can be used to write a program for a particular computer.

voder A speech synthesizer.

voice communications The transmission of sound in the human hearing range. Voice or audio sound can be transmitted either as analog or digital signals.

voice grade channel A channel that permits transmission of speech. Accommodates frequencies from 300 to 3000 Hz.

voice input An input device that permits a human voice to be used as input to a computer.

voice output An audio response output device that permits the computer to deliver answers by the spoken word.

voice recognition See *speech recognition*.

voice response Computer output in spoken form.

voice synthesis The ability of the computer to use stored patterns of sounds within its memory to assemble words that can be played through a loudspeaker.

volatile storage A storage medium whose contents are lost if power is removed from the system.

voltage Electrical pressure. High voltage in a computer circuit is represented by a "1"; low (or zero) voltage is represented by a "0."

voltage regulator A circuit that holds an output voltage at a predetermined value or causes it to vary according to a predetermined plan, regardless of normal input-voltage change or changes in the load impedance.

volume A physical unit of a storage medium (disk pack, diskette, tape reel, etc.) capable of having data recorded on it and subsequently read.

von Neumann, John (1903–1957) One of the outstanding mathemeticians of this century. He built one of the first electronic computers, contributed much to game theory, and introduced the stored program concept. See *stored program concept. (Illus. p. 205)*

John von Neumann

von Neumann machine The machine as defined by John von Neumann in 1946 in a report titled "Preliminary Discussion of the Logical Design of an Electronic Computing Instrument." Central to the von Neumann machine is the concept of the stored program—the principle that instructions and data are to be stored together intermixed in a single, uniform storage medium. See *stored program concept* and *von Neumann, John*.

VRC An acronym for Vertical Redundancy Check.

VS An acronym for *virtual storage*.

W

wafer The thin, round piece of silicon from which integrated circuits are made.

wait state A condition in which the central processing unit is idle, not executing instructions.

wait time The time during which a program or a computer waits for the completion of other activities.

WAMI An acronym for World Association for Medical Informatics.

wand A penlike device able to read optically coded labels.

WATFIV See *WATFOR*.

WATFOR A version of FORTRAN developed at the University of Waterloo in Ontario, Canada. WATFIV is a revision of WATFOR.

WATS An acronym for *Wide Area Telephone Service*. A service that permits an unlimited number of calls from one point to any location in a large area. The United States is divided into six WATS zones.

Watson, Thomas J. (1874–1956) The guiding spirit of the IBM Corporation. He was a superb salesman and the president of IBM until 1952. His motto was THINK, and he has made a lot of people, in particular IBM competitors, think long and hard.

weed To discard currently undesirable or needless items from a file.

weighted code A code where each bit position of the code has a weighted value. In the 8-4-2-1 weighted code system, the decimal numeral 529 = 0101 0010 1001.

wheel printer A printer with a printing mechanism that contains the print-

Thomas J. Watson

ing characters on metal wheels. A type of *line printer*.

whole number A number without a fractional part (e.g., 63, −47, 88.0).

Wide Area Telephone Service A service provided by telephone companies that permits a customer, by use of an access line called a WATS line, to make data communications in a specific zone on a dial basis for a flat monthly charge. Abbreviated WATS.

wideband In data communications, a channel wider in bandwidth than a voice grade channel.

Wiener, Norbert (1894–1964) An American scientist who coined the term cybernetics. The founder of a new branch of science, he believed that many thought processes in the human brain could be determined mathematically and adapted for computers. Pioneer in the theory of automata. See *automata* and *cybernetics*.

Maurice Vincent Wilkes

Norbert Wiener

Wilkes, Maurice Vincent (born 1913) Headed the team of people at the University of Cambridge (Great Britain) who built the Electronic Delay Storage Automatic Calculator (EDSAC) in 1949. See *EDSAC*.

Winchester disk A fast, auxiliary storage device. Consists of a rigid magnetic disk in a sealed container.

window A portion of the video display area that is dedicated to some specific purpose.

wire board See *control panel*.

wired program computer A computer in which the instructions that specify the operations to be performed are specified by the placement and interconnection of wires. The wires are usually held by a removable control

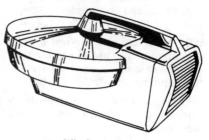

Winchester disk

panel, allowing limited flexibility of operation. The term is also applied to permanently wired machines that are then called fixed program computers.

wire wrap A type of circuit board construction. Electrical connections are made through wires connected to the posts that correspond to the proper component lead.

word A group of bits, characters, or bytes considered as an entity and capable of being stored in one storage location. See *keyboard*.

word length The number of bits, characters, or bytes in a word.

word processing A technique for electronically storing, editing, and manipulating text using an electronic keyboard, computer, and printer. The text is recorded on a magnetic medium, usually floppy disks, except for the final output which is on paper.

working storage Same as *temporary storage*.

workspace A loosely defined term that usually refers to the amount of internal storage available for programs and data.

work station A configuration of computer equipment designed for use by one person at a time. This may have a terminal connected to a computer, or it may be a "stand alone system" with local processing capability.

work year The effort expended by one person for one year. This term is used to estimate the personnel resources needed to complete a specific task.

WP An acronym for Word Processing. Involves the use of computerized equipment and systems to facilitate the handling of words and text.

WPM An acronym for Words Per Minute. A measure of data transmission speed.

WPS An acronym for Word Processing Society. This organization encourages word processing educational programs in school to promote word processing as a profession.

wraparound The continuation of an operation such as a change in the storage location from the largest addressable location to the first addressable location; or a visual display cursor movement from the last character position to the first position.

write (1) The process of transferring information from the computer to an output medium. (2) To copy data,

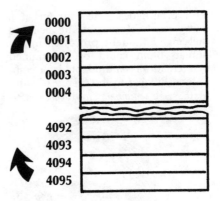

wraparound

usually from internal storage to auxiliary storage devices.

write head A magnetic head that is designed and used to write data onto the media. Contrast with *read head*.

write-inhibit ring Used to prevent data from being written over on magnetic tapes.

write protect notch Floppy disks (diskettes) may be protected from the possibility of undesired recording of data by application of a gummed tab over the "write protect notch." An uncovered write protect notch will allow writing to the diskette. See *file protection*.

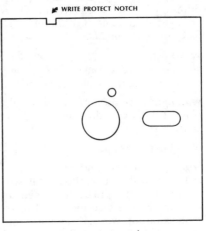

write protect notch

xerographic printer A device for printing an optical image on paper in which light and dark areas are represented by electrostatically charged areas on the paper. A powdered ink is dusted on the paper which adheres to the charged areas and is melted into the paper by heat.

XOR An acronym for *Exclusive OR.*

X-punch A punch in the eleventh punching position (row 11) of a Hollerith punched card. Synonymous with *eleven-punch.*

X-Y plotter See *plotter.*

Y-punch A punch in the twelfth position (row 12) of a Hollerith card. Also called a high-punch. Synonymous with *twelve-punch.*

zero A numeral normally denoting lack of magnitude. In many computers, there are distinct representations for plus and minus zero.

zero flag A flip-flop that goes to logic 1 if the result of an instruction has the value zero.

zero suppression The suppression (e.g., elimination) of nonsignificant zeros in a numeral, usually before or during a printing operation. For example, the numeral 00004763, with zero suppression, would be printed as 4763.

zone bits These are used along with numeric bits to represent alphanumeric characters.

zone punch A punch in the O, X, or Y row on a Hollerith card.

Zuse, Konrad (born 1910) A German pioneer in the development of computing equipment. In 1941, he completed the Zuse Z-3, a machine with some remarkable advanced features. The speed of this machine was about the same as the Mark I.

Konrad Zuse